Lecture Notes in Computer Science 8735

Commenced Publication in 1973
Founding and Former Series Editors:
Gerhard Goos, Juris Hartmanis, and Jan van Leeuwen

Bart De Decker   André Zúquete (Eds.)

Communications and Multimedia Security

15th IFIP TC 6/TC 11 International Conference, CMS 2014
Aveiro, Portugal, September 25-26, 2014
Proceedings

 Springer

Volume Editors

Bart De Decker
KU Leuven, Department of Computer Science, iMinds-DistriNet
Celestijnenlaan 200A, 3001 Leuven, Belgium
E-mail: bart.dedecker@cs.kuleuven.be

André Zúquete
University of Aveiro, DETI/IEETA
Campus Universitário de Santiago, 3810-193 Aveiro, Portugal
E-mail: andre.zuquete@ua.pt

ISSN 0302-9743   e-ISSN 1611-3349
ISBN 978-3-662-44884-7   e-ISBN 978-3-662-44885-4
DOI 10.1007/978-3-662-44885-4
Springer Heidelberg New York Dordrecht London

Library of Congress Control Number: 2014948333

LNCS Sublibrary: SL 4 – Security and Cryptology

Typesetting: Camera-ready by author, data conversion by Scientific Publishing Services, Chennai, India

Printed on acid-free paper

Springer is part of Springer Science+Business Media (www.springer.com)

Preface

It is with great pleasure that we present the proceedings of the 15th IFIP TC-6 and TC-11 Conference on Communications and Multimedia Security (CMS 2014), which was held in Aveiro, Portugal during September 25–26, 2014. The meeting continues the tradition of previous CMS conferences which were held in Magdeburg, Germany (2013), Canterbury, UK (2012), Ghent, Belgium (2011) and Linz, Austria (2010).

The Program Committee (PC) received 22 submissions, comprising 16 full papers, 3 short papers and 3 extended abstracts, out of which only 4 full papers were accepted (25% acceptance rate). In this edition, we have included 6 short papers, which describe valuable work-in-progress, as well as 3 extended abstracts, which describe the posters that were discussed at the conference. Some of the latter two categories are shortened versions of original full or short paper submissions respectively, which the PC judged to be valuable contributions but somewhat premature for submission under their original category.

We are grateful to Paulo Mateus, of the Instituto Superior Técnico/University of Lisbon and Rui Melo Biscaia, of Watchful Software, for accepting our invitations to deliver keynote addresses, the abstracts of which can be found at the end of these proceedings.

We would also like to say a word of appreciation to our sponsors, the Institute of Electronics and Telematics Engineering of Aveiro (IEETA) and the University of Aveiro, for hosting the conference and providing all the human and material support requested by the Organizing Committee.

Finally, special thanks go to the Organizing Committee who handled all local organizational issues and provided us with a comfortable and inspiring location and an interesting evening event. For us, it was a distinct pleasure to serve as program chairs of CMS 2014.

We hope that you will enjoy reading these proceedings and that they may inspire you for future research in communications and multimedia security.

September 2014

Bart De Decker
André Zúquete

Organization

CMS 2014 was the 15th Joint IFIP TC6 and TC11 Conference on Communications and Multimedia Security. It was organized by the University of Aveiro, Portugal.

Executive Committee

Conference Chair

André Zúquete   University of Aveiro, Portugal

Program Co-chairs

Bart De Decker   KU Leuven, Belgium
André Zúquete

Organizing Chair

Carlos Costa   University of Aveiro, Portugal

Organizing Committee

Carlos Costa   Fábio Marques
André Zúquete   Cláudio Teixeira

Program Committee

Anas Abou El Kalam	Cadi Ayyad University, ENSA of Marrakesh, Morocco
Eric Alata	LAAS-CNRS, France
Patrick Bas	CNRS-Lagis, France
Jan Camenisch	IBM Research - Zurich, Switzerland
David W. Chadwick	University of Kent, UK
Howard Chivers	University of York, UK
Isabelle Chrisment	LORIA-University of Nancy, France
Gabriela F. Ciocarlie	Computer Science Lab, SRI International, USA
Dave Clarke	Uppsala University, Sweden & KU Leuven, Belgium
Frédéric Cuppens	Télécom Bretagne, France

Italo Dacosta	KU Leuven, Belgium
Hervé Debar	Télécom SudParis, France
Sabrina De Capitani di Vimercati	Università degli Studi di Milano, Italy
Bart De Decker	KU Leuven, Belgium
Yvo Desmedt	University of Texas at Dallas, USA and University College London, UK
Lieven Desmet	KU Leuven, Belgium
Lieven De Strycker	KU Leuven, Technology Campus Ghent, Belgium
Jana Dittmann	Otto-von-Guericke University Magdeburg, Germany
Stelios Dritsas	Athens University of Economics and Business, Greece
Gerhard Eschelbeck	Sophos, USA
Simone Fischer-Hübner	Karlstad University, Sweden
Steven Furnell	Plymouth University, UK
Jürgen Fuß	University of Applied Sciences Upper Austria, Austria
Sébastien Gambs	Université de Rennes 1 - Inria/IRISA, France
Dieter Gollmann	Hamburg University of Technology, Germany
Rüdiger Grimm	University of Koblenz, Germany
Eckehard Hermann	University of Applied Sciences Upper Austria, Austria
Jens Hermans	KU Leuven, Belgium
Alejandro Hevia	University of Chile, Chile
Andreas Humm	University of Fribourg, Switzerland
Christophe Huygens	KU Leuven, Belgium
Sushil Jajodia	George Mason University, USA
Günter Karjoth	Lucerne University of Applied Sciences and Arts, Switzerland
Stefan Katzenbeisser	TU Darmstadt, Germany
Ella Kolkowska	Swedish Business School, Örebro University, Sweden
Robert Kolmhofer	University of Applied Sciences Upper Austria, Austria
Christian Kraetzer	Otto-von-Guericke University Magdeburg, Germany
Romain Laborde	Institut de Recherche en Informatique de Toulouse (IRIT), France
Jorn Lapon	KU Leuven, Technology Campus Ghent, Belgium
Herbert Leitold	Secure Information Technology Center (A-SIT), Austria

Javier Lopez   University of Malaga, Spain
Keith Martin   Royal Holloway, University of London, UK
Chris Mitchell   Royal Holloway, University of London, UK
Yuko Murayama   Iwate Prefectural University, Japan
Vincent Naessens   KU Leuven, Technology Campus Ghent,
                                   Belgium
Eiji Okomoto   University of Tsukuba, Japan
Chandrasekaran
   Pandurangan   Indian Institute of Technology, India
Günther Pernul   University of Regensburg, Germany
Alessandro Piva   University of Florence, Italy
Franz-Stefan Preiss   IBM Research - Zurich, Switzerland
Jean-Jacques Quisquater   Université catholique de Louvain, Belgium
Kai Rannenberg   Goethe University Frankfurt, Germany
Carlos Ribeiro   Instituto Superior Técnico, Portugal
Sergi Robles   Universitat Autònoma de Barcelona, Spain
Pierangela Samarati   Università degli Studi di Milano, Italy
Riccardo Scandariato   KU Leuven, Belgium
Ingrid Schaumüller-Bichl   University of Applied Sciences Upper Austria,
                                   Austria
Jörg Schwenk   Ruhr University Bochum, Germany
Stefaan Seys   KU Leuven, Belgium
Herman Sikora   Johannes Kepler University of Linz, Austria
Einar Snekkenes   Gjøvik University College, Norway
Andreas Uhl   University of Salzburg, Austria
Umut Uludag   Scientific and Technological Research
                                   Council (TUBITAK), Turkey
Pedro Veiga   University of Lisbon, Portugal
Claus Vielhauer   Brandenburg University of Applied Sciences,
                                   Germany
Tatjana Welzer   University of Maribor, Slovenia
Andreas Westfeld   Dresden University of Applied Sciences,
                                   Germany
Ted Wobber   Microsoft Research Silicon Valley, USA
Shouhuai Xu   University of Texas at San Antonio, USA
Gansen Zhao   South China Normal University, China
Ge Zhang   Karlstad University, Sweden
André Zúquete   IEETA, University of Aveiro, Portugal

Reviews

Cristina Alcaraz   University of Malaga, Spain
Philippe De Ryck   KU Leuven, Belgium
Michael Diener   University of Regensburg, Germany
Jingtao Li   Fudan University, China

Tarik Moataz	Télécom Bretagne, France
Roel Peeters	KU Leuven, Belgium
Sarah Louise Renwick	Royal Holloway, University of London, UK
Ahmad Sabouri	Goethe University Frankfurt, Germany
Thomas Zefferer	Graz University of Technology, Austria

Sponsoring Institutions

DETI / IEETA, University of Aveiro, Portugal.

Table of Contents

Part III: Extended Abstracts

Part IV: Keynotes

Part I

Research Papers

Malicious MPLS Policy Engine Reconnaissance

Abdulrahman Al-Mutairi[2] and Stephen Wolthusen[1,2]

[1] Norwegian Information Security Laboratory,
Department of Computer Science,
Gjøvik University College, Norway
[2] Information Security Group,
Department of Mathematics,
Royal Holloway, University of London, UK
{Abdulrahman.Almutairi.2009,stephen.wolthusen}@rhul.ac.uk

Abstract. *Multi-Protocol Label Switching* (MPLS) is widely used on telecommunications carrier and service provider backbone networks, complex network infrastructures, and also for the interconnection of distributed sites requiring guaranteed quality of service (QoS) and service levels such as the financial services sector, government and public safety, or control networks such as the electric power grid.

MPLS is a policy-based system wherein router behaviour is determined not only by the base protocols, but also by a set of further policies that network operators will typically wish not to reveal. However, sophisticated adversaries are known to conduct network reconnaissance years before executing actual attacks, and may also wish to conduct *deniable* attacks that may not be visible as such that appear as service degradation or which will cause re-configuration of paths in the interest of the attacker. In this paper we therefore describe a *probing algorithm* and a model of MPLS state space allowing an adversary to learn about the policies and policy state of an MPLS speaker. In spite of the restrictions on the adversary, our probing algorithm revealed the policy states of non-directly connected routers. Also, we analyse the confirmed information using a Bayesian network and provide simulative validation of our findings.

Keywords: Multi-protocol Label Switching, Real-Time Networks, Quality of Service, Reconnaissance, Bayesian networks.

1 Introduction

The *Multi-Protocol Label Switching* (MPLS) protocol provides a highly efficient mechanism for packet forwarding based on a *label switching* approach that seeks to reduce the need for explicit per-packet routing in wide-area networks by pre-identifying optimum paths to the final destination, thereby allowing intermediate routers to forward information traffic based on a once-applied label rather than an explicit lookup at each intervening router. This is of interest not only for network operators seeking to improve the effective throughput of routers and

B. De Decker and A. Zúquete (Eds.): CMS 2014, LNCS 8735, pp. 3–18, 2014.
© IFIP International Federation for Information Processing 2014

overhead required, but also particularly for applications where so-called *flows* can be identified. Consequently flows that share common characteristics such as source and destination as well as other service characteristics could be treated in the same way. By analysing flow requirements and characteristics, it is thus possible to also provide a defined *quality of service* (QoS) for a flow, typically through a process of resource reservation. This is crucial for network operators seeking to accommodate traffic on consolidated IP networks that may also be sensitive, e.g., to real-time characteristics.

Where adversaries seek to analyse and ultimately disrupt service availability such as by disabling and impeding links or routers, a first step will need to be the analysis of network behaviour, which is determined not only by the basic MPLS protocol and real-time or QoS extensions, but also by a number of policies. The revelation of the used policies may not be considered as a vulnerability, but that would make the attack more easy for an adversary and assist or enable the adversary to launch accurate attacks against the policy engines as this type of attacks is referred to as foot-printing attacks [1]. For example, such information would assist the attacker to estimate to what extent the manipulation of labels would propagate or the sensitivity of MPLS networks to sudden changes in specific MPLS nodes. A main purpose of this paper is therefore to study the ability of attackers to learn about the configured policies on MPLS routers whilst having access to limited resources using a limited and legitimate probing within the MPLS network.

The remainder of this paper is structured as follows: we review related work on MPLS security analyses and policy reverse engineering in section 2, followed by a description of the MPLS policy engine in general. A simplified policy model employed for subsequent analysis is introduced in section 3. We then provide a description of the policy state analysis framework in section 4 and study the validity and mapping of our model onto a simulated instantiation in section 5. Then, we introduce a probability model for the confirmed traces left by each of the MPLS policies as well as the relationships among MPLS policies themselves in section 6. We conclude with a brief discussion and summary of our findings as well as an outlook on on-going research in section 7.

2   Related Work

In policy-based protocols among peer networks, the policy under which a network operates must be considered sensitive as this may, e.g., reveal commercial information for operators or can have security implications as it allows adversaries to deliberately target policy behaviour. Research in this area has been largely limited to the exterior Border Gateway Protocol (BGP) [2] where a more state information is revealed in a larger body of security analysis [3–5].

However, few research studies have been conducted on MPLS, generally in the field of integrity and availability. The MPLS label distribution protocol (LDP) was analysed by Guernsey *et al.* [6]. Guernsey *et al.* demonstrated several exploits that may cause route modification, traffic injection and Denial-of-Service

(DoS) mainly by BGP update messages poisoning or directly injecting malicious traffic into Label Switched Paths (LSPs). Grayson *et al.* [7] provided a further analysis of MPLS security with special emphasis on the use of MPLS to realise Virtual Private Networks (VPNs). Mainly, the authors focused on route injection and traffic injection attacks and paid some attention to DoS-type attacks, but placed less emphasis on the reconnaissance and targeted quality of service (QoS) degradation resulting in policy-driven attacks that we are considering in this paper. It should be noted that DoS or integrity violations might not be the main objectives of attacks where the adversary aims to affect the QoS of the routed traffic. The failure to realise such facts in networks operation may have long-lasting impacts on QoS and the direction of flows that go far beyond transitive faults [8].

The main alternative for the MPLS control plane to LDP is the extension of existing protocols for signalling; this is realised both in the form of Traffic Engineering extension of Resource Reservation protocol (RSVP-TE) and Multi-Protocol Extension for BGP (MP-BGP). The security properties of RSVP-TE were studied by Spainhower *et al.* [11]. The authors demonstrated some reconnaissance and DoS attacks. The introduced reconnaissance attacks aim to reveal the record route object (RRO) in the reservation message that contains some topology information, e.g., core addresses as well as the identification of MPLS ingress. However, in our work we aim to reveal the MPLS nodes' states rather than the network topology.

The security properties of MP-BGP, on the other hand, were studied by Liorens and Serhouchni [12]. The authors introduced the notion of using Bayesian networks for defining an approach to penetrate VPNs in order to rank the VPNs perimeter and deciding the probability of the best VPN perimeter to ensure VPNs isolation and integrity in MP-BGP protocol. We are going to use the Bayesian network in slightly different way to demonstrate the probability of different MPLS policies and the relationships amongst them.

The analysis and reverse-engineering of inter-domain routing policies has, e.g., been studied by Machiraju and Katz [2] who proposed a technique for BGP routing policies' reverse engineering by examining the BGP updates in order to reveal local preferences used by Autonomous Systems (ASs). Similarly, Wang and Gao [13] introduced a method to characterise routing policies used in the Internet. Wang and Gao could infer the route preference that influences route selection in import policies by associating local preference values to the inferred relationships among ASs. In addition, the author could infer the export policies that are used for controlling the inbound traffic. Furthermore, Liang *et al.* [14] developed a model to infer routing policy for individual ISPs. Basically, Liang *et al.* aimed to abstract the policy patterns from BGP routing tables and then group the collected data for translation into the high-level policy objectives as a method of routing policy reverse engineering. Liang *et al.* claimed that the developed model achieves over 78.94% average accuracy in routing policy inference.

Siganos and Faloutsos [3] developed a tool (Nemesis) to infer business relationships of ASs by parsing and restoring the information found in Internet Routing

Registries (IRRs) in an easy relational database. Basically, the authors' methodology was to convert the simple text polices into equivalent link-level policies, infer the business relations of ASs (customers, peers and providers), then validate the results against the BGP routing updates to check the consistency of IRRs. Alternatively, Ming et al. [15] applied reverse engineering techniques in order to reveal the actions taken by certain ASs in response to false announcements in false Multiple Origin AS (MOAS) events using BGP updates. Ming et al. concluded that the bad announcements are not only arising from the originating AS, but other ASs took early actions to withdraw such bad announcements.

To the best of our knowledge, all of the existing studies on routing policy inference are based on BGP updates and mostly aim to reveal the import and export routing policies rather than the other policies that might affect the routing operation such as the MPLS policies, thereby making a direct application of these results difficult. Going beyond this, our aim is to reveal the more limited MPLS state information by analysing the actual effects on signalling behaviour.

3   MPLS Policy Engine

Network operators and service providers employ routing policies not only for the sake of efficiency, e.g., load balancing, but also for business relationships or other operational and political factors that are hard to consider in the classic shortest path routing. Unfortunately, there are many routing policies to be considered and hard to be defined in addition to the complexity of the policies implementation which is well known as an error prone process [16,17].

In addition, MPLS networks are associated with other mechanisms such as Differentiated Services (DiffServ) or Traffic Engineering (TE) in order to deliver QoS [18] which would result in more complicated policies other than those found in IP based routing networks. However, there is a certain number of policies in the pure implementation of MPLS and included in the MPLS architecture design [19] as well as in LDP specification [20].

Mainly, MPLS networks treat packets based on common classes which are known as Flow Equivalent Classes (FECs) where each FEC presents a group of packets to be treated in the same manner. Furthermore, each FEC is bound to a unique label before each MPLS enabled router or what is known as Label Switch Routers (LSR) could treat them differently as configured. For that reason, there are certain policies used to govern the way of binding labels to FECs and exchanging of the bindings among LSRs as well as the way of treating packets differently.

Policies in MPLS could be divided into two main classes. The first class is *traffic policy* class which governs the operation carried by LSRs on traffic as per packet by packet. Generally, once each LSR receives a packet, it would carry one of the label operations (push, swap, pop or drop) on it based on the configured policies. It should be noted that the only label operations could be done on unlabeled packets, usually by the MPLS ingress LSRs, are push and drop operation. Then, each packet is scheduled and buffered according to the experiment field (EXP) of MPLS label which has 3 bits (8 values) that could be sorted as different classes of services to be delivered in each LSR separately which is defined by Per-Hop-Behaviour (PHB). Moreover, each LSR could readjust that field depending on the configured policies. The other type is the label policies that are related to the management of labels inside the MPLS domain.

The other class of policies is the *label management* class. The label bindings could be distributed to other LSRs that have not explicitly requested them when *Unsolicited Downstream* (UD) label distribution policy is configured. Alternatively, the upstream LSR has to explicitly request the label bindings from the next LSR when *Downstream on Demand* (DD) label distribution policy is used. In addition, there are two policies govern label allocation in each LSR. The first policy is called *Independent Label Allocation* (ILA) where each LSR assigns a label to the recognised FEC whether or not it received the label assignment from the next hop. However, LSRs need to receive a label assignment for specific FEC in order to create and propagate their own label bindings in the *Ordered Control* (OC) label allocation policy. Also, there are two policies control labels retention strategy as LSRs may receive multiple labels but only use one of them. The *Liberal Retention* (LR) policy keeps the received labels even if they are unused. Alternatively, the *Conservative Retention* (CR) policy leads the LSR to only keep the labels those are used previously and discard the unused ones.

State Space Reduction
As the two MPLS policy classes mentioned above have essential differences in functionality, setting a restriction on the MPLS policy engine state space by focusing on one of the policy classes would unify and increase the accuracy of the analysis in later sections. While, traffic policies could be generalised by how the LSPs are managed as the routing in MPLS is based on per-flow basis rather than per-packet basis and influences certain flows rather than the MPLS environment, analysis of such policies is beyond the scope of this work and would be investigated in future work. Instead, we concentrate on the analysis of the label management policies that concern with label distribution, allocation and retention strategies.

In addition, the label management policy state space could be reduced due to the limitation of our simulation tool as well as the dynamical nature of certain policies which leave a unified trace. According to Andersson et al. [20], when implementing DD policy with ILA policy which we refer to as ID policy, LSR would answer the requested label binding immediately without waiting for label binding from next hop. On the other hand, LSR would advertise label bindings to its LSR peers whenever it is prepared to label switch those FECs when it is operating in ILA policy with UD policy which we refer to as IU. However, a LSR that is operating in OC policy must only issue a label mapping after receiving a label mapping from the egress LSR.

The label retention policy is going to be addressed only in section 6 due to the limitation of our simulation tool where only CR policy is applicable. Knowledge of retention policy is critical for our analysis because it represents one of the three main operation policies in MPLS network. Also, there are some dependency could be drawn among these MPLS operation policies. For example, CR policy is typically implemented with DoD policy unlike the case with UD which may implement one of the retention policies fairly [20].

Therefore, the state space we are interested in is restricted in our simulation to a set of three policy states which we denote by S. The set of policy states are Independent Unsolicited (IU), Independent Downstream on Demand (ID) and Ordered Control (OC). Formally, each policy state s is an element of the policy state set S as $s \in S : IU, ID, OC$. All of the three policy states mentioned above are mutually exclusive. Moreover, two of the policy states which are (IU & ID) represent four policies combined together as the IU policy represents ILA policy and UD policy, also the ID policy represents ILA policy and DD policy. However, the third policy state (OC) represents only one policy for two reasons. The first reason is due to the limitation of our simulation tool which only implements OC policy with UD policy. The second reason that the allocation policy OC was taken as an independent state is because the implementation of OC policy dominates other policies, particularly the label distribution policies, i.e., UD & DD. In other words, if any label request message was sent to the egress LSR, each LSR in MPLS domain receive that message would forward it towards the egress LSR as well as forwarding the response, i.e., mapping message from the egress towards the ingress LSR.

4   Policy Engine State Analysis Design

In this part of the paper, we would like to introduce the analysis framework which includes the assumptions and facts that our analysis of MPLS policy engine states is based on. We used NS-2 [21] network simulator in our analysis study. NS-2 is a discrete events simulator that has an extension model for MPLS. Our analysis design consists of the network model, adversary model, probing elements and simulation scenario as follows:

4.1   Network Model

Our network is based on pure MPLS implementation for the sake of simplicity and generality. Network topology is assumed to be stable and unchanged throughout the analysis process, e.g., no new addition or removal of nodes). Each LSR is trusted to process and response accurately to the received LDP signals, also the possibility of signals loss is excluded as well as all cases of channel errors, e.g., channel loose). Even though, the instability, connectivity or changing of nodes states could benefit our adversary to observe most of the needed information passively, the same assumption could affect the accuracy of our probing process.

There are two sources of traffic represented by node-0 and node-1 to two destinations presented by node-14 and node-15 respectively. Also there are twelve LSRs represented by LSR-2,...,LSR-13 where the network ingress

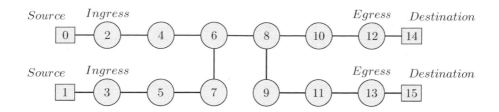

Fig. 1. MPLS Network Topology

and egress edges are LSR-2&3 and LSR-12&13 respectively as shown in figure 1. Each two adjacent LSRs are connected by at most one link. There are two flows which are assigned to FEC-14&15 and pass through the path on node-0→LSR-2→LSR-4→LSR-6→LSR-8→LSR-10→LSR-12→node-14 and the path on node-1→LSR-3→LSR-5→LSR-7→LSR-6→LSR-8→LSR-9→LSR-11→LSR-13→node-15 respectively. It should be noted that this simple network has been chosen for illustration purposes, also to distribute flows throughout the MPLS domain without using traffic engineering which would add a complex routing decision possibility according to the configured policies.

For example, in case of a resource release scenario, different back-up LSPs could be used for forwarding the affected flows, the ingress LSR could communicate with the LSRs alongside the torn-down LSP immediately or different actions could be taken by each LSR that receives the affected flows according to the configured policies on it. Also, the added restrictions on our adversary, as we will see later, limit the ability of probing non-directly connected node. However, there is a possibility that our adversary could discover and manipulate the non-directly connected LSRs by using different exist signalling mechanisms which is beyond the scope of this work and have been avoided by our network model. For example, the adversary could use the LDP extended discovery mechanism which is a mechanism that allows LSRs to establish sessions with potential LDP peers [20], otherwise the adversary could just trick the non-directly connected LSR to exchange fake labels for malicious intents.

4.2 Adversary Model

Most of the service providers and network operators make sure that their network edges and core nodes are well configured and physically secured which reduces the chances of the compromised node scenario [22], hence the compromised node scenario is excluded from our adversary model. We are going to extract a restricted adversary model which we refer to as a probing adversary following the same method that was introduced by Al-Mutairi and Wolthusen [23] to extract MPLS adversary models. Basically, the method was to extract a specific

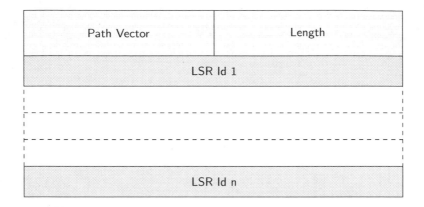

Fig. 2. Path Vector TLV

adversary model for a specific analysis purposes from an abstracted framework for the adversarial properties of any adversary that could emerge in MPLS networks.

Therefore, we assume the adversary to have knowledge about the physical information of the network topology, e.g., topological address information. Also, the adversary has access to control information regarding the labels of related flows and can identify them. Moreover, we assume the probing adversary to have access to at most one arbitrary chosen core link which is the link between LSR-6 and LSR-8 with a write/read operation. Also, the probing adversary is capable of fabricating and sending LDP signalling messages to the LSRs that are attached to the compromised link.

4.3   Probe Elements

The main task of LDP is the establishment of adjacency relationships among peer LSRs and mapping the FECs into the established LSPs [20]. Therefore, we are going to use LDP messages, particularly, label withdraw and release messages in our probing processes to stimulate LSRs to communicate among each other for adversarial analysis. It should be noted that the label withdraw message is sent towards the ingress (imposing) LSR of the withdrawn label and the label release message is sent towards the egress (deposing) LSR of the released label. Also, LDP signalling messages have a common structure that uses type length value (TLV) encoding scheme which would typically include path vector TLV. Path vector TLV records the path of LSRs that label request and mapping messages have traversed [20]. Basically, the path that the message has traversed is presented as a list of router-Ids as shown in figure 2. Each LSR Id is the first four octets of the LDP Identifier for the corresponding LSR for the sake of uniqueness within the MPLS network.

4.4   Simulation Scenarios

We configured all of the LSRs with the policy engine states (IU, ID, OC) one by one in order to analyse the traces left by each state and the ability of our adversary to reveal the LSRs policy engine state. In each one of the above scenarios, the adversary sent release messages for the label related to FEC-14&15 towards LSR-6 as well as withdraw messages for the label related to the same FECs towards LSR-8 and waits for replies from the affected LSRs for analysis purposes in order to reveal the LSRs policy engine states as every policy engine state has a different allocation process.

5   Analysis Results

In this part of the paper we are going to introduce a description of the validation of the probing process and the affect that was noticed on LSRs. Then, we are going to show the ability of our adversary to reveal LSRs policy engine states.

5.1   Probing Process Validation

The probing messages that were sent by our adversary propagated differently through LSRs according to the method that was used to allocate the related labels, i.e., upstream or downstream allocation. While, label withdraw messages were successfully propagated to the ingress LSRs in all cases and the label entries were removed from the upstream nodes (LSR-2,3,4,5,6,7), released messages only propagated in case the released label was upstream allocated and the label entries were removed from downstream nodes (LSR-8,9,10,11,12,13). However, label release messages failed to propagate in case the label was downstream allocated. This problem could be mitigated by our adversary by sending a downstream label mapping or request message depending on the configured policy for the downstream node which is LSR-8. Consequently, after the label entries were removed, the affected LSRs responded differently according to the configured policy as following:

- **Independent Unsolicited (IU):** Label mappings for the withdrawn and released labels were sent independently from LSR-2,3,4,5,6,7,8,9,10,11,12,13.
- **Independent Downstream on Demand (ID):** Label requests for the withdrawn and released label were sent from LSR-2,3,4,5,6,7,8,9,10,11,12,13 and independent label mappings were sent by the peer LSRs in response to the request messages.
- **Ordered Control (OC):** Label requests for the withdrawn labels were sent from the ingress LSR-2&3 to LSR-8. It should be noted that LSR-8 did not forward the request messages for the withdrawn labels because it already has received the label binding from the egress LSRs, hence LSR-8 answered the request messages immediately and sent the label bindings for FEC-14&15. However, a label request for the released label were sent only from LSR-10&11 for the penultimate hop popping mechanism [19]. Clearly, sending a request message to LSR-8 would mitigate this problem by stimulating the downstream LSRs to intervene in the label allocation processes.

5.2 Policy Reveal

Our simulation has showed different responses to the used probes which we used to reveal the policy states for directly connected LSRs. For the non-directly connected peers we analysed the TLV path vector that is included in the mapping or request messages to discover the LSRs that the messages propagated through. The following policy reveal algorithm 1 was used to analyse the response by the direct LSRs and try to reveal the policy states of other LSRs in the MPLS domain.

Given the LDP signals, the algorithm outputs the policy states for specific LSRs. The algorithm takes the LDP message LDP_m related to the withdrawn/released label l as an input and checks if it is a request for the label REQ_l where the request message is processed to check if the TLV entry includes the ingress LSR to assign all of the LSRs found in TLV entry to the OC state otherwise the LSRs in the TLV entry are set to ID state. However, if it was a mapping message MAP_l, all of LSRs found in TLV entry are set to IU state.

Algorithm 1. Policy Reveal Algorithm

Require: LDP messages LDP_m on the compromised link
Ensure: The policy states S of LSRs
  $S[n]$ where n is the number of LSRs
  if $LDP_m = REQ_l$ **then**
    if $TLV[1] = 1$ **then**
      for all $i \in TLV$ **do**
        $x = TLV[i]$;
        $S[x] = OC$
      end for
    else
      for all $i \in TLV$ **do**
        $x = TLV[i]$;
        $S[x] = ID$;
      end for
    end if
  else if $LDP_m = MAP_l$ **then**
    for all $i \in TLV$ **do**
      $x = TLV[i]$;
      $S[x] = IU$;
    end for
  end if
  return S

The results that our adversary gained from the reconnaissance probing using the policy reveal algorithm 1 to reveal the policy state of LSRs in MPLS domain are listed below for each one of the configured policy states with a brief description of the results:

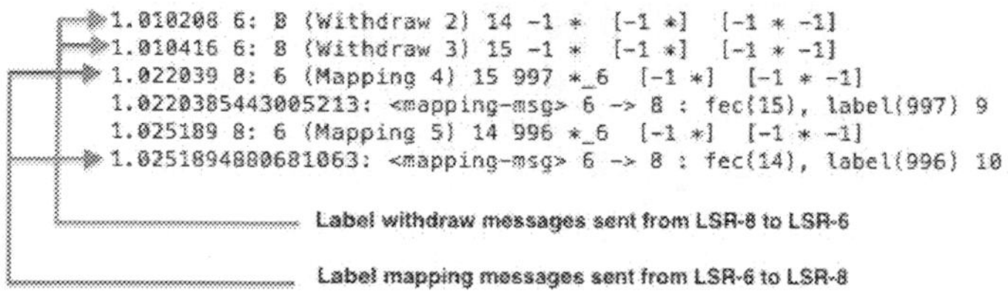

```
1.010208 6: 8 (Withdraw 2) 14 -1 *  [-1 *]  [-1 * -1]
1.010416 6: 8 (Withdraw 3) 15 -1 *  [-1 *]  [-1 * -1]
1.022039 8: 6 (Mapping 4) 15 997 *_6  [-1 *]  [-1 * -1]
1.0220385443005213: <mapping-msg> 6 -> 8 : fec(15), label(997) 9
1.025189 8: 6 (Mapping 5) 14 996 *_6  [-1 *]  [-1 * -1]
1.0251894880681063: <mapping-msg> 6 -> 8 : fec(14), label(996) 10
```

Label withdraw messages sent from LSR-8 to LSR-6

Label mapping messages sent from LSR-6 to LSR-8

Fig. 3. Independent Unsolicited state response to the probing withdraw message

```
1.010208 6: 8 (Withdraw 5) 14 -1 *  [-1 *]  [-1 * -1]
1.010416 6: 8 (Withdraw 6) 15 -1 *  [-1 *]  [-1 * -1]
1.021975 8: 6 (Request 5) 15 -1 *_6  [-1 *]  [-1 * -1]
1.025125 8: 6 (Request 6) 14 -1 *_6  [-1 *]  [-1 * -1]
1.032311 6: 8 (Mapping 7) 15 3 *  [5 *]  [-1 * -1]
1.0323105443005214: <mapping-msg> 8 -> 6 : fec(15), label(3) 8
1.032775 6: 7 (Request 4) 15 -1 *_7  [-1 *]  [-1 * -1]
1.034859 6: 4 (Request 4) 14 -1 *_4  [-1 *]  [-1 * -1]
1.035461 6: 8 (Mapping 8) 14 4 *  [6 *]  [-1 * -1]
1.0354614880681063: <mapping-msg> 8 -> 6 : fec(14), label(4) 8
1.046279 8: 6 (Request 7) 14 -1 *_4_6  [-1 *]  [-1 * -1]
```

Label withdraw messages sent from LSR-8 to LSR-6

Label request messages sent from LSR-6 to LSR-8
including TLV path vector

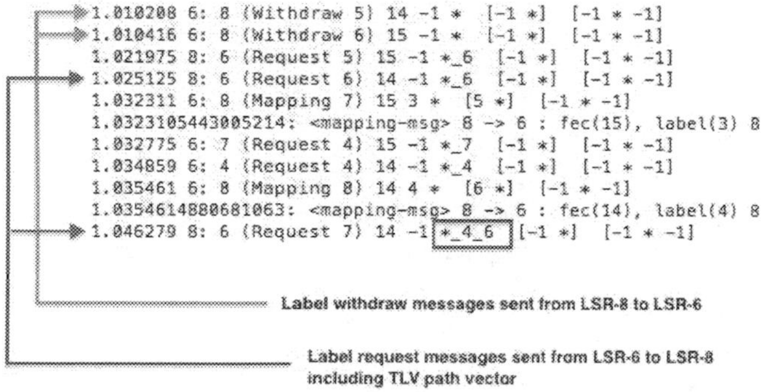

Fig. 4. Independent Downstream on Demand state response to the probing withdraw message

- **Independent Unsolicited (IU):** Only LSR-6 state has been confirmed as shown in figure 3. Theoretically, at least LSR-8 state should be confirmed too in case it sends a mapping message to LSR-6 [1].
- **Independent Downstream on Demand (ID):** The upstream LSRs (LSR-6&4) states have been confirmed as shown in figure 4. Theoretically, even the downstream LSR (LSR-8) state should be revealed by sending a request message to LSR-6.
- **Ordered Control (OC):** The upstream LSRs (LSR-2,3,4,5,6,7) states have been confirmed as shown in figure 5.

Obviously, the reported results have been captured by a restricted adversary with a limited ability and a very simple and stable environment, i.e., network model where some relaxation of restriction on both models (adversary or network model) would reveal more information about other LSRs in MPLS domain. For example a slight change on the network model such as assuming there is another

---

[1] All or some of the upstream LSRs states could be revealed depending on the time that LSR-6 takes to send the mapping messages for the withdrawn labels.

```
 →1.010208 6:  8 (Withdraw 5) 14 -1 *   [-1 *]   [-1 * -1]
 →1.010416 6:  8 (Withdraw 6) 15 -1 *   [-1 *]   [-1 * -1]
  1.054896 6:  4 (Request 5) 14 -1 * 2 4   [-1 *]   [-1 * -1]
 →1.065723 8:  6 (Request 7) 14 -1 * 2 4 6  [-1 *]   [-1 * -1]
  1.076039 6:  7 (Request 5) 15 -1 * 3 5 7  [-1 *]   [-1 * -1]
  1.076059 6:  8 (Mapping 7) 14 0 *   [7 *]   [-1 * -1]
  1.0760588214014397: <mapping-msg>  8 -> 6 : fec(14), label(0) 8
 →1.087671 8:  6 (Request 8) 15 -1 * 3 5 7 6  [-1 *]   [-1 * -1]
 ───────────── Label withdraw messages sent from LSR-8 to LSR-6

 ───────────── Label request messages sent from LSR-6 to LSR-8
                including TLV path vector
```

Fig. 5. Order Control state response to the probing withdraw message

source of flow that is routed in the opposite direction would reveal at least the policy state of LSR-8 in case it was running on IU policy state, the policy states of LSR-8,9,10 in case they were running on ID policy state and LSR-8,9,10,11,12,13 in case they were running on OC policy state. Alternatively, making a relaxation of restrictions on adversary model by giving the adversary a read access on more links (in the worst case n/2 links where n denotes the number of LSRs) would reveal the policy state of all LSRs in all cases with no need to analyse the TLV entry that is included in each LDP messages.

6   MPLS Policy States Probability

The results we gained from the simulation in addition to the knowledge we have about different policy states in MPLS network could be represented in Bayesian Network (BN). Our main aim here is to be able to give approximate estimation about how much to reveal about the policy state by getting some information related to them and to what extent in order to demonstrate the probability of revealing MPLS policies with zero or less prior information.

The BN could answer some useful questions about the probability of the policy states, for example, if a label allocation for the origin LSR's FEC was observed what is the probability that the origin LSR is on independent unsolicited mode. Therefore, we need to define the random variables those playing the roles in MPLS policies after describing the scenario we are interested to model.

Problem Domain
There are three mutually exclusive states that we suppose each LSR in MPLS domain to have, which are: Independent Unsolicited (IU), Independent Downstream on Demand (ID) or Ordered Control (OC). By having the first state implemented on any LSR, the label allocation of a known FEC will highly be sent to the directly connected peer independently, however a request for label mapping of that FEC will never be sent. On the other hand, a label allocation will not be sent from a node with ID or OC states (except as an answer for a request), however a label request will be sent for the recognised FEC. The

other involved concept is whether the node implements the liberal or conservative retention mode because as we mentioned in section 3 that typically ID will include conservative retention mode other than the liberal mode.

Consequently, the LSR policy state could be presented in various methods, but, the simplest method is to use the graph structure of Bayesian Network to represent policy states (IU, ID, OC) as well as the retention policy and traces found on the simulation where the root node is State (S) and the leaf nodes under the root node are Label Allocation (L) and Label Retention as shown in figure 6. The theoritcial foundation of BN is the Bayes rule:

$$p(h|e) = \frac{p(e|h).p(h)}{p(e)} \tag{1}$$

As $p(h)$ is the prior probability of hypothesis h, $p(e)$ is the prior probability of evidence e, $p(h|e)$ is the probability of h given e and $p(e|h)$ is the probability of e given h. Our BN has a root node S that has three values (IU, ID or OC). The probability of a node having an explicit state is represented by $p(S = IU)$, $p(S = ID)$ and $p(S = OC)$ respectively. Unfortunately, the prior probability for the our root nodes is not available. Therefore, we are going to chose an equi-probable condition for each node. It should be noted that when we reduced the state space for MPLS policies, we specified the three policies based on the label allocation policies, i.e., ILA & OC policy. Which means that the prior probability for each one of the label allocation policy is set to 0.5. Hence, the prior probability of ILA policy should be equally divided between the other two policies, i.e, IU & ID and set to 0.25 for each policy. The prior probability of each root node is calculated as per the following equation:

$$p(S) = p(S = IU) + p(S = ID) + p(S = OC) = 1 \tag{2}$$

The leaf nodes under the root node represent the other policy (retention mode) that would be associated with the MPLS state and the traces observed on MPLS simulation (label allocation). Each leaf node is associated with a conditional probability table (CPT). The retention mode node, denoted by R, includes two values as "Conservative" and "Liberal". The label allocation node, denoted by L, includes two values as "Label Assignment" and "Request". The CPTs correspond to both nodes are shown in Table: 1 and Table: 2 respectively. Each column follows one constraint, which corresponds to one value of the root node. The sum of values of each column is equal to 1. $p(R = "Conservative"|S = IU)$ is the conditional probability with the condition that the state is independent unsolicited which is 0.5 in the first entry of Table: 1. It measures the probability that the MPLS node is implementing conservative retention mode, given the state as independent unsolicited and so on with the other entries in both CPTs.

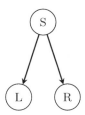

Fig. 6. Bayesian network model

Table 1. The CPT for node R

State	S=IU	S=ID	S=OC
Conservative	0.5	0.9	0.5
Liberal	0.5	0.1	0.5

By filling the entries in CPTs of MPLS node states BN, the probability of the MPLS node's state could be computed in different aspects by using the Bayes rules. For example, $p(S = IU|R = "Conservative")$ gives the probability that the MPLS node's state is IU by knowing that it is in conservative mode, $p(S = IU|R = "Liberal")$ gives the probability that the MPLS node's state is IU by knowing that it is in liberal mode, while, $p(S = IU|R = "Conservative", L = "LabelAssignment")$ gives the probability that the MPLS node's state is independent unsolicited by knowing that it is in conservative mode and a label assignment has been observed.

Therefore, we could now fully specify the joint distribution for MPLS policy states using the following general equation:

$$p(S, R, L) = p(S)p(R|S)p(L|S) \qquad (3)$$

Using equation 6 we could calculate the possible twelve entries for the joint distribution over the three relevant variables S, R and L as shown in Table 3.

Table 2. The CPT for node L

State	S=IU	S=ID	S=OC
Label Assignment	1	0	0
Request	0	1	1

Table 3. The probability table for MPLS policy states

State	Retention Mode	Label Assignment	Probability
IU	Conservative	Label Allocation	$0.25 \times 0.5 \times 1 = 0.125$
IU	Conservative	Request	$0.25 \times 0.5 \times 0 = 0$
IU	Liberal	Label Allocation	$0.25 \times 0.5 \times 1 = 0.125$
IU	Liberal	Request	$0.25 \times 0.5 \times 0 = 0$
ID	Conservative	Label Allocation	$0.25 \times 0.9 \times 0 = 0$
ID	Conservative	Request	$0.25 \times 0.9 \times 1 = 0.225$
ID	Liberal	Label Allocation	$0.25 \times 0.1 \times 0 = 0$
ID	Liberal	Request	$0.25 \times 0.1 \times 1 = 0.025$
OC	Conservative	Label Allocation	$0.5 \times 0.5 \times 0 = 0$
OC	Conservative	Request	$0.5 \times 0.5 \times 1 = 0.25$
OC	Liberal	Label Allocation	$0.5 \times 0.5 \times 0 = 0$
OC	Liberal	Request	$0.5 \times 0.5 \times 1 = 0.25$

7 Conclusions

In this paper we analysed the problem of revealing the internal MPLS policy
engine state. We have, particularly, paid attention to policy parameters that are
based on a pure MPLS implementation. We analysed the ability of an adversary
with a limited capability to reveal MPLS policy engine states with simulation.
Also, based on our simulation findings as well as knowledge of MPLS specification, we modelled a Bayesian network to illustrate to what extent we could gain
information about some policies by getting information about other policies or
about the traces founds on MPLS networks.

Future work will seek to extend the policy model and states which could
be captured on one hand, but also will investigate different adversary models
and capabilities to understand how policy state information can best be kept
private. Building on this we are also developing novel attacks aiming to degrade
and disrupt MPLS flows both overtly and in deniable form, also focusing on
performance parameters relevant for quality of service.

References

1. McClure, S., Scambray, J., Kurtz, G.: Hacking exposed: network security secrets
   and solutions. McGraw-Hill (2009)
2. Machiraju, S., Katz, R.H.: Leveraging BGP Dynamics to Reverse-Engineer Routing
   Policies. Technical report (May 2006)
3. Siganos, G., Faloutsos, M.: Analyzing BGP Policies: Methodology and Tool. In:
   Proceedings of the Twenty-Third Annual Joint Conference of the IEEE Computer
   and Communications Societies (INFOCOM 2004), pp. 1640–1651 (March 2004)
4. Battista, G.D., Erlebach, T., Hall, A., Patrignani, M.: Computing the Types of the
   Relationships Between Autonomous Systems. IEEE/ACM Transactions on Networking 15(2), 267–280 (2007)

5. Cittadini, L., Battista, G.D., Rimondini, M., Vissicchio, S.: Wheel + Ring = Reel: The Impact of Route Filtering on the Stability of Policy Routing. IEEE/ACM Transactions on Networking 19(8), 1085–1096 (2011)
6. Guernsey, D., Engel, A., Butts, J., Shenoi, S.: Security Analysis of the MPLS Label Distribution Protocol. In: Moore, T., Shenoi, S. (eds.) Critical Infrastructure Protection IV. IFIP AICT, vol. 342, pp. 127–139. Springer, Heidelberg (2010)
7. Grayson, D., Guernsey, D., Butts, J., Spainhower, M., Shenoi, S.: Analysis of Security Threats to MPLS Virtual Private Networks. International Journal of Critical Infrastructure Protection 2(4), 146–153 (2009)
8. Bilski, T.: Fluctuations and Lasting Trends of QoS on Intercontinental Links. In: Bartolini, N., Nikoletseas, S., Sinha, P., Cardellini, V., Mahanti, A. (eds.) QShine 2009. LNICST, vol. 22, pp. 251–264. Springer, Heidelberg (2009)
9. Alkahtani, A.M., Woodward, M.E., Al-Begain, E.: An Overview of Quality of Service (QoS) and QoS Routing in Communication Networks. In: 4th PGNET 2003 Symposium, pp. 236–242 (2003)
10. Braden, B., Clark, D., Shenker, S.: Integrated service in the internet architecture: an overview. Program on Internet and Telecoms Convergence (1994)
11. Spainhower, M., Butts, J., Guernsey, D., Shenoi, S.: Security Analysis of RSVP-TE Signaling in MPLS Networks. International Journal of Critical Infrastructure Protection 1(1), 68–74 (2008)
12. Llorens, C., Serhrouchni, A.: Security Verification of a Virtual Private Network over MPLS. In: Network Control and Engineering for QoS, Security, and Mobility IV, pp. 339–353 (November 2007)
13. Wang, F., Gao, L.: On inferring and characterizing internet routing policies. In: Proceedings of the 3rd ACM SIGCOMM Conference on Internet Measurement, pp. 15–26. ACM (October 2003)
14. Liang, W., Bi, J., Xia, Y., Hu, C.: RPIM: Inferring BGP Routing Policies in ISP Networks. In: Global Telecommunications Conference (GLOBECOM 2011), pp. 1–6 (December 2011)
15. Ming, S., Wu, S., Zhao, X., Zhang, K.: On reverse engineering the management actions from observed BGP data. In: INFOCOM Workshops 2008, pp. 1–6 (April 2008)
16. Caesar, M., Rexford, J.: BGP routing policies in ISP networks. IEEE Network 19(6), 5–11 (2005)
17. Mahajan, R., Anderson, T.: Understanding BGP misconfiguration. ACM SIGCOMM Computer Communication Review 32(4), 3–16 (2002)
18. Awduchea, D.O., Jabbarib, B.: Internet traffic engineering using multi-protocol label switching (MPLS). Computer Networks 40(1), 111–129 (2002)
19. Rosen, E., Viswanathan, A., Callon, R.: Multiprotocol label switching architecture. IETF, RFC 3031 (January 2001)
20. Andersson, L., Doolan, P., Feldman, N., Fredette, A., Thomas, B.: LDP specification (October 2007)
21. Isi.edu: The Network Simulator - ns-2, http://www.isi.edu/nsnam/ns/ (accessed June 17, 2014)
22. Palmieri, F., Fiore, U.: Securing the MPLS control plane. In: Yang, L.T., Rana, O.F., Di Martino, B., Dongarra, J. (eds.) HPCC 2005. LNCS, vol. 3726, pp. 511–523. Springer, Heidelberg (2005)
23. Al-Mutairi, A.A., Wolthusen, S.D.: A Security Analysis of MPLS Service Degradation Attacks Based on Restricted Adversary Models. In: Information Security in Diverse Computing Environments. IGI Global (2014) (Print)

USB Connection Vulnerabilities on Android Smartphones: Default and Vendors' Customizations

André Pereira[1], Manuel Correia[1], and Pedro Brandão[2]

[1] Center for Research in Advanced Computing Systems (CRACS-INESC LA), Portugal
[2] Instituto de Telecomunicações, FCUP/UP, Portugal
{apereira,mcc,pbrandao}@dcc.fc.up.pt

Abstract. We expose an USB vulnerability in some vendors' customization of the android system, where the serial AT commands processed by the cellular modem are extended to allow other functionalities. We target that vulnerability for the specific vendor system and present a proof of concept of the attack in a realistic scenario environment. For this we use an apparently inoffensive smartphone charging station like the one that is now common at public places like airports. We unveil the implications of such vulnerability that culminate in flashing a compromised boot partition, root access, enable adb and install a surveillance application that is impossible to uninstall without re-flashing the android boot partition. All these attacks are done without user consent or knowledge on the attacked mobile phone.

Keywords: Android, Security, USB vulnerability, privileges escalation, vendor vulnerabilities.

1   Introduction

Nowadays the extended features that smartphones possess are crucial to explaining its success, we see a yearly increase of its market share over traditional phones. The extra features like phone banking, e-mail, GPS, together with the traditional features of phone calling and SMS make the smartphone essential to our daily lives and ease our existence in this day and age. These benefits lead us to expose our personal data increasingly more, as such, the security associated with these systems is essential.

The Android system composes 80% [1] of the worldwide market share, making it a big player on the smartphone business. Since it is an open source Operating System (OS), the research of vulnerabilities on the system is in the best interest of the community.

Vendor customization is one of the advantages of the Android ecosystem, but this is a double-edged sword, since it can introduce security breaches. Attackers could exploit different attack vectors on many of the different ROMs, as vendors add software, such as applications and system owned processes, for dealing with things like USB pairing. According to a recent study [2], vendor customization accounts for 60% of the vulnerabilities found in the Android ecosystem. We researched Samsung's Android customization and discovered the possibilities introduced to exploit the system.

B. De Decker and A. Zúquete (Eds.): CMS 2014, LNCS 8735, pp. 19–32, 2014.
© IFIP International Federation for Information Processing 2014

In this paper we present a newly found vector to exploit the USB connection, more precisely to a vendor customization that extends the AT commands[1]. The system understands and lets these commands be sent by USB. We also describe a proof of concept of the attack and a scenario where this attack could be used.

In the proof of concept, we were able to effectively flash a compromised boot partition without the user consent. This enabled the three main objectives of the attack: gain root access, enable adb[2] and install a surveillance application that is impossible to uninstall without re-flashing the android boot partition.

2   Attack Scenario

The main purpose of the attack is to explore the vulnerabilities found on the Android OS, namely the vulnerabilities found in its USB connection. This mandates that the attacker must possess a physical USB connection linking the computer of the attacker to the victim's device.

A practical scenario would be the installation of a public kiosk for charging devices' batteries. However, the true purpose would be to inject malicious code into the devices. Unbeknownst to this malicious purpose, the victim would willingly place its device in a compromised situation, hoping that it would charge the phone's batteries.

Such scenario could be very fruitful, as we expect easy acceptance by the victim to place the phone in such a manner. There are a couple of reasons for this. First the lack of knowledge of the dangers of an exposed USB connection. As this is such an uncommon practice, even an IT experienced user could possibly lack this knowledge. The second reason is the emergency state in which the victim is in. Nowadays our cellphone is an extension of ourselves, it is completely implanted in our daily life and the lack of it is unthinkable. This is even truer for smartphones, since you can perform additional tasks on it, like phone banking and e-mails. So a situation where the cellphone battery is empty or almost empty, would easily lead the victim to expose its device to the charging kiosk.

Given the nature of such an attack, a script is necessary on the computer holding the other end of the USB cable. A script capable of accurately detecting the smartphone, match its vulnerabilities and proceed with the attack. For example we would execute a different type of attack for different Android versions, for different firmware versions, as well as different brands and different products of those brands. As an example, in the Samsung smartphone family, we could have an attack for the Galaxy S2 and another attack using different vulnerabilities found for the Galaxy S4.

3   Vulnerabilities

The following vulnerabilities are used in the proof of concept described in the next section. We will first elaborate on said weaknesses and then describe the overall attack. Some vulnerabilities are documented commands, like the standard AT commands and others were discovered in our work. AT commands by themselves are not the vulnerability, but the vendors' implementation of them make them so.

---

[1] Serial commands for modem configuration and management.
[2] Android Debug Bridge [10].

3.1   AT COMMANDS

The AT commands (ATC) define a command language that was initially developed to communicate with Hayes Smartmodem. Nowadays it stands as the standard language to communicate with some types of modems. For example, protocols like GSM and 3GPP use this type of commands as a standard way of communicating with the modem. With ability to issue these commands to the modem, we are able to [3]:

- Issue calls;
- Send SMSs;
- Obtain contacts stored inside the SIM card;
- Alter the PIN.

In order to understand this attack vector, we need to comprehend how a modern smartphone works. A modern smartphone is built with two OSs, running in two very different environments [4]. On one hand we have the AP, Application Processor, where the android OS and all the applications with which the user interacts run. On the other we have the Baseband/Cellular Processor (BP/CP), where the entire cellular (ex.: GSM) communication is done and where the modem lies. Issuing AT commands is not the only way to communicate with the modem, but it is the most popular way, together with RPC (Remote Procedural Calls).

The RIL, Radio Interface Layer [5], is the layer on the OS responsible for establishing a communication between the android OS and the modem. If a component in the application framework needs to send messages or make calls, it uses the RIL in the application framework to do so.

Fig. 1 details the communication stack, from the applications to the baseband. Where in the application framework, the RIL uses the Linux IP stack as a way of communicating with the baseband, establishing the communication channel.

In our scenario we can use the USB connection to issue such commands. This vulnerability is only made possible due to the fact that some Android smartphone manufacturers, like Samsung and HTC, enable this through the USB channel. This means that it is possible to send, using the USB connection, AT commands directly to the baseband. We stress the fact that this is not a default feature of the Android OS, but manufacture added.

In a practical scenario, upon the detection of a new USB device, the driver responsible for that device recognizes that the device has a modem type of interface through the USB, notifying the OS of such. Hence forward the OS has a way of communicating with the modem, which can be used in our attack scenario. We can thus send AT commands to make phone calls or send SMS to premium cost numbers. This way making the attacker earn money, or more accurately stealing it.

Complementing this, some manufacturers extend this list, adding some proprietary commands, with the purpose of enabling control and capabilities that they want to have on the system. These commands are private and manufacturers do not publish them. But without the use of some form of encryption, anyone is able to eavesdrop the communication channel and try to understand, what lies under the system.

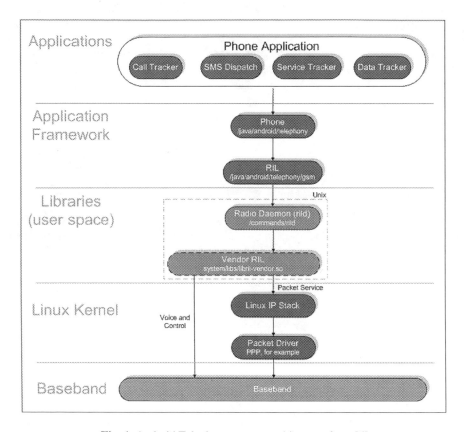

Fig. 1. Android Telephony system architecture from [6]

3.2   Vulnerabilities Discovered and AT Samsung Proprietary Commands

In the case of Samsung, a vast list of its family of smartphones has this vulnerability, where it is possible to communicate with the modem through the USB channel, without any previous configuration on the smartphone. This is something that does not happen with `adb`.

Samsung extends the standard AT command set that comes with the 3GPP and GSM standards adding their proprietary commands. This extends the capabilities of interaction that their computer software (Kies) has on the device.

In fact Kies for Windows uses both the standard set and the extended proprietary AT command set, to at least achieve the following operations:

- Obtain the contact book;
- Obtain the files in the SD card;
- Update the firmware on the cellphone.

Through eavesdropping methods[3], on the USB channel and watching the android `logcat`[4], it was possible to discover the way in which the Kies software interacts with the device to accomplish those tasks.

As mentioned, the Kies software uses a proprietary set of AT commands. To achieve this, several processes inside the smartphone parse the commands received, to know if it is just an ordinary AT command or a proprietary Samsung command. According to the result, it issues or not the command to the modem. The smartphone must be a Samsung phone and contain a valid Samsung ROM. The ROM has a chain of processes that intercept the commands sent by USB and send them or not to the modem.

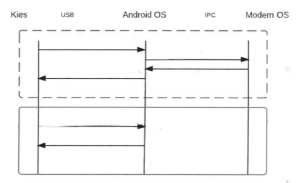

Fig. 2. Chain of communication when AT commands is sent through USB

In **Fig. 2** we are able to see in the red dashed box a non-proprietary AT command that the OS intercepts and sends to the modem. In the blue box we have an example of a flow for a proprietary command that is not sent to the modem.

If we use a program to communicate using the serial port (eg.: Realterm[5]), we can send commands to the modem through a virtual COM type, instantiated by the driver. When we issue the proprietary command AT+DEVCONINFO and analyze the Androids' `logcat`, we can see that there is a process with a tag dun_mgr that is listening to the USB channel. Initially it receives the command and delegates it to the process with the AT tag. This process executes it and responds to the original process, which forwards the response through the USB channel.

dun_mgr	AT command: at+devconinfo
at	ATcmd:0 at+devconinfo 14
at	AT_ProcessCharParserDataInd at cmd sent state=4
dun_mgr	atx response: ...

Fig. 3. `Logcat` of issuing AT command

---

[3] `http://www.sysnucleus.com/`, USBTrace: USB Protocol Analyzer.
[4] Android Logging System [19].
[5] Realterm is a terminal program specially designed for capturing, controlling and debugging binary and other data streams. [20].

This led us to conclude that there is an interception by the OS, before deciding whether to send the command to the modem or to the Android OS.

Command "AT+DEVCONINFO"

The execution of the proprietary command AT+DEVCONINFO, in addition to obtaining all the information displayed in **Fig. 4**, also triggers the smartphone to mount the SD card on the computer as a mass storage device. When we eavesdropped the USB connection, we could confirm that this was one of the firsts commands sent to the phone by the Kies software. This assists the program in gathering all the necessary information in order to work properly. As it can be seen in **Fig. 4**, the information includes the smartphones' firmware version, the phone model and IMEI.

Fig. 4. Response message from issuing AT+DEVCONINFO

With this functionality, it is possible to make an attack to steal all the information inside the SD card.

Command "AT+FUS?"

With the execution of AT+FUS? the smartphone is placed in download mode, which is the mode where all Samsung smartphones need to be in order to flash their internal partitions and thus update the smartphones' firmware. Normally putting the phone in download mode involves mechanical key pressing, i.e., input from the user, which implies acceptance to flash the phone. This is not the case when it is triggered by the AT command, no user intervention is needed, which enables an automation of this process. The discovery of this command, led us to conclude that this is the way that the Kies software uses to update the phone firmware. Download mode is similar to fastboot mode that you find in other Android smartphones, but in download mode we cannot use the fastboot tool included inside the android SDK, only Odin [7] and Heimdall [8] serve that purpose. They are both popular flashing software for Samsung devices. Odin is closed-source free flashing tool for windows and Heimdall is a cross-platform open-source tool suite.

This is the most damaging of the vulnerabilities, since we can alter the partitions inside the phone, explicitly injecting code on the partition that we want. The novelty of this attack, like the AT+DEVCONINFO command, is that no prior configuration is needed on the phone. We can do this, just right after the phone is bought. Placing the phone in download mode enables us to use Odin to flash the phone with malicious partitions.

3.3   ADB Enabled

It is important to mention `adb`, the android debug bridge, since later we use it to gain further capabilities on the system.

The `adb` serves as a means of communication between a computer (host) and a smartphone (device). The communication is done via USB, but it is also possible to configure the device so that the connection is made through WiFi.

An USB connection and an `adb` enabled Android, could pose a serious security threat to the smartphone, so serious that since Android version 4.2.2 [9] Google made a security enhancement to the `adb` connection. Making sure that every USB connection has an accepted RSA key pair with the host computer the android is connected to. So every new USB host the android smartphone tries to connected, needs to be previously accepted by the user.

With `adb` enabled we can [10]: **a)** get shell access to the device; **b)** install applications that were not verified by the Google app store bouncer[6]; **c)** uninstall applications; **d)** mount the SD card; **e)** read the contents of `logcat`; and **f)** start an application.

Shell access through `adb` could also unveil new attack vectors has shown in [11], were it is possible to gain privileged access, with rooting techniques like Super One-Click root [12] and also Cyndia impactor [13].

In fact Kyle Osborn presented in Derbycon 2012, a shell script suite[7] that uses `adb` to injected several rootkit malwares and tools, to help in the extraction of the screen pattern, user information and other data. Prior to that, in Defcon 2011, Joseph Mlodzianowski and Robert Rowley built a public charging kiosk, to raise awareness about the dangers with USB connections. The users would plug the device, and the kiosk would prompt the device id of the user, with no other malicious intent.

4   Anatomy of the Attack (Script)

As mentioned in section 3.3.2 we developed a script to automate the attack process in our proof of concept development. We will describe it in this section.

4.1   Architecture

The script has to be fast, fully automated, effective and able to perform operations on numerous levels of the OS stack.

We had the need to make use of the functionalities of two different OSs, Windows and Linux. For that we deployed the script in a guest virtual machine containing Xubuntu that is able to communicate with its Windows7 host machine. We use a Xubuntu virtual machine so that the script can take advantage of the Linux OS scripting environment. Linux comes with libusb[8] as a generic driver to handle USB devices, which in turn is used by the usbutils, making it more practical for scripts like this to be developed. We will detail its functionalities further down.

---

[6]   Dynamic heuristic malware detection system, for the Google app store.
[7]   `https://github.com/kosborn/p2p-adb`: p2p-adb Framework
[8]   `http://www.libusb.org/`

As virtualization software we used Virtual Box[9]. This program enables us to create guest virtual machines and at running time exchange the control of the USB device from guest to host and vice-versa. In order to give the guest control over the USB device, it presents a virtual USB controller to the guest, and as soon as the guest starts using the USB virtual device, the USB device will appear as unavailable to the host. So only one OS has access to, and thus can control, the USB connection at a time.

It is essential that the guest machine is Linux and the host Windows and not the other way around. This guarantees that the Samsung device drivers have direct access to the USB device, which would not work inside a guest machine, because the devices are emulated by Virtual Box. The type of attacks done by the guest machine cope with this emulation process.

We have a host with Windows 7 so that we can have access to Odin that is used to flash Samsung devices. This tool is unable to work on Linux, because of the dependence that it has on the Windows' Samsung drivers. Other tools are able to flash firmware on Samsung phones on Linux, like Heimdall, but it is only able to target a limited number of Samsung smartphones, whereas in the case of Odin we are able to target all Samsung smartphones.

A communication channel between the host and the guest is needed, in order that the guest, which is doing most of the work, can tell the host when and which smartphone to flash. For that we use a shared file between the guest and the host OS, so when the guest needs to communicate it writes the file. The host is polling the file for changes. The roles are exchanged when the communication is in the opposite direction.

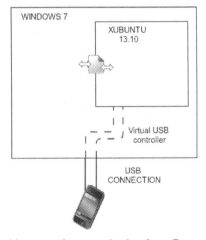

Fig. 5. Architecture of communication from Guest to Host

In the guest machine, a full list of the USB devices that we want to attack is needed, in order to tell the guest machine which devices to filter, so that they can be controlled inside the guest and not on the host. This is done by identifying the product id and the vendor id, which together identify all USB devices. The vendor id identifies the brand, for example Sony, and the product id identifies the product, for example Xperia.

---

[9] https://www.virtualbox.org/

The script running on the Xubuntu (guest) is responsible for:

- Detecting plugged USB devices;
- Identifying the type of device;
- Identifying the vulnerabilities known for that device;
- Attacking using the known vulnerabilities;
- Communicating with the host, in case the vulnerabilities require the use of the Odin tool;
- Identifying the mounted external cards of USB devices.

The Windows 7 (host) is responsible for:

- Communicating with the guest, to know which device to flash;
- Identifying the flash image that matches the device and its firmware ;
- Identifying the correct version of Odin for flashing ;

It uses GUI automation libraries, namely Pywinauto [14], to control Odin without human intervention.

4.2   Using the Vulnerabilities Found

As we mentioned in the previous sub-section, the guest machine detects plugged devices, identifies them, matches them to the vulnerabilities found and executes the attacks that target those vulnerabilities. We will now cover the vulnerabilities and the attacks.

Device Identification

The purpose of this attack is firstly to identify the firmware version of the smartphone with the command AT+DEVCONINFO, as it was shown in Fig. 4. Enabling us to identify the firmware version of the smartphone in question. In Fig. 4 it is identifiable by VER (S5839iBULE2/ EUR_CSC /S5839iBULC1/ S5839iBULE2) that shows the following details as per the format PDA CSC Modem Boot:

- **PDA:** The build version, which includes the system partition.
- **CSC:** (Country Sales Code): Language and country parameters.
- **Modem:** Identifying the modem firmware version.
- **Boot:** For the version of the Boot partition.

Changing the Boot Image

As we described in 3.3.2 the AT command AT+FUS? places the phone in download mode and allows flashing a new boot partition.The primary functions of the boot partition are:

- Mount the primary partitions necessary for the system to boot;
- Start the first process of all OSs based on Linux, i.e. the init process;
- Read and execute the init.rc boot configuration file;
- Load the kernel and the ramdisk.

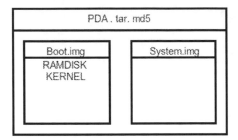

Fig. 6. Structure of a typical PDA file

Fig. 6 illustrates a firmware file to be flashed on a device. The boot partition is placed in a `boot.img` type file, which is inside of the PDA file. This file in turn is a tar file with a checksum, usually a .tar.md5. Usually inside the PDA file there is also the System partition. In order to flash we only need the `boot.img` file. For our proof of concept we re-constructed a stock boot partition.

The bootloader [15] is very different from the boot image. The bootloader is the very first piece of software that gets executed on a device. One of its roles is to check the integrity and signatures of the partitions before it starts them. This prevents any modification of the partitions, such as the boot or the system, by an un-authorized third party. When a bootloader is unlocked, like in some Samsung devices', it does not check the signatures of the partitions, which means a further modification of the partitions is possible, thus enabling our attack.

Normally the `boot.img` file is divided in two parts, the Kernel and the ramdisk. The ramdisk is the first file system mounted on the root of the system. There we can find files like the `init` file and the `init.rc`, the image that is used in the booting process of the smartphone and various other folders needed for good performance of the system.

In the `init.rc` [11] file we can find several shell type instructions for the initial configuration of the system. Instructions that will be executed with root access by the `init` process. It is in this file that we will alter the ramdisk of the boot partition, adding malicious instructions.

In this scenario we want to show three different things that can be done by altering just the boot partition, first make the `adb` debug over USB option always enabled, second obtain root access, third install a surveillance application, in this case Androrat [12].

For the first objective, we have to alter the `on property:persist.service.adb.enable=0`. This system property tells the system, what operations to do when disabling `adb`. In the original file, when `adb` was disabled, we had that it would `stop adbd`, effectively stopping the `adb` daemon on the smartphone. We changed this from `stop adbd` to `start adbd`, rendering it impossible to disable the `adb` from configuration, even thought it might appear disabled in the systemss' options.

For the second objective, we want to obtain root access on the smartphone using the binary tool `su` [18]. The binary configured with permissions of execution for eve-ryone, and with the owner as root, enables every user to have root access. We put the su file inside the ramdisk, being placed on the root of the system and then copying it to /sytem/xbin/. This is done adding these lines to the init.rc file.

- COPY /SU /SYSTEM/XBIN/SU
- CHMOD 06755 /SYSTEM/XBIN/SU
- CHOWN ROOT /SYSTEM/XBIN/SU

This will allow root access to any operation, for example when adb is enabled it will have root access.

For the third objective we want to install a surveillance application, in this case Androrat which stands for Android RAT (Remote Access Tool), in a way that the user does not know of its existence. First we place the application .apk file in the ramdisk directory, so that once it boots, it places the .apk in the root of the system, similar to what we did for su. Then we add again to the init.rc script, the following code:

COPY /ANDRORAT.APK /SYSTEM/APPS/ANDRORAT.APK

Once the phone boots, the application is installed as a system app. This makes the removal of the application extremely difficult for regular users even with root access. As described the application gets installed each time the phone boots.

The AndroRat application enables several remote surveillance capabilities on the phone, such as get contacts, get call logs, get all messages, GPS location.

AndroRat is composed of a client and a server, the client is the application that gets installed on the phone, the server runs on a PC, regardless if it is a Windows, Linux or Mac, since it runs in a java virtual machine. The client communicates with the server by TCP/IP. We altered the AndroidManifest.xml of the original application, deleting the following lines:

```
<intent-filter>
    <action android:name="android.intent.action.MAIN" />
    <category android:name="android.intent.category.LAUNCHER" />
</intent-filter>
```

This way making the icon is not visible in the app section of the phone, so an inexperienced user would not detect the malicious application.

Installing the New Boot Image

For a successful attack we need to create a dictionary of previously altered boot partitions, to encompass all the different smartphones that we want to attack. For example, for the bundle version presented in VER(S5839iBULE2/ EUR_CSC/ S5839iBULC1/ S5839iBULE2), we have to specifically map this bundle version to a boot previously altered that matches it.

After an initial identification of the smartphone version from the Linux guest machine, it is necessary that we place the smartphone in download and notify the host machine, handing over the control of the USB device to the host. When putting the device in download mode, its product Id and vendor Id gets altered, to a non-filtered combination of vendor Id and product id by Virtual Box, rendering the process of handing over the control of the USB device automatic. The guest machine saves the IMEI of the smartphone, so that once the phone reboots, it already knows that it is a compromised smartphone, which would enable the guest to do other types of attacks, since the `adb` is on and we have root access.

After the host is notified to flash the device with the firmware version, it maps the given version to a previously altered boot image that is ready to be flashed. It also maps the correct version of Odin.

Using a GUI automation tool for Windows, the host commands Odin to choose the correct image file folder and name and then to flash the phone. The smartphone proceeds with the flashing of the partitions and reboots normally. After rebooting, its product id and vendor id changes once more to the previous ones, handing over again the control of the USB connection to the guest machine, so that it can proceed with the attack.

First the Guest Linux does:

1. Detection of plugged USB devices.
2. Matching of its vulnerability.
3. Checks if it has a compromised boot partition.
4. Notifies the boot image to flash the device and saves the IMEI.
5. Places the phone in download mode.

Then the Host Windows does:

6. Identification of which file matches give version.
7. Makes use of GUI automation tools to control Odin and flash the phone

And again the guest Linux finishes with:

8. Proceeds with the rest of the attack, now that it possesses root access and `adb` enabled.

List of Phones Tested with the Vulnerabilities Found
We successfully verified the attack on the following phones:

- Samsung GT-S5839i
- Samsung GT-I5500

And it was also possible to confirm that the attack was possible, by issuing AT commands that the fallowing phones had the vulnerability:

- Samsung GT-S7500
- Samsung GT-S5830
- Samsung I9100
- Samsung S7560M

It is necessary that the smartphone has an original ROM from Samsung. We expect that the span of vulnerable versions of Samsung smartphones be much more wide than this, since in our assumption, having the vulnerability or not is implicitly related with the ability that the smartphone has on communicating with Kies software. So as far as we now, most (if not all) Samsung smartphones are supported by Kies.

List of Tested Anti-Virus Apps
AVG, **Avast** and **Virus Scanner** were the anti-virus chosen for testing. First we examined if any of them detected/prevented the attack, and later, after the attack if any of them detected malicious software on the phone.

The results are that none of them prevented the attack at first. After the attack, and after a scan had been performed, AVG detected that `androrat` was installed and informed the user that it could be malicious. However, upon trying to uninstall the threat it states that it cannot. Nothing more has been detected by AVG, or by the other two anti-viruses. They did not detect alterations to the `init.rc` file, or that `su` binary was added when compared to the previous state.

5   Conclusion

We exposed a serious vulnerability on some vendor customization of the android OS. We described our proof-of-concept with which we were able to explore the implications of that vulnerability, such as gaining root access by flashing a compromised boot partition. As the extended functionalities are intended to be used by the computer application of the vendor to configure and manage the smartphone, they were developed knowingly and with the mentioned intent. In our view, implementation of such "features" should be at least disclosed to users, in order that they understand the risks of an exposed USB connection. Our future work will involve developing a smartphone application to warn and advise the user regarding these possibilities. Depending on the smartphone's root access it can also be possible to allow the charging by possible hibernating the process responsible for handling the AT commands. Another future investigation will be to confirm that the "features" are still present in the latest version of the Samsung Kies software and the latest version of Android.

Acknowledgments. This work is financed by the ERDF – European Regional Development Fund through the COMPETE Programme (operational programme for competitiveness) and by National Funds through the FCT – Fundação para a Ciência e a Tecnologia (Portuguese Foundation for Science and Technology) within project *«FCOMP-01-0124-FEDER-037281»*.

References

1. Android Pushes Past 80% Market Share While Windows Phone Shipments Leap 156.0% Year Over Year in the Third Quarter, According to IDC - prUS24442013, http://www.idc.com/getdoc.jsp?containerId=prUS24442013
2. Wu, L., Grace, M., Zhou, Y., Wu, C., Jiang, X.: The impact of vendor customizations on android security. In: Proc. 2013 ACM SIGSAC Conf. Comput. Commun. Secur., CCS 2013, pp. 623–634 (2013)
3. Technical Specification Group Terminals: AT command set for 3GPP User Equipment (UE) (3G TS 27.007 version 2.0.0) 4, 17–18 (1999)

4. Mulliner, C., Liebergeld, S., Lange, M., Seifert, J.-P.: Taming Mr Hayes: Mitigating signaling based attacks on smartphones. In: IEEE/IFIP Int. Conf. Dependable Syst. Networks (DSN 2012), pp. 1–12 (2012)
5. Singh, A.J., Bhardwaj, A.: Android Internals and Telephony. Int. J. Emerg. Technol. Adv. Eng. 4, 51–59 (2014)
6. Module, H.: Android RIL Integration Guide- Huawei (2014)
7. Odin 3.09 - Odin download with Samsung ROM Flashing Tool, http://odindownload.com/
8. Heimdall | Glass Echidna, http://glassechidna.com.au/heimdall/
9. Security Enhancements in Android 4.3 | Android Developers, http://source.android.com/devices/tech/security/enhancements43.html
10. Android Debug Bridge | Android Developers, http://developer.android.com/tools/help/adb.html
11. Vidas, T., Cylab, E.C.E., Votipka, D., Cylab, I.N.I., Christin, N.: All Your Droid Are Belong To Us: A Survey of Current Android Attacks. In: WOOT (2011)
12. SuperOneClick Root v2.3.3, http://www.superoneclickdownload.com/
13. Cydia Impactor, http://www.cydiaimpactor.com/
14. pywinauto - Windows GUI automation using Python - Google Project Hosting, https://code.google.com/p/pywinauto/
15. Hoog, A.: Android Forensics: Investigation, Analysis and Mobile Security for Google Android. Elsevier (2011)
16. Android Init Language Google Git, https://android.googlesource.com/platform/system/core/+/master/init/readme.txt
17. VRT: Androrat - Android Remote Access Tool, http://vrt-blog.snort.org/2013/07/androrat-android-remote-access-tool.html
18. Superuser, http://androidsu.com/superuser/
19. Gargenta, M.: Learning Android. O'Reilly Media, Inc. (2011)
20. Terminal Software, http://realterm.sourceforge.net/

Free Typed Text Using Keystroke Dynamics for Continuous Authentication

Paulo Pinto, Bernardo Patrão, and Henrique Santos

Watchful Software, Coimbra, Portugal
Universidade do Minho - Dep. de Sistemas de Informação, Braga, Portugal
prpinto@itgrow.pt, bernardo.patrao@watchfulsoftware.com,
hsantos@dsi.uminho.pt
http://www.watchfulsoftware.com, http://www.uminho.pt

Abstract. Information is increasingly in a digital-only format and almost everything we do nowadays depends on a digital identity for authentication and authorization. No matter how strong the authentication system is, after the authentication phase, there is no continuous verification that user is still the same human being that successfully logged in, thus leaving the system unprotected. This paper presents a usable breakthrough approach for continuous authentication with free typed text through the use of biometric techniques based on keystroke dynamics. Our main purpose is to achieve a reduction of the required sample size, while improving (or at least not worsen) precision performance, by adapting and improving parameters on a keystroke dynamics algorithm.

Keywords: Identity verification, User authentication, Biometrics, Keystroke dynamics, Host-based intrusion detection, Security.

1 Introduction

In a world governed by digital information, computing is the main activity and user authentication plays an important role in access control. One of the most common situations of intrusion occurs when a worker leaves his/her workstation unlocked or when someone knows a user password and tries to use a false identity to do something malicious (for example, to send an e-mail, to change a document, to write on facebook or twitter)[1,2].

Keystroke dynamics, as a biometric for authentication, can be used to mitigate the above threat, continuously detecting intrusions[3]. But false alarms in such intrusion detection systems are quite common[4] and the european standard for access-control systems (EN-50133-1) specifies a false alarm rate of less than 1% for this type of solution [5]. For that reason, it is crucial to optimize algorithms to achieve low false rejection rate (FRR) and false acceptance rate (FAR).

In this paper, we present an heuristic optimization of an algorithm based on keystroke dynamics and results obtained from a real experiment, for validation purposes.

The rest of the paper is organized as follows. Section 2 is dedicated to the study of keystroke dynamics and how it can be used to verify user identity and

B. De Decker and A. Zúquete (Eds.): CMS 2014, LNCS 8735, pp. 33–45, 2014.

section 3 is the state of the art. In section 4, we start defining main functions used for the intrusion detection and we also define the decision criterion. In section 5 we present techniques that will allow us to improve the algorithm as well as how these techniques can be implemented. On the same section we describe a new decision criterion that will allow us to get FRR lower than 1% (validated with results on a real environment) and in section 6 we write the main conclusions of this work.

2   Biometrics and Keystroke Dynamics

Using biometrics, each individual can be uniquely identified by physical and behavioural characteristics and, unlike passwords, biometrics can not be lost, stolen or copied. There are several biometric techniques such as fingerprints, the way you walk, your eye geometry or even the way you speak[6]. Each one can be used to identify or to authenticate. In a very simplified way, identification involves the comparison of a given biometric pattern with all of previously stored patterns. Authentication is similar but involves only one comparison with the pattern belonging to someone claiming identity checking. In both cases, one main concern is to avoid false rejections and false acceptances: for access control the objective of the application is to not allowing access to unauthorized individuals under all circumstances while granting access to all legitimate users. It is clear that the surveillance software has to be set up with a very low FAR even if it comes at the price of a higher FRR. On the other hand, identification within surveillance software has to be set up with a low FRR even if FAR gets higher.

Keystroke dynamics is a technique aiming to find patterns based on timing information from pressed and released keys when a person is typing at a keyboard. Most common features are dwells (time between key down and key up of a specific key), flights (time between key up and key down of two consecutive keys), digraphs, trigraphs and fourgraphs[3]. Weather conditions, fatigue, stress or any sort of influence, can drastically impact the result but with a constant user profile update, even the effect of these weird behaviours can be drastically reduced.

3   State of the Art

Keystroke dynamics is a behavioural based furtive biometric technique[7] that does not require any special resources (hardware), besides a normal keyboard and the support low-level software usually available in any PC like system. These properties make it a good candidate for continuous authentication[8]. Recently this research topic received some important contributions, being evident that one of the main issues is the training data used. Solami et. al present a generic model for a Continuous Biometric Authentication System (CBAS), discussed some proposed solutions and propose a classification based on the type of target scenario: class I, when legitimate users' profiles are available and the identities of all possible impostors are known (i.e., a closed system); class II, otherwise[9]. In this work we are targeting a class I system, aiming to improve only its performance over the internal user universe.

4   Software Design and Algorithm

4.1   Architecture

The base of the software architecture is the one proposed in[8,10]. It is composed of a central server, a database where user profiles are saved and a constant validation mechanism for each sample produced by the user (see above references for more detailed information).

The mechanism receives an attempt sample and needs to decide whether it is an intrusion or not (see Fig. 1). The decision algorithm is the heart of the mechanism and, as we will see later, with a generalization of the scores function proposed in [3] (by defining new parameters and new metrics), varying acceptance thresholds and implementing a dynamic decision criterion, it is possible to substantially decrease the FRR, the FAR and the attempt sample size.

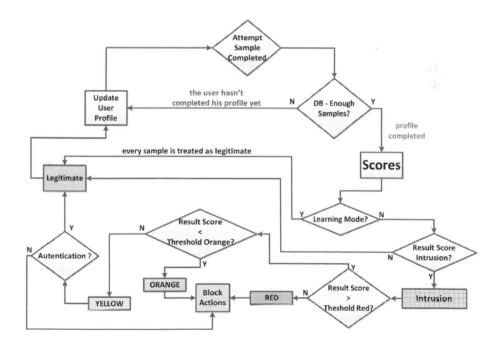

Fig. 1. Algorithm architecture

4.2   Absolute Scores

The user profile, stored in the database, consists essentially in one merged sample with all characteristic user features. This profile is constructed and constantly updated every time the user produces a new valid sample.

Let us define $AS(l)$ as the set of all features from an **attempt sample** with length l and DB as the set of all features from the **merged sample** stored on the database. Let us also define, if exist, $DW(x(y))$ as the average of $x(y)$ where

$$x(y) \in I_{DW}(y) = \{all\ dwells\ in\ y\}$$

and

$$y \in J = \{AS(l), DB\}.$$

Intuitively, we define $FL(x(y))$, $DI(x(y))$, $TR(x(y))$ and $FR(x(y))$ for flights, digraphs, trigraphs and fourgraphs, respectively, and the corresponding sets $I_{FL}(y) = \{all\ flights\ in\ y\}$, $I_{DI}(y) = \{all\ digraphs\ in\ y\}$, $I_{TR}(y) = \{all\ trigraphs\ in\ y\}$ and $I_{FR}(y) = \{all\ fourgraphs\ in\ y\}$.

For each feature x on the merged sample ($x(DB)$), we define the **acceptance neighbourhood** as

$$V(x(DB)) = [(2 - p(z))z(x(DB)), p(z)z(x(DB))],$$

where

$$z(x(y)) = \begin{cases} DW(x(y)) & if\ x\ is\ a\ dwell\ in\ y, \\ FL(x(y)) & if\ x\ is\ a\ flight\ in\ y, \\ DI(x(y)) & if\ x\ is\ a\ digraph\ in\ y, \\ TR(x(y)) & if\ x\ is\ a\ trigraph\ in\ y, \\ FR(x(y)) & if\ x\ is\ a\ fourgraph\ in\ y. \end{cases}$$

and $p(z) \in [1, 2]$ is a parameter that defines the interval around $z(x(y))$. Note that we write z without arguments in $p(z)$ because we are referring to the type of feature and not to some specific feature, meaning that features of the same type (for example dwells) all have the same parameter value to define his acceptance neighbourhood.

For each feature $x \in AS(l)$ that is shared with the merged samples, the acceptance feature function is defined as

$$A(x) = \begin{cases} 1 & if\ z(x(AS(l))) \in V(x(DB)), \\ 0 & otherwise. \end{cases}$$

Defining $N(z)$ as the number of shared features between $AS(l)$ and DB of the type z (for example, if $z = DW$ then $N(z)$ is the number of all shared dwells between the attempt sample and the merged sample), we write the **absolute score** as

$$Ab(AS(l)) = \sum_{z \in Z} \left(w(z) \left(\frac{1}{N(z)} \sum_{x \in I_z} A(x) \right) \right),$$

with $\sum w(z) = 1$, where $w(z)$ is the weight parameter associated to each type of feature. Note that the formula proposed by Monrose and Rubin[3] is a particular case of the absolute score defined here.

4.3   Relative Scores

The relative score value is based in time disorder divided by the maximum disorder. For each type of features in our $AS(l)$, a list is created ordering all features by time. Then this order is compared with the one from DB. Let us define $D(z, AS(l))$ as the function that give us the disorder between all shared features of the type z in $AS(l)$ with DB(see [8], 5.3.2 for more details). Then, the **relative score** is written as

$$Rl(AS(l)) = 1 - \sum_{z \in Z} \frac{D(z, AS(l))}{D_m(z, AS(l))},$$

where $D_m(z, AS(l))$ is the maximum possible disorder between $AS(l)$ and DB for some z type of feature.

4.4   Decision Criterion

The value to compare with a fixed threshold is a linear combination of the two quantities defined before:

$$S(AS(l)) = w_{Ab}Ab(AS(l)) + w_{Rl}Rl(AS(l)), \tag{1}$$

where w_{Ab} and w_{Rl} are weights.

We define 3 thresholds for different intrusion levels: yellow, orange and red level represented by th_y, th_o and th_r, respectively. The intrusion is detected when

$$S(AS(l)) < th_y.$$

4.5   Parameter Space

The parameter space is composed by $p(z) \; \forall z \in Z$, $w(z) \; \forall z \in Z$, th_y, w_{Ab}, w_{Rl} and l. The **trivial configuration** is the configuration where each event has the same weight as well as each score function.

5   Validation

All results presented in this section come from a real environment composed, most of the times, by more than 10 users. The users are, for the most part, software developers, meaning their input can result from coding and/or writing, both formally and informally, in English and Portuguese, in several distinct software environments. In some sense it is the worst case scenario to classify behaviour since there is a great variety on the user actions.

According to initial requirements we assume no other users have access, i.e., intruders are internal users trying to circumvent access control rules.

5.1 Tool Description for Artificial Attacks

On the database, each user has his own merged sample with all characteristic features. This merged sample is the user profile previously saved and constructed using the user samples also saved on the database.

With all samples from the database we can test the algorithm. For a particular user, we can simulate authentications using the samples from the database against the merged sample of the same user. In that way we can calculate the FRR. Also, we can calculate the FAR of the entire group using all samples against each merged sample. It is an *artificial attack* because people are not intentionally attacking but it is the easiest way to simulate a large number of attacks and it is according to the scenario specification.

5.2 Acceptance Neighbourhoods Study

Acceptance neighbourhoods are controlled by the parameters $p(z)$. Considering $w(z) = 0.2 \ \forall z \in Z$, $w_{Ab} = 0.5$ and $w_{Rl} = 0.5$ (trivial configuration), what we study first is the "best" (heuristically speaking) acceptance neighbourhoods for each type of features looking at the FRR and FAR calculated from artificial attacks. Fig. 2 is a summary of the best scenarios tested with $l = 750$. The first column of the second table represents different thresholds to detect intrusion.

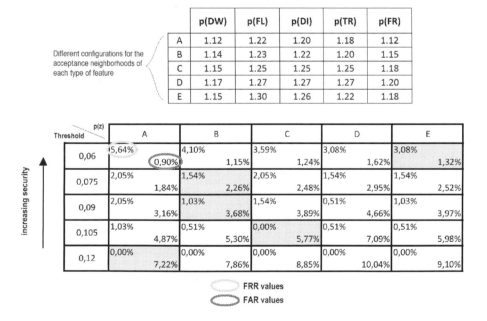

	p(DW)	p(FL)	p(DI)	p(TR)	p(FR)
A	1.12	1.22	1.20	1.18	1.12
B	1.14	1.23	1.22	1.20	1.15
C	1.15	1.25	1.25	1.25	1.18
D	1.17	1.27	1.27	1.27	1.20
E	1.15	1.30	1.26	1.22	1.18

Different configurations for the acceptance neighborhoods of each type of feature

Threshold	A		B		C		D		E	
0,06	5,64%		4,10%		3,59%		3,08%		3,08%	
		0,90%		1,15%		1,24%		1,62%		1,32%
0,075	2,05%		1,54%		2,05%		1,54%		1,54%	
		1,84%		2,26%		2,48%		2,95%		2,52%
0,09	2,05%		1,03%		1,54%		0,51%		1,03%	
		3,16%		3,68%		3,89%		4,66%		3,97%
0,105	1,03%		0,51%		0,00%		0,51%		0,51%	
		4,87%		5,30%		5,77%		7,09%		5,98%
0,12	0,00%		0,00%		0,00%		0,00%		0,00%	
		7,22%		7,86%		8,85%		10,04%		9,10%

increasing security

FRR values
FAR values

Fig. 2. Summary of the acceptance neighbourhoods study. All FRR and FAR values, for each fixed configuration $(A, B, C, D \ and \ E)$ and for each fixed threshold, were obtained from 11 users each with 15 samples of 750 keys.

As an example, for the value 0.06, th_y is defined as $th_y = (S(DB) - 0.06)$, where $S(DB)$ is the score from the user profile.

As we can see from Fig. 2, when we increase the threshold we get a high FRR and when we decrease the threshold the FAR tends to increase. Situation A produces a very high FRR with high security level (threshold= 0.06) and situation E produces a very low FAR with low security level (threshold= 0.12). The table shows that situation B is the one that produces the best results to minimize FAR and FRR.

5.3   Transients Study for Sample Reduction

This part of the study allows us to understand if it is possible to reduce the size of the attempt sample and how much we can reduce. The more information we have, the more accurate are our decisions. On the other hand, the fewer keys the intruder types, the less damage the intruder does before being detected. The aim is always to find best of both parts.

Transient is a common term in differential equations theory and essentially represents states that actually are not the common states on some dynamical system. A simple example is throwing a rock to a lake: The waves produced by the rock is a transient state since most of the time the lake has no waves. The classical example for transients is the harmonic oscillator[11]. In our mechanism, we have

$$S(AS(l))_{l \to \infty} \longrightarrow a$$

with a representing the characteristic value for the user (in theory close to 1). Here, the transients are the values we get when l is too small and, consequently, are not user representative. Identifying the minimum l for which we do not have any more transients means identifying the minimum size of the sample to get a reasonable value for a.

Fig. 3 shows the transients study using 3 samples with 750 keys each from 3 different users. The horizontal axis represents sample reduction process and the vertical axis is the score defined in (1). In each iteration of the reduction process, we erase 11 or 12 features from the samples (on the same proportion as they exist for any sample with length l). This figure shows that after 11 sample reductions, the value of $S(AS(l))$ starts to be a bit unstable. Using 11 as the maximum number of reductions for the trivial configuration means that we can reduce the sample size in 40% (around less 300 keys) but 450 keys is still a considerable number for an attempt sample.

The question we would like to answer is: It is possible to get a better reduction result with a different parameter configuration? Next section we answer this question with an heuristic study of the weights.

5.4   Weights Study

The study of weights has three distinct phases. The first one is the absolute and relative weights study. With the good weights from the first phase a study

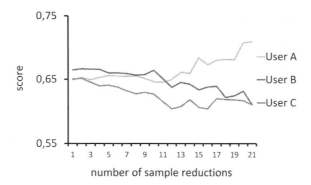

Fig. 3. Transients study. The horizontal axis represents the number of reductions that were made on each sample. The vertical axis represents the scores defined in (1) for each sample in different reduction phases. The more reductions we do, the smaller is the sample. The initial sample size is 750 keys and this picture shows samples from 3 different users, the reduction process and the score in each reduction phase.

of the weights of each type of feature in the absolute score is done (the reason we are only considering the absolute score is justified by the first phase study). Finally, we check if, after the second phase, we still have the same weight results for absolute and relative scores. There might be more efficient ways to conduct this study like using genetic algorithms[12] but, apart from the fact that this approach takes much less time, even using this simplified technique, the results should be very similar to the ones from a genetic algorithm strategy.

In Fig. 4, the chart on the left shows how the gap between the average intrusion score and the average user score increases at the same time as we increase the weight of the absolute score. On the horizontal axis, we start with $S(AS(l))$ calculated using only the relative score. Then we increase the weight of the absolute score until we have $S(AS(l))$ calculated using only the absolute score. The gap represents how much separate is the intrusion score region and the user score region. The chart on the right shows some stability when the absolute score weight is more than 70%. We conclude, among all the distinct combinations, that $70\% - 30\%$ or even $80\% - 20\%$ are the best configurations for $w_{Ab} - w_{Rl}$ to get an higher gap and, at the same time, to consider the relative score in our evaluation.

Fig. 5 shows a summary of many simulations, using $80\% - 20\%$ for $w_{Ab} - w_{Rl}$, for many different parameters $w(z)$ $\forall z \in Z$. From here we observe an important fact: dwells, flights and digraphs are the most efficient type of features to identify or to authenticate the user. On the other hand, in a real environment, when we try to isolate the most important type of feature (dwell) the FAR typically tends to increase because the validation mechanism tends to be more sensible. We conclude that $(42\% - 24\% - 16\% - 10\% - 8\%)$ is, heuristically speaking, the best configuration for $w(z)$ and with this configuration the results from the first phase (Fig. (4)) were exactly the same.

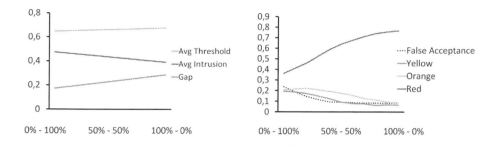

Fig. 4. Absolute and relative weights study for user samples with 750 keys. The gap between the typical intrusion score and the typical user score increases whenever we increase the importance (weight) of the absolute score. On the other hand, it is important to have more than one measure to evaluate identities, we should not ignore the relative score at all. Instead of ignoring it, we should decrease his importance.

weights (dwell-flight-di-tri-four)	20-20-20-20-20	40-25-18-12-5	20-40-23-12-5	8-22-40-22-8	5-12-23-40-20	5-12-18-25-40
Avg Threshold	0,67	0,70	0,67	0,65	0,64	0,63
Average Intrusion	0,40	0,40	0,40	0,41	0,41	0,40
Gap	0,26	0,30	0,26	0,24	0,23	0,23

weights (dwell-flight-di-tri-four)	60-15-10-8-7	50-20-12-10-8	42-24-16-10-8	34-27-19-11-9
Avg Threshold	0,74	0,72	0,70	0,69
Average Intrusion	0,39	0,40	0,40	0,40
Gap	0,34	0,32	0,30	0,29

Fig. 5. Features weights study

Finally, the transient study was repeated but this time taking into account the previous best configurations (the best acceptance neighbourhood parameters and the best weights previously presented). Fig. 6 shows $S(AS(l))$ for different values of l. As we can see, the value stays stable during all the reduction process (starting with $l = 750$). After 20 reductions, the value shows no relevant fluctuations. This means a reduction of 80%, equivalent to a reduction of around 600 keys. At this point we are able to use attempt samples with 150 keys.

5.5   ROC Curve

The Receiver Operating Characteristics (ROC) curve illustrates the performance as its discrimination threshold is varied. We present, in Fig. 7, a pseudo ROC curve using the best parameters configuration presented here and attempt samples with 250 keys ($l = 250$). At this point we are able to produce rates close to 2%. Next section we present a simple way to reduce even more these rates.

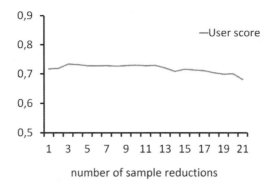

Fig. 6. Transients study with an improved configuration and considering only one user. The initial sample size is 750 keys.

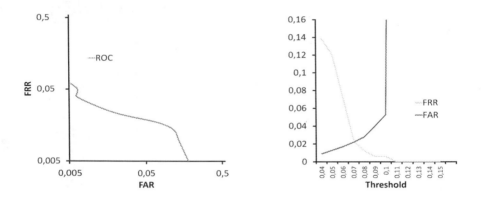

Fig. 7. Pseudo ROC curve (left) with logarithmic scale and DET curve (right) for an improved configuration. The sample size is 250 keys and all simulations were done using a group of 11 real users.

5.6   Evaluations Scheme

One of the main focus in any continuous detection system using keystroke dynamics is to reduce the size of the required sample to detect intrusions and, at the same time, not increase FRR and FAR. For a static biometric system it is important to know how often a wrong decision is made but the purpose of a performance evaluation for a continuous biometric authentication system is not to see if an impostor is detected, but how fast he is detected[13].

An interesting way to detect intrusions fast is dividing the evaluation process in more than one part. Let us suppose that, after each l keys, we want intrusion detection probability p. So, p is what we want after l keys and the question is: What should we have in $l/2$ keys to achieve p in l keys?

To simplify our example, let us divide the process in only two parts and let us assume that $l/2 \in N$. If we define $X = "number\ of\ authentications\ in\ 2\ attempts"$ then $X - Bi(2, m)$ with

$$P(X = k) = \binom{2}{k}m^k(1 - m)^{2-k},\ k = \{0, 1, 2\}$$

If we define $Y = "detect\ intrusion"$ then we want to know m for $P(Y) \approx p$:

$$P(X \geq 1) \approx p \Leftrightarrow 1 - P(X = 0) \approx p \Leftrightarrow 1 - (1 - m)^2 \approx p \Leftrightarrow m \approx 1 - (1 - p)^{1/2}.$$

So, $m < p$ for $p \neq \{0, 1\}$ meaning that we do not need p probability after each $l/2$ keys but usually much less! As a consequence, we do not need to be so accurate with $l/2$ keys to have probability p in l keys and we have the opportunity to catch the intrusion in less than l keys(in our example, in $l/2$). Another direct consequence of not being so accurate is the fact that the FRR decreases.

As a conclusion, if we divide the process in two parts then we just need to have intrusion probability m (less than p) and we automatically have a lower FRR. Also, during this process, the yellow (th_y) and orange (th_o) warnings are ignored and only red warnings are considered intrusion. At the end of the process (in this example after each 2 evaluations) some particular situations with yellow and orange warnings are considered intrusion. All these considerations on the yellow and orange warnings will help us on the FRR reduction.

We already have some good and stable results using this approach and considering evaluations after each 125 keys but it is still a work in progress. Fig. 8 shows DET curve for 125 keys and for 250 keys (process divided in two parts) from a real scenario of users (11 users) and considering the best configuration, presented here, for the parameters.

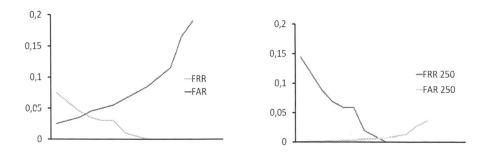

Fig. 8. DET curve at the middle of the evaluation process and with 125 keys (left) and DET curve at the end of the process and with 250 keys (right). In this example the process was only divided in two parts.

6   Conclusions

The purpose of this paper is to present improvements of some of the keystroke dynamics biometrics to identify/authenticate users and to detect intrusions, using data from a real environment to validate.

The main conclusions of this work are the huge importance of dwells (time difference between key up and key down for any key) to identify/authenticate users. Also, the importance of the right weights on all features to reduce the size of the attempt sample (sample used to verify user identity or to detect intrusion) and to reduce FAR and FRR at the same time. In our particular scenario, we were able to get an amazing reduction of the sample size from 750 keys to 150 keys with FRR and FAR close to 2%. Also, using an evaluation scheme we were actually able to get an impressive FRR and FAR lower than 1% with the strong possibility to detect the intrusion after only 125 keys.

It is important to refer that in [8] all the presented simulations are with samples of 750 keys and what we present here is a huge reduction of the sample size which is crucial to have an earlier intrusion detection. Also, Kevin Killourhy and Roy Maxion [4] referred, in a recent study, that at present no anomaly detector has archived a false alarm rate specified in the european standards which makes our results even more interesting.

We believe that the strategy presented here to calculate the weights in order to improve the FAR, FRR and attempt sample reduction is something that can be implemented in any group of users. Also, the weights study can be done periodically, continuously calculating the best parameters for an specific group of users.

Acknowledgements. This work has been supported by FCT - Fundação para a Ciência e Tecnologia within the Project Scope: PEst-OE/EEI/UI0319/2014. We would like also to thank Watchful for supporting this work and the Software Development Team for helpful comments and data. The authors had financial support from Watchful Software.

References

1. Lynch, D.M.: Securing Against Insider Attacks. Information Security Journal: A Global Perspective 15, 39–47 (2006)
2. Schulz, E.E.: A Framework for Understanding and Predicting Insider Attacks. Computers and Security 21, 526–531 (2002)
3. Monrose, F., Rubin, A.: Keystroke dynamics as a biometric for authentication. Future Generation Computer Systems 16, 351–359 (2000)
4. Killourhy, K., Maxion, R.: Comparing Anomaly-Detection Algorithms for Keystroke Dynamics. In: Dependable Systems and Networks, pp. 125–134 (2009)
5. CENELEC European standard EN 50133-1, Alarm systems. Access control systems for use in security applications, European Committee for Eletrotechnical Standardization (2002)

6. Bergadano, F., Gunetti, D., Picardi, C.: User authentication through keystrokes dynamics. ACM Transactions on Information and Systems Security 5, 367–397 (2002)
7. Magalhães, S.: Keystroke dynamics - stepping forward in authentication. GESTS International Transactions on Computer Science and Engineering 29 (2006)
8. Ferreira, J., Santos, H., Patrão, B.: Intrusion detection through keystroke dynamics. In: 10th European Conference on Information Warfare and Security (2011)
9. Al Solami, E.: Continuous Biometric Authentication: Can It Be More Practical? In: 12th IEEE International Conference on High Performance Computing and Communications, pp. 647–652 (2010)
10. Ferreira, J., Santos, H.: Keystroke dynamics for continuous access control enforcement. In: Proceedings of the International Conference on Cyber-Enabled Distributed Computing and Knowledge, pp. 216–223 (2012)
11. Serway, R.A., Jewett, J.W.: Physics for Scientists and Engineers (2003)
12. Mitchell, M.: An Introduction to Genetic Algorithms (Complex Adaptive Systems) (1998)
13. Boruc, P.: Continuous keystroke dynamics: A different perspective towards biometric evaluation. Information Security Technical Report 17, 36–43 (2012)

Secure Storage on Android
with Context-Aware Access Control

Faysal Boukayoua[1], Jorn Lapon[1], Bart De Decker[2], and Vincent Naessens[1]

[1] KU Leuven, Dept. of Computer Science, Ghent Technology Campus, Belgium
[2] KU Leuven, Dept. of Computer Science, iMinds-DistriNet, Belgium
`firstname.lastname@cs.kuleuven.be`

Abstract. Android devices are increasingly used in corporate settings. Although openness and cost-effectiveness are key factors to opt for the platform, its level of data protection is often inadequate for corporate use. This paper presents a strategy for secure credential and data storage in Android. It is supplemented by a context-aware mechanism that restricts data availability according to predefined policies. Our approach protects stored data better than iOS in case of device theft. Contrary to other Android-based solutions, we do not depend on device brand, hardware specs, price range or platform version. No modifications to the operating system are required. The proposed concepts are validated by a context-aware file management prototype.

Keywords: secure storage, context-aware security, mobile devices, Android, interoperability.

1 Introduction

For years mobile devices have mainly been used privately. More recently, their potential has become apparent to enterprises. For instance, a sales representative could retrieve product information on-site to convince prospective clients and, in case of success, sign an agreement. Similarly, home care nurses could use their tablet or smartphone to consult a patient's dietary prescriptions. Additionally, in confined setups like retirement communities, nurses may also be granted controlled access to the locks of serviced flats. The result is a myriad of sensitive data becoming present on these devices, which are at the same time prone to theft and loss. In the end, this increases the risks of data compromise.

Nevertheless, many companies are issuing smartphones or tablets to their employees. The iOS platform is often selected for its built-in security features, offering protection against malware and theft. This is mainly due to strong application vetting and tight hard- and software integration. For instance, data protection is based on a crypto engine with keys fused into the application processor, making offline attacks to retrieve data very hard - even for jailbroken devices. Moreover, iOS supports multiple availability levels for data and credentials (i.e. *data protection classes*). On the other hand, opting for an Android device also offers benefits. A broad range of prices and specifications is available.

B. De Decker and A. Zúquete (Eds.): CMS 2014, LNCS 8735, pp. 46–59, 2014.
© IFIP International Federation for Information Processing 2014

The hard- and software costs are typically lower than iOS devices. However, regarding data protection, Android does not impose hardware constraints on device crypto, which makes asset protection (i.e. *sensitive data and credentials*) more difficult. Optionally, the file system can be encrypted, using a passcode-derived key. As a result, offline brute force and dictionary attacks remain possible.

Contribution. This paper presents a secure asset storage mechanism for Android-based devices. It is supplemented by a context-aware mechanism that further limits asset exposure. The secure storage mechanism is backed by a secure element, which is readily or optionally available for most Android tablets and smartphones. On-device passcode attacks are made infeasible, as opposed to iOS. The context-aware module provides decision support by automating asset management tasks and only releasing data to external apps, according to predefined policies. Note that no modifications to the operating system are required. This work is validated through the development of a context-aware file-management system.

The rest of this paper is structured as follows. Section 2 presents related work. Our general approach is described in section 3. Thereafter, the secure storage strategy and the context-aware management module are presented in section 4. The prototype is described in section 6. Both components are evaluated in section 7. Finally, conclusions are drawn and future work is suggested in section 8.

2   Related Work

Many security-sensitive applications, across mobile platforms, use custom, weak storage mechanisms [7, 10]. Yet platform-provided facilities offer strong crypto as well as MDM integration [1, 2, 4].

Device encryption in Android can optionally be enabled since version 3. Even so, the external storage is never encrypted. From Android 4 onwards, the KeyChain introduces per-app private key storage. This component is still prone to offline attacks on the user's passcode. Version 4.3 further improves the KeyChain by adding hardware backing, although not many devices currently support this. It relies on the ARM TrustZone extensions, an implementation of GlobalPlatform's Trusted Execution Environment (TEE). The same approach is introduced in Windows Phone 8 and iOS 4. The hardware-enforced OS isolation allows the three platforms to partly implement their credential storage as trustworthy code. Passcode attacks are thus throttled, since they are confined to the device. Nevertheless, the number of attempts can be unlimited. Windows Phone and iOS also apply the above approach in how they implement file system encryption, a feature not yet supported by Android.

Android has two types of persistent memory. The internal storage is sandboxed and provides each app with exclusive access to its files. The external storage, on the other hand, is accessible to every application with the corresponding Manifest permission(s). It is used by many popular apps to keep permanent and temporary data and copies of IPC-obtained data [12, 17]. Relying on the user to meticulously manage this data, is not only user-unfriendly, it would likely lead to the increased exposure of sensitive information. This is a key motivator for the context-aware management module in section 5.

In the light of an integrated user experience, Android offers developers numerous IPC capabilities. However, this leads to heightened security risks [8], which are made worse by the BYOD trend in corporate mobile computing. In anticipation, Samsung has been equipping Android with the KNOX extension [3]. It divides the OS into *application containers*, f.i. in a private and a work-related one. IPC and data sharing are only allowed within the same container. This separation is hardware-enforced, also relying on the TrustZone extensions. Moreover, the use of hardware-based certificates is supported, notably CAC cards (used by the US Department of Defense). Apps can access them through a PKCS interface. Other uses include setting up VPN connections and unlocking the screen.

Context-aware resource protection is a well-discussed topic in scientific literature. ConUCON [5] presents an Android-based model for resource usage and access control. It provides both specification and enforcement. However, being merely OS-based, information is left vulnerable in case of device theft or loss.

Saint [13] provides Android apps with mechanisms to restrict their interfaces towards other applications. Its decision making is context-aware. As Saint modifies the OS, it succeeds in providing far-reaching enforcement. Secure storage is not considered.

The approach by Feth and Jung [11] uses TaintDroid's [9] capability to analyse data flows throughout the device. Here as well, the approach is purely OS-based.

Bubbles [16], by Tiwari et al, allows users to assign resources like data, applications, cameras and network connections, to one or more *bubbles*. The authors describe these as representations of different social contexts, separated by digital boundaries. A combination of bubble-assigned resources can only be used within that particular bubble. Administration is user-centric, and therefore less suitable for corporate use.

Riva et al propose a user authentication model based on a contextual learning component [14]. It implements different forms of authentication, each of which is assigned a *confidence level*. Depending on how sensitive a resource is deemed, a higher confidence level is required to access it. Contrary to this work, the focus lies on making authentication more usable, rather than on resource protection.

In a nutshell, we observe that iOS and Windows Phone devices tend to outperform many of their Android counterparts regarding secure storage. Much can be attributed to the device requirements imposed by platform vendors. The choice that organisations are left with, is either to adopt a different platform or to be limited to a specific subset of Android devices. This restriction is stringent, bearing in mind that Android accounts for a 78.9% marketshare (source: Strategy Analytics, 2013 Q4). At the same time, it goes without saying that approaches that modify the platform, are less likely to be adopted. In this work we explicitly aim not to change the OS. From thereon, we explore the data protection level that can be offered.

3   General Approach

Prior to introducing the architecture, we list the requirements it must satisfy and the assumptions it is subject to.

3.1   Security Requirements

S1 Assets on the mobile device can be managed and selectively disclosed according to specified policies.

S2 Following device theft or loss, computational attacks to retrieve the assets, are infeasible. Physical attacks are more difficult than against the state of the art (see section 2).

3.2   Usability Requirements

The approach should not impose an insurmountable burden on the user, f.i. by requiring a long, complex passcode.

3.3   Interoperability Requirements

I1 Our solution must be deployable on a device base that is representative of existing Android versions, hardware specifications and price ranges.

I2 No platform modifications are allowed.

I3 Standard platform building blocks are preferred over custom-made components.

3.4   Assumptions

A1 The security controls of the OS are enforced correctly during legitimate use.

A2 The user does not weaken platform security, f.i. by rooting the device.

Given that installation channels other than the trusted repositories are disabled by default, it is reasonable to assume A1. An internal corporate store only contains trusted applications, while Google Play has several mechanisms to fend off malware outbreaks: automated scanning, manual removal from the Store and over-the-air updates. Assumption A2 implies that eligible users are not considered potential adversaries.

3.5   Architecture

To address the Android shortcomings listed in section 2, we propose 2 complementary approaches. First, a context-aware management module provides soft security by managing assets semi-automatically. It thereby relieves the user from this task. In addition, it selectively discloses them to trusted apps under predefined contextual conditions. The second, hard security approach introduces secure storage that is backed by tamper-resistant hardware.

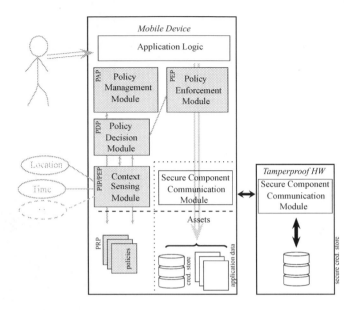

Fig. 1. Overview of the modules for both the soft (grey) and strong (white) security approaches

The architecture is depicted in figure 1. Five components make up the context-aware module. The *Policy Management Module* allows the user or corporate administrator to manage its policies. A policy event may be triggered when an application tries to access an asset. As a result, the *Policy Enforcement Module* inquires the *Policy Decision Module*. It thus obtains and enforces an access decision, along with actions that must be carried out before or afterwards, if any. The *Context Sensing Module* serves as a policy information point, as it is responsible for retrieving policies and sensory information and making them known to the PDP. The *Policy Retrieval Point* exists in the form of a database on the device, in conjunction with a remote policy server with which it synchronises. The context may change, potentially triggering additional operations. For instance, when a tablet leaves the company premises, certain assets might be erased. In such cases, the Context Sensing Module is also a Policy Enforcement Module.

The second approach improves secure storage on the mobile device. App-controlled encryption is provided, backed by a secure element. The latter ensures that only predefined users and apps can access protected assets: it only exposes cryptographic key material upon successful user and app authentication. The component implementing this –the *Secure Component Communication Module*– resides on both the device and the secure element. Since communication between the app and the secure element takes place over a secure channel, a contactless smartcard can be used without concessions regarding confidentiality and data authentication.

4   Secure Asset Storage

The first part of our approach is application-controlled secure storage. The important concerns are access control, data authentication and confidentiality. We propose using a secure element for hardware backing. Different types are available: a SIM card, a secure microSD card, a contactless smartcard or an embedded secure element. This makes our solution deployable on nearly every Android device. The tamper-resistance property also provides better security guarantees than solutions based on a Trusted Execution Environment (see section 2).

Cryptographic keys on the secure element can be used to encrypt assets, to authenticate to a server or for digital signatures. For the encryption of large amounts of data, symmetric keys are the method of choice. Different strategies are conceivable. A first one is for all crypto operations to take place on the secure element. This provides the highest level of protection, but is not feasible due to the computational and bandwidth constraints of such tamper-resistant hardware. In a second option, the secure element maintains a key pair for each application, while wrapped symmetric keys are stored on the persistent memory of the mobile device. Upon an app's request, the secure element unwraps and returns these keys. Alternatively, symmetric keys can be stored and retrieved directly. While the latter approach imposes less overhead, the former allows confidential asset sharing on untrusted servers, using a PKI-based approach.

The threats we take into account, are the following.

Eavesdropping. The communication between the app and the secure element cannot necessarily be trusted (e.g. when using a contactless smartcard). To address this, the secure element exposes a –certified– public key, designated to set up a secure channel.

Illegitimate Access. Authorised apps have exclusive access to their keys. Before being granted access, two conditions must be fulfilled. First, the user must authenticate using a personal passcode. Since the number of entry attempts is limited, this can safely be a PIN. Second, the app must prove knowledge of a secret that it obtained during an initial pairing phase.

Denial of Service Against PIN Entry. The aforementioned PIN limit precludes brute-force attacks. However, illegitimate applications could perform trials until the allowed attempts are exhausted. To prevent this, the secure element first verifies the application secret and subsequently authenticates the user. Only then, a PIN attempt is counted. The application secret is a 128-bit pseudorandom string, making resilient enough against unlimited trials from unauthorised apps.

4.1   Protocols

This section elaborates on the protocols, used by our approach.

Pairing. In this phase, the application registers to the secure element. Upon success, the latter creates an app-specific credential store. Both parties now also share the same app secret $K_{SE,A}$. Furthermore, the application obtains the secure element's public key pk_{SE}. The most simple approach is for the user to express his consent using a long PUK code. Alternatively, a third party can mediate between the app and the secure element.

Access to Assets. Once the pairing phase is complete, the application can access its credential store upon user consent. This is depicted in protocol 1. First, a session key is established using the secure element's public key [step 1]. The key agreement protocol used, is *dhOneFlow*, from the NIST 800-56A specification [6]. Next, the app requests the user's passcode and transfers it together with its secret $K_{SE,A}$ (N_{SE} represents a nonce) [steps 3-4]. Subsequently, the secure element verifies $K_{SE,A}$ and the user's passcode [steps 5-6]. The secure channel is now set up and the app can retrieve its credentials.

Protocol 1 (setupSecureChannel).

(1) SE $\leftrightarrows$ A : $K_{sess} \leftarrow$ authKeyAgreement(sk_{SE}; pk_{SE})
        % further communication is encrypted with key K_{sess}
(2) SE $\rightarrow$ A : N_{SE}
(3) U $\rightarrow$ A   : $passcode \leftarrow$ enterPasscode()
(4) SE $\leftarrow$ A : $h(K_{SE,A}||N_{SE}+1), passcode$
(5) SE   : if (not verify$_A(K_{SE,A})$) abort
(6) SE   : if (not verify$_U(passcode)$) abort

5   Context-Aware Asset Management

The rationale behind the second part of our approach is to selectively constrain the availability and the presence of assets towards apps. Note that the context-aware component provides soft, *user-assistive security*. It assumes the user is already authenticated, a concern addressed in section 4. If this is not the case, the app's symmetric key is not released by the secure element and the stored assets cannot be decrypted.

Each asset is accompanied by a policy, which specifies the apps that can access it and under what contextual conditions. Apart from access control for apps, actions executed before or after such a request or following the triggering of an event, are also part of the policy. Typical examples are asset download, synchronisation and removal. Metrics that qualify as context include time, location, application white- or blacklists and the presence of nearby wireless networks. The party acting as policy administrator can vary, depending on the application scenario: an individual user, a corporate administrator or a third party service provider. The policies described here, are related to both *access control* and *device self-management*. Prominent languages in these domains are XACML and Ponder2, respectively. Regardless of the overlapping expressiveness in each other's domains, we have opted for XACML. There are advantages to using a standardised policy language: portability across platforms, tool support, extensibility and familiarity among security administrators.

To further illustrate the intended approach, two example policies are demonstrated below. To get around XACML's extensive syntax, they are shown in pseudocode. The first one constrains the availability of door credentials on a home nurse's tablet. Door credential Y is removed if it has not been used for over one hour or if the device is away from the residence of patience X.

```
If location offsite "Residence of patient X"
OR unused > 1hr
Then Remove "DoorCredential Y"
```

In the second policy, access to a contract on a sales representative's tablet, is restricted. The contracting app is only granted read and write access during working hours.

```
If 8:00 <= time <= 18:00
Then App.Contract has R/W-access
            to "Contract Z"
```

Lastly, access to privileged code invocation can also be controlled. The exact implementation of the above concepts is platform-specific and is therefore described along with the prototype in section 6.

6   Prototype: Context-Aware File Management

The proof-of-concept implements a corporate file management system, consisting of three parts: a corporate file server, an administration component and a mobile component on a phone or tablet.

6.1   File Server

The file server is considered to be legacy infrastructure. State of the art file management solutions offer a myriad of functionality. However, to validate the interoperability of our approach, we limit ourselves to a simple FTP server with confidentiality and mutual authentication over a TLS layer (FTPS). Apache Commons Net 3.2 is used for this purpose.

6.2   Administration Component

The MDM server resides on the same machine as the file server. In more complex deployments, they can be hosted separately. The administration component allows to create and modify policies and to push them to the file server and to affected mobile devices. A notification is sent to each of these devices. Consequently, their mobile component connects to the file server and retrieves the policies involved. Push notifications serve to relieve mobile devices from listening to incoming connections. The push service we use, is Google Cloud Messaging.

6.3   Mobile Component

The mobile component –a file management app– uses the mechanisms described in section 4, to protect its files.

File Synchronisation and Secure Storage. The secure element is a Giesecke & Devrient Mobile Security Card. It runs Java Card 2.2.2 and offers tamper-resistant storage of key material. A symmetric key belonging to the mobile component, is housed in it. This key is created when the pairing phase is successfully completed (see section 4.1). The Mobile Security Card can be easily addressed using the `MSC SmartcardService` from the SEEK4Android project, installable in the same way as any app.

Managed files must be confidential and authentic, while policies are not considered confidential. To fulfill both, AES-GCM (AES in Galois Counter Mode) is used. Not only do authentication and encryption take place in a single step, GCM takes better advantage of parallellism than f.i. the more frequently-used CBC mode. To quantify the performance of our approach, we executed 100 encryptions and decryptions of 10KB, 100KB, 500KB, 1MB, 5MB and 10MB files from the internal app storage to the external storage and vice versa. We compared our results to Android's file system encryption, which uses Linux's `dm-crypt`. To obtain meaningful test results, we switched to AES-CBC, the algorithm used by `dm-crypt`. Table 1 lists the mean values of four setups: unencrypted I/O, Android's file system encryption and two versions of the proposed secure storage mechanism: a Java-based (Bouncy Castle v1.47) and a C-based one (PolarSSL v1.3.2) that is accessed through the Java Native Interface. The tests were run on a Samsung Galaxy Tab 2, with Android 4.1.2. Note that dm-crypt is nearly as fast as having no encryption at all. The Java-based implementation, on the other hand, is prohibitively slow: between 7 and 27 times. This has led us to create a native implementation. A performance gain can clearly be observed. For 10MB, the C implementation with a 20KB buffer encrypts and decrypts only 1.5 and 3 times slower than dm-crypt, which operates at the kernel-level. The C-based implementation can be further optimised by not only executing the cipher operations natively, but the I/O as well.

Confidentiality and authenticity are also a concern when files are in transit between the file server and the mobile component. We address this using a TLS layer with mutual authentication. For prototyping purposes, trust is established by exchanging and trusting public keys offline. In large-scale setups, this is typically realised using a public key infrastructure. The app's private authentication key is stored in the secure element.

Setting up a secure channel between the mobile component and the secure element involves an authenticated key agreement step. 192-bit ECDH (Elliptic Curve Diffie-Hellman) is chosen over RSA, as it is less computationally intensive. This is particularly a point of attention for resource-constrained secure elements. A performance test of 100 runs shows that the average time to set up the secure channel and retrieve the app encryption key is 1667ms. Note that this step only

Table 1. Secure storage performance: comparative test results (milliseconds)

File size	10KB	100KB	500KB	1MB	5MB	10MB
No encryption						
Outgoing stream	1.17	5.06	24.14	48.56	239.83	638.28
Incoming stream	2.13	17.73	86.23	171.53	871.87	1784.20
Android file system encryption (dm-crypt)						
Outgoing encryption	1.18	5.58	23.95	49.78	250.13	903.48
Incoming decryption	2.61	17.69	95.65	181.22	937.48	1962.45
Java-based AES (Bouncy Castle)						
Outgoing encryption	19.46	140.98	644.34	1309.11	6940.81	13801.72
Incoming decryption	18.78	147.93	688.69	1438.58	7222.27	14607.33
C-based AES through JNI (1K buffer)						
Outgoing encryption	3.84	37.90	194.22	402.09	1977.56	4138.84
Incoming decryption	6.93	55.89	272.75	539.62	2678.56	5333.50
C-based AES through JNI (20K buffer)						
Outgoing encryption	15.50	45.95	143.60	277.94	1384.46	2799.56
Incoming decryption	15.32	45.98	158.44	308.13	1491.25	2957.24

takes place when the app is started: the key remains available as long as the it is running. A usability-security tradeoff exists in how frequently a user is asked to enter his PIN.

Our secure storage API consists of two layers. The first one is specific to the storage of cryptographic keys. It enables the developer to interchangeably use different technologies. As a validation case, we created an implementation with the Mobile Security Card as well as with the Android KeyChain. The biggest challenge in the adding the latter, was how to deal with its asynchronous invocation. The second layer encrypts and decrypts the stored items and exposes them to the application. It is realised as an intuitive key-value store.

Contextual Sensing, Decision and Enforcement. The Context Sensing Module is built on top of a generic codebase, which can be extended to contain various types of context. The internal policy representation is hierarchical and event-driven. Monitoring change events is necessary, as policy decisions do not only occur in relation to an access request, but also as a result of context change. This proof of concept incorporates the following contextual metrics: location, absolute and recurring time intervals and application black- and whitelists. Multiple implementations of the same contextual variable are supported. For instance, time can be retrieved from the mobile device or through a trusted time server, for more critical uses.

The Context Sensing Module interfaces with a `ContentProvider` that is extended to act as a Policy Decision Module and a Policy Enforcement Module. A `ContentProvider` is a flexible Android building block that offers dynamically assignable and revocable permissions. It can essentially supply any structured data type, including files. Two-way context-aware synchronisation is implemented between local files and their remote counterparts.

To denote the type and id of a requested file, an external app constructs and sends an `Intent` with a local URI to the `ContentProvider`. This allows per-file decisions and enforcement. Note that nothing prevents receiving apps from saving a copy of acquired files. Determining which apps to trust, is seen as part of the administrator's task. This trust preference is specified as an application white- or blacklist in the policy. The beneficial result of this approach is that neither Android nor the requesting app need modification: secure storage and policy enforcement are handled transparently by the `ContentProvider`.

Automatic download, synchronisation and deletion tasks are executed by a subclassed Android `Service`. It also interacts with the Context Sensing Module. The tasks are executed in two different manners: relative to a user's workflow (e.g. deleting a credential one hour after last use), or completely automated (e.g. periodic cleanup of assets not used for more than a given time span).

More advanced functionality can be realised if we allow modifications to external applications. `ContentProvider`'s API provides a `call` function for the invocation of custom methods it exposes. Similarly, RPC interfaces can be offered by extending the above Android `Service` implementation. External applications can bind to it and invoke its exposed set of methods. The `Service` enforces controlled access in much the same way as the `ContentProvider`. This approach allows support for credential-based operations without releasing the secrets (e.g. signing and proof generation).

7 Evaluation

This section evaluates the added value of the context-aware management module (CAM) and the secure storage module (SST). It mainly focuses on the added security that CAM and SST offer in comparison to major mobile platforms. Moreover, we argue that the interoperability and the usability of our approach, positively contribute to its adoption. Table 2 summarises the main benefits.

For the security analysis, we assume that the sandboxing mechanism works correctly on both Android and iOS. More specifically: malware without root privileges cannot steal data that is stored in an app's context. We also assume this malware cannot intercept entered passwords. Similar assumptions are taken in [15] and are reasonable if a user does not root or jailbreak his device. However, a skilled adversary can access the –encrypted– file system on a stolen device and launch dictionary and brute-force attacks on the passcode.

Android's file system encryption uses `dm-crypt`. It wraps the file system key with a passcode-derived one using the `PBKDF2` algorithm. A adept attacker can extract the contents of the encrypted file system and perform offline passcode attempts, thus exploiting additional computing power. iOS' file encryption keys are derived from a passcode as well as a hardware-backed secret (i.e. the device `UID`). This precludes offline passcode attacks. If configured by the user or the mobile device management admin (MDM), Android and iOS can automatically

Table 2. Comparison of security and usability properties of Android, iOS, the context-aware management module (CAM), and the secure storage module (SST)

	Android	iOS	CAM	SST	SST + CAM
Security					
-Factors	passcode	passcode, device	n/a	passcode, SE	passcode, SE
-Attack barriers	PBKDF2	PBKDF2 (Δt)	n/a	attempt limit	attempt limit
-Local asset mgmt	app/user	app/user	semi-auto	app/user	semi-auto
-Data revocation	wipe	wipe	n/a	implicit	implicit
Prerequisites	*Internet*	*Internet*		*none*	*none*
Usability					
-Passcode complexity	high	medium	high	low	low
-Hardware reqs?	no	yes: on board	no	yes	yes
-Context mgmt gran.	none	coarse	fine	none	fine

wipe themselves after a specified number of failed attempts. However, this circumventable if the device is rooted or jailbroken. As a result, iOS' key derivation function and its hardware backing only slow down passcode attacks (the imposed time delay is denoted by Δt in table 2).

SST surpasses the security offered by both platforms. It is based on a PIN and a tamper-resistant secure element (SE). The attempt limit cannot be circumvented without successfully tampering with the SE. This protection holds, regardless if the device is rooted or not. The remaining possibility is to attack the cryptosystem, a computationally infeasible option. Also note that an Internet connection is needed to initiate a wipe on a default Android or iOS device. The secure element in our approach is blocked after a number of failed PIN attempts, de facto wiping the device. Initiating this requires no network connectivity. Furthermore, unauthorised applications cannot exhaust the PIN entry limit, since an attempt is only counted after successful verification of the app secret. An attacker with physical access to the device, cannot decrypt the data for lack of the PIN. A blocked secure element can be conveniently reactivated by the organisation when the device is back in the hands of the eligible user.

Although CAM is not resistant to physical and rooting attacks, it does minimise the presence of temporary and residual data during its uncompromised use. This means that less sensitive information is harvestable in general. It also provides an effective countermeasure against information-hungry greyware, a significant problem in today's app ecosystem.

Although SST and CAM increase protection level of corporate assets, they do not impose high usability barriers. On the contrary. Passcode complexity is reduced: the attempt limit makes a 4-digit PIN acceptable. Adding to that, asset management is partly automated, which relieves the user from doing this manually.

As for interoperability, the secure element in our solution is –readily or optionally– available in different forms: a SIM card, a secure microSD card, a contactless smartcard or an embedded SE. This makes deployment possible on nearly every Android device. This is in contrast to Android 4.3 and Samsung

KNOX, where an organisation would be limited to a handful of devices with hardware support or to Samsung's high-end range, respectively. The operating system is never altered, lowering the adoption barrier even further. If a `ContentProvider`-based approach is taken, as described in section 6, our approach is interoperable with many third-party apps without having to modify them.

8   Conclusions and Future Work

This paper has presented a secure asset storage strategy for the Android platform. It is backed by a secure element that verifies the eligibility of the user and the app before key material can be accessed. This approach is supplemented by a semi-automated context-aware, management module. It selectively constrains the availability and the presence of assets according to predefined policies. Our approach protects stored data better than iOS in case of device theft and requires no modifications to the operating system. The secure element-based approach ensures that nearly every Android phone can be equipped, contrary to Samsung KNOX or Android 4.3. The proposed concepts have been validated by a context-aware file management prototype.

An interesting extension to this work, is to integrate the secure element in the Android KeyChain, so that API-level support is offered to any application using Android's standard credential storage. Additionally, this would allow the integration of our secure storage strategy into the Device Administration (i.e. MDM) API. A limitation to this approach is that the KeyChain has only been publicly available since Android 4.

Another promising track is trustworthy PIN entry on smartphones and tablets. An increasing number of mobile devices are equipped with a Trusted Execution Environment. Implementing the PIN input as a trusted application, would prevent malware with root access from intercepting it. In addition, trust indicators, such as a blinking LED when the TEE is active, would empower users to appraise the trustworthiness of a PIN input prompt. However, this extension must be traded off against deployability on a more narrow range of devices.

References

1. iOS security (October 2012),
   https://ssl.apple.com/iphone/business/docs/iOS_Security_Oct12.pdf
2. Android Security Overview - Android Open Source (May 2013),
   https://source.android.com/tech/security/
3. Samsung Knox (June 2013),
   http://www.samsung.com/global/business/business-images/resource/
   white-paper/2013/06/Samsung_KNOX_whitepaper_June-0.pdf
4. Windows Phone 8 Security Guide (September 2013),
   http://go.microsoft.com/fwlink/?LinkId=266838

5. Bai, G., Gu, L., Feng, T., Guo, Y., Chen, X.: Context-aware usage control for android. In: Jajodia, S., Zhou, J. (eds.) SecureComm 2010. LNICST, vol. 50, pp. 326–343. Springer, Heidelberg (2010),
   http://dx.doi.org/10.1007/978-3-642-16161-2_19
6. Barker, E.B., Johnson, D., Smid, M.E.: NIST SP 800-56A. Recommendation for Pair-Wise Key Establishment Schemes Using Discrete Logarithm Cryptography. Technical report, Gaithersburg, MD, United States (2013)
7. Belenko, A., Sklyarov, D.: secure password managers" and "military-grade encryption. on smartphones: Oh, really? Technical report, Elcomsoft, Amsterdam (March 2012)
8. Chin, E., Felt, A.P., Greenwood, K., Wagner, D.: Analyzing inter-application communication in android. In: Proceedings of the 9th International Conference on Mobile Systems, Applications, and Services, MobiSys 2011, pp. 239–252. ACM, New York (2011)
9. Enck, W., Gilbert, P., Chun, B.-G., Cox, L.P., Jung, J., McDaniel, P., Sheth, A.N.: Taintdroid: an information-flow tracking system for realtime privacy monitoring on smartphones. In: Proceedings of the 9th USENIX Conference on Operating Systems Design and Implementation, OSDI 2010, pp. 1–6. USENIX Association, Berkeley (2010)
10. Fahl, S., Harbach, M., Oltrogge, M., Muders, T., Smith, M.: Hey, you, get off of my clipboard. In: Sadeghi, A.-R. (ed.) FC 2013. LNCS, vol. 7859, pp. 144–161. Springer, Heidelberg (2013)
11. Feth, D., Jung, C.: Context-aware, data-driven policy enforcement for smart mobile devices in business environments. In: Schmidt, A.U., Russello, G., Krontiris, I., Lian, S. (eds.) MobiSec 2012. LNICST, vol. 107, pp. 69–80. Springer, Heidelberg (2012)
12. May, M.J., Bhargavan, K.: Towards unified authorization for android. In: Jürjens, J., Livshits, B., Scandariato, R. (eds.) ESSoS 2013. LNCS, vol. 7781, pp. 42–57. Springer, Heidelberg (2013)
13. Ongtang, M., McLaughlin, S., Enck, W., McDaniel, P.: Semantically rich application-centric security in android. Security and Communication Networks 5(6), 658–673 (2012)
14. Riva, O., Qin, C., Strauss, K., Lymberopoulos, D.: Progressive authentication: deciding when to authenticate on mobile phones. In: Proceedings of the 21st USENIX Conference on Security Symposium, Security 2012, p. 15. USENIX Association, Berkeley (2012)
15. Teufl, P., Zefferer, T., Stromberger, C.: Mobile device encryption systems. In: Janczewski, L.J., Wolfe, H.B., Shenoi, S. (eds.) SEC 2013. IFIP AICT, vol. 405, pp. 203–216. Springer, Heidelberg (2013)
16. Tiwari, M., Mohan, P., Osheroff, A., Alkaff, H., Shi, E., Love, E., Song, D., Asanović, K.: Context-centric security. In: Proceedings of the 7th USENIX Conference on Hot Topics in Security, HotSec 2012, p. 9. USENIX Association, Berkeley (2012)
17. Wei, X., Gomez, L., Neamtiu, I., Faloutsos, M.: Malicious android applications in the enterprise: What do they do and how do we fix it? In: 2012 IEEE 28th International Conference on Data Engineering Workshops (ICDEW), pp. 251–254 (2012)

Part II

Work in Progress

A Study on Advanced Persistent Threats

Ping Chen, Lieven Desmet, and Christophe Huygens

iMinds-DistriNet, KU Leuven
3001 Leuven, Belgium
{firstname.lastname}@cs.kuleuven.be

Abstract A recent class of threats, known as Advanced Persistent Threats (APTs), has drawn increasing attention from researchers, primarily from the industrial security sector. APTs are cyber attacks executed by sophisticated and well-resourced adversaries targeting specific information in high-profile companies and governments, usually in a long term campaign involving different steps. To a significant extent, the academic community has neglected the specificity of these threats and as such an objective approach to the APT issue is lacking. In this paper, we present the results of a comprehensive study on APT, characterizing its distinguishing characteristics and attack model, and analyzing techniques commonly seen in APT attacks. We also enumerate some non-conventional countermeasures that can help to mitigate APTs, hereby highlighting the directions for future research.

Keywords: advanced threat, APT, sophisticated attacks, cyber security.

1 Introduction

Cyber attacks have existed since the adoption of the Internet and have evolved a lot in the past decades, from viruses and worms in the early days to malware and botnets nowadays. In recent years, a new class of threat, the "Advanced Persistent Threat" (APT) has emerged. Originally used to describe cyber intrusions against military organizations, the APT has evolved and is no longer limited to the military domain. As highlighted in several large-scale security breaches [12,15,1,29], APTs are now targeting a wide range of industries and governments.

While APT has drawn increasing attention from the industrial security community, a comprehensive and clear understanding of the APT research problem is lacking. This paper presents the result of a detailed study of the APT phenomenon, and contributes a taxonomy of phases, mechanisms, and countermeasures. In this paper, we first identify the characteristics of APT, and compare it to traditional threats in Section 2. In Section 3, we dissect a typical APT attack into six phases, analyzing the techniques that are commonly used in each stage. We also enumerate various countermeasure that can be applied to defend against APT attacks. In Section 3.2, we provide case studies of four APTs, illustrating the adversaries' tactics and techniques by applying our presented taxonomy and technical analysis.

B. De Decker and A. Zúquete (Eds.): CMS 2014, LNCS 8735, pp. 63–72, 2014.
© IFIP International Federation for Information Processing 2014

2   Definition: What Is APT?

APTs frequently made global headlines in recent years, and many feel that this term is overloaded, since different people refer to it as different things. Because so many different opinions of what constitutes an APT exist in the commercial market [2,14,23], a clear definition is needed. In this paper, we adopt the definition given by US National Institute of Standards and Technology (NIST), which states that an APT is [17]:

"An adversary that possesses sophisticated levels of expertise and significant resources which allow it to create opportunities to achieve its objectives by using multiple attack vectors (e.g., cyber, physical, and deception). These objectives typically include establishing and extending footholds within the information technology infrastructure of the targeted organizations for purposes of exfiltrating information, undermining or impeding critical aspects of a mission, program, or organization; or positioning itself to carry out these objectives in the future. The advanced persistent threat: (i) pursues its objectives repeatedly over an extended period of time; (ii) adapts to defenders' efforts to resist it; and (iii) is determined to maintain the level of interaction needed to execute its objectives".

This definition provides a good base for distinction between traditional threats and APTs. The distinguishing characteristics of APTs are: (1) specific targets and clear objectives; (2) highly organized and well-resourced attackers; (3) a long-term campaign with repeated attempts; (4) stealthy and evasive attack techniques. We elaborate on each of these characteristics below.

Specific Targets and Clear Objectives. APT attacks are highly targeted attacks, always having a clear goal. The targets are typically governments or organizations possessing substantial intellectual property value. Based on the number of APT attacks discovered by FireEye in 2013 [11], the top ten industry vertical targets are education, finance, high-tech, government, consulting, energy, chemical, telecom, healthcare, and aerospace. While traditional attacks propagate as broadly as possible to improve the chances of success and maximize the harvest, an APT attack only focuses on its pre-defined targets, limiting its attack range.

As for the attack objectives, APTs typically look for digital assets that bring competitive advantage or strategic benefits, such as national security data, intellectual property, trade secrets, etc., while traditional threats mostly search for personal information like credit card data, or generically valuable information that facilitates financial gain.

Highly Organized and Well-Resourced Attackers. The actors behind APTs are typically a group of skilled hackers, working in a coordinated way. They may work in a government/military cyber unit [15], or be hired as cyber mercenaries by governments and private companies [9]. They are well-resourced from both financial and technical perspectives. This provides them with the ability to work for a long period, and have access (by development or procurement) to zero-day vulnerabilities and attack tools. When they are state-sponsored, they may even operate with the support of military or state intelligence.

A Long-Term Campaign with Repeated Attempts. An APT attack is typically a long-term campaign, which can stay undetected in the target's network for several months or years. APT actors persistently attack their targets and they repeatedly adapt their efforts to complete the job when a previous attempt fails. This is different from traditional threats, since traditional attackers often target a wide range of victims, and they will move right on to something less secure if they cannot penetrate the initial target.

Stealthy and Evasive Techniques. APT attacks are stealthy, possessing the ability to stay undetected, concealing themselves within enterprise network traffic, and interacting just enough to achieve the defined objectives. For example, APT actors may use zero-day exploits to avoid signature-based detection, and encryption to obfuscate network traffic. This is different from traditional attacks, where the attackers typically employ "smash and grab" tactics that alert the defenders.

In Table 1, we summarize the differences between traditional threats and APTs for several attack attributes.

Table 1. Comparison of traditional and APT attacks

	Traditional Attacks	APT Attacks
Attacker	Mostly single person	Highly organized, sophisticated, determined and well-resourced group
Target	Unspecified, mostly individual systems	Specific organizations, governmental institutions, commercial enterprises
Purpose	Financial benefits, demonstrating abilities	Competitive advantages, strategic benefits
Approach	Single-run, "smash and grab", short period	Repeated attempts, stays low and slow, adapts to resist defenses, long term

3   Attack Model: How Does APT Work?

APT attacks are meticulously planned, and typically have multiple steps involved. While a specific APT attack may have its unique features, the stages of APT attacks are similar and they differ mostly in the techniques used in each stage. To describe the phases of an APT attack, we adopt a six-stage model based on the concept of an "intrusion kill chain" introduced in [7]. Using such a kill chain model helps to understand threat actors' techniques in each stage, and provides guidance for defense against APT attacks as well.

3.1   Phases of an APT Attack

A typical ATP attack will have the following six phases: (1) reconnaissance and weaponization; (2) delivery; (3) initial intrusion; (4) command and control; (5) lateral movement; (6) data exfiltration.

(1) Reconnaissance and Weaponization. Reconnaissance is also known as information gathering, which is an important preparation step before launching attacks. In this stage, attackers identify and study the targeted organization, collecting as much as information possible about the technical environment and key personnel in that organization. This information is often gathered via open-source intelligence (OSINT) tools and social engineering techniques.

- **Social Engineering.** Social engineering refers to psychological manipulation of people into accomplishing goals that may or may not be in the target's best interest. In cyber attacks, it is often used for obtaining sensitive information, or getting the target to take certain action (e.g. executing malware).
- **OSINT.** OSINT is a form of intelligence collection from publicly available sources, and nowadays it typically refers to aggregating information about a subject via either paid or free sources on the internet. Various information can be collected via OSINT, ranging from the personal profile of an employee to the hardware and software configurations in an organization.

Besides simply grabbing information from the web, attackers may also employ data mining techniques and big data analytics to automatically process the gathered data, in order to produce actionable intelligence. Based on the gathered intelligence, APT actors construct an attacking plan and prepare the necessary tools. In order to be successful, attackers typically prepare various tools for different attack vectors, so that they can adapt tactics in case of failure.

(2) Delivery. In this stage, attackers deliver their exploits to the targets. There are two types of delivery mechanisms: direct and indirect delivery. For direct delivery, the attackers send exploits to their targets via various social engineering techniques, such as spear phishing.

Indirect delivery is stealthy. In this approach the attackers will compromise a 3rd party that is trusted by the target, and then use the compromised 3rd party to indirectly serve exploits. A trusted 3rd party can be a supplier of software/hardware used in the targeted organization, or a legitimate website that is frequently visited by the targeted persons (watering hole attack).

- **Spear Phishing.** Spear phishing is a targeted form of phishing in which fraudulent emails only target a small group of selected recipients. It typically use information gathered during reconnaissance to make the attack more specific and "personal" to the target, in order to increase the probability of success. The recipient is lured to either download a seemingly harmless attachment that contains a vulnerability exploit, or to click a link to a malicious site serving drive-by-download exploits [27]. In APT attacks, malicious attachments are used more often than malicious links, as people normally share files (e.g., reports, business documents, and resumes) via email in the corporate or government environment.
- **Watering Hole Attack.** The concept of a watering hole attack is similar to a predator waiting at a watering hole in a desert, as the predator knows that the victims will have to come to the watering hole. Similarly, rather

than actively sending malicious emails, the attackers can identify 3rd party websites that are frequently visited by the targeted persons, and then try to infect one or more of these websites with malware. Eventually, the delivery accomplishes when the infected webpages are viewed by victims [18]. The use of watering hole attacks have been seen in several APT campaigns [5,6,10].

(3) Initial Intrusion. Initial intrusion happens when the attacker get a first unauthorized access to the target's computer/network. While the attackers may obtain access credentials through social engineering, and simply use them for "legitimate" access, the typical way for intrusion is executing malicious code that exploits a vulnerability in the target's computer. The attackers first deliver malicious code in the delivery stage, and then in the intrusion stage gain access to target's computer when the exploit is successfully executed.

In APT attacks, the attackers often focus on vulnerabilities in Adobe PDF, Adobe Flash and Microsoft Office as well as Internet Explorer. While several APT attacks [12,20] have leveraged zero-day exploits for initial intrusion, many APT attacks also employ older exploits that target unpatched applications.

The initial intrusion is a pivotal phase in an APT attack, since the APT actors establish a foothold in the target's network in this stage. A successful intrusion typically results in the installation of a backdoor malware. From this point, the threat actors connects to the targets' network. As a result, network traffic is generated, and file evidences are left on the victims' computers, which gives defenders the chance to detect an APT in an early phase.

(4) Command and Control. Upon successfully establishing a backdoor, APT actors use Command and Control (C2) mechanisms to take control of the compromised computers, enabling further exploitation of the network. In order to evade detection, the attackers increasingly make use of *various legitimate services* and *publicly available tools*.

- **Social Networking Sites.** The attackers register accounts on various social networking sites, and put control information into blog posts or status messages [16].
- **Tor Anonymity Network.** Servers configured to receive inbound connections only through Tor are called hidden services. Hosting C2 servers in Tor as hidden services makes them harder to identify, blacklist or eliminate.
- **Remote Access Tools (RATs).** Although often used for legitimate remote administration, RATs are often associated with cyber attacks [3,28]. A RAT contains two components: a "server" residing on a victim's endpoint, and a "client" that is installed on the attackers machine. In order to make it work, the "server" component needs to be delivered to the target's machine first, which is often accomplished via spear-phishing emails.

(5) Lateral Movement. Once the communication between the compromised systems and C2 servers is established, threat actors move inside the network, in order to expand their control over the targeted organization, which in turn enables them to discover and collect valuable data. Lateral movement usually involves the following activities: (1) performing internal reconnaissance to map the network and acquire intelligence; (2) compromising additional systems in order to harvest credentials and gain escalated privileges; (3) identifying and collecting valuable digital assets, such as development plans, trade secrets, etc..

This stage typically lasts a long period, because (1) the attackers want to harvest a maximum of information over a long term; (2) the activities are designed to run low and slow in order to avoid detection. As APT actors move deeper into the network, their movements become difficult to detect. APT actors often utilize legitimate OS features and tools that are typically used by IT administrators, and they may also crack or steal credentials to gain legitimate access, which both make their activities undetectable or even untraceable.

(6) Data Exfiltration. The primary goal for an APT attack is to steal sensitive data in order to gain strategic benefits, thus data exfiltration is a critical step for the attackers. Typically the data is funneled to an internal staging server where it is compressed and often encrypted for transmission to external locations under the attackers' control. In order to hide the transmission process, APT actors often use secure protocols like SSL/TLS, or leverage the anonymity feature of Tor network [16].

3.2   Case Study of APT Attacks

In order to better understand the APT attack model, we studied four APT attacks reported in various sources [12,20,29,10], mapping the attackers' action into our six-stage model. The results are shown in Table 2.

3.3   Countermeasures

Due to the complexity and stealthiness of APTs, there is no single solution that offers effective protection. The current best practice is a wide range of security countermeasures resulting a multi-layered defense. However, due to the specific nature of APTs, some of the existing defense systems need to be reengineered to work in the APT context, hereby requiring additional research. For example, while genetic algorithms have been proved useful for malware detection, their applicability in a large dataset is subject of further study. We elaborate on some defense techniques below.

Security Awareness Training. Considering the wide use of social engineering techniques (e.g., spear-phishing emails) in APT campaigns, security awareness training plays an important role in defense. Besides the general best security practices, the training should also provide education about APT attacks. According to an APT awareness study [8], more than half of the industries are not awareness of the differences between APTs and traditional threats, and 67% of respondents report the lack of awareness training relative to APTs.

Traditional Defense Mechanisms. Traditional defense mechanisms are necessary since they block known attack vectors, and hence increase the difficulty

Table 2. Comparison of different APTs

Name	Operation Aurora [12]	RAS Breach [20]	Operation Ke3chang [29]	Operation SnowMan [10]
Active Time	June 2009 - December 2009	Unknown - March 2011	May 2010 - December 2013	Unknown - February 2014
Recon. and Weaponization	employees' emails, zero-day exploits, backdoor, and C2 tools	employees' emails, zero-day exploits, trojanized docs, backdoor, RAT	officials' emails, trojanized docs, backdoor, and C2 tools	identify weakness in vfw.org, RAT, backdoor
Delivery	spear phishing (malicious links)	spear phishing (malicious xls file)	spear phishing (malicious zip file)	watering hole attack (compromise & infect vfw.org)
Initial Intrusion	drive-by download (CVE-2010-0249)	xls vulnerability (CVE-2011-0609)	victims open the executable file	drive-by download (CVE-2014-0322)
Command and Control	custom C2 protocol, operating on TCP port 443	Poison Ivy RAT	custom C2 protocol, based on HTTP protocol	ZxShell, Gh0st RAT
Lateral Movement	compromise SCM, and obtain source code	Perform privilege escalation, gather SecureID data	compromise internal systems, collect data	unknown
Data Exfiltration	upload data to C2 servers	compress, encrypt data as RAR files, use FTP for transmission	compress, encrypt data as RAR files	unknown, could be US military intelligence

for APT actors. Common countermeasures that must be used are: patch management, anti-virus software, firewalls, host-based intrusion detection systems (HIDS), network-based intrusion detection systems (NIDS), intrusion prevention system (IPS), Security Information and Event Management (SIEM), content filtering software, etc..

Security awareness training and traditional defense mechanisms do not adequately address APTs. Defenders should combine them with the following state-of-the-art countermeasures that are proposed to mitigate APTs.

Advanced Malware Detection. Malware is critical for the initial intrusion. Since APT actors often leverage zero-day exploits or custom-developed evasive tools that bypass traditional defenses, the ability to detect advanced malware is important for defense against APTs. Sandboxing execution is a proven technique for analyzing malware's behavior, which allows defenders to identify unknown advanced malware [19]. As advanced malware may leverage various sandbox-evasion techniques [22] to detect the VM environment, it is important to take these sandbox-evasion techniques into consideration when using sandboxing execution. Also, the research challenge in this area is to perform the malware analysis on-line, and in a non-intrusive fashion.

Event Anomaly Detection. Since APT actors use various stealthy and evasive techniques, there is no "known bad" pattern that traditional signature-based defense mechanisms could use. Instead of looking for "known bad" item, an effective APT detection approach is to study normal behavior and search for anomalous activities. Anomaly detection includes the detection of suspicious network traffic and suspicious system activities, or "irregular" clusters of activities (potentially obtained through machine learning). Due to the massive amount of data the need to be analyzed in a reasonable time, anomaly detection typically relates to the research problem of big data analytics. There are several researchers proposing the use of big data analytic for APT detection. In [4], Giura & Wang implemented a large-scale distributed computing framework based on MapReduce to process all possible events, which can be used to detect APT attacks. Liu et. al. [13] proved that analyzing a huge volume of HTTP requests with Hadoop and Lucene can help to quickly uncover potential victims based on a known APT victim.

Data Loss Prevention. Since the ultimate goal of an APT attacks is the transmission of valuable data from the target's network to outside, a fully contextually aware data loss prevention (DLP) solution can be deployed as the last line of defense to protect sensitive data against exfiltration. A DLP solution is a system that is designed to detect and·prevent potential data breach by monitoring and blocking sensitive data while in-use, in-motion, and at-rest. It requires the defender to identify its sensitive and critical data first, and define policies and rules in a DLP application for protection. An example research solution is [21].

Intelligence-Driven Defense. Intelligence-driven defense is not a specific defense solution, it is a defense strategy that leverage the knowledge about the adversaries, and adapt defense based on the gathered intelligence [7]. Since APT actors are determined, and typically launch repeated attacks against the target, defenders can create an intelligence feedback loop, which allow them to identify patterns of previous intrusion attempts, understand the adversaries' techniques, and then implement countermeasures to reduce the risk of subsequent intrusions.

In Table 3, we summarize the attack techniques and tools that commonly seen in each stage of an APT attack. Additionally, we also identify the countermeasures that can be applied in each stage.

4 Related Work

Existing research on APTs are mostly from industrial security community. Traditional security service providers (e.g., McAfee, Symantec) and emerging APT-focused companies (e.g., FireEye, Mandiant) regularly publish technical reports that document cases of APT attacks [18,1,15,11]. In [26], Thonnard et al. conducted an in-depth analysis of of 18,580 email attacks that were identified as targeted attacks by Symantec, and through the analysis, they showed that a targeted attack is typically a long-running campaign highly focusing on a limited number of organizations.

Table 3. Attack techniques and countermeasures in each stage of an APT attack

Stages	Attack techniques/tools	Countermeasures
Reconnaissance and Weaponization	OSINT, Social engineering Preparing malware	Security awareness training, Patch management, Firewall
Delivery	Spear phishing, Watering hole attack	Content filtering software, NIDS, Anti-virus software
Initial Intrusion	Zero-day exploits, Remote code execution	Patch management, HIDS, Advanced malware detection
Command and Control	Exploiting legitimate services, RAT, Encryption	NIDS, SIEM, Event Anomaly detection
Lateral Movement	Privilege Escalation, Collecting data	Access control, HIDS, NIDS, Event Anomaly detection
Data Exfiltration	Compression, Encryption, Intermediary Staging	Data Loss Prevention

There are several articles [24,25] that briefly explained APT attacks and discussed the detection techniques. However, they are not as comprehensive as our presented analysis. As for the countermeasures, several academic researchers proposed the use of big data analytics for APT detection [4,13].

5 Conclusion

APTs are sophisticated, specific and evolving threats, yet certain patterns can be identified in the their process. In this paper, we focused on the identification of these commonalities. Traditional countermeasures are needed but not sufficient for the protection against APTs. In order to mitigate the risks posed by APTs, defenders have to gain a baseline understanding of the steps and techniques involved in the attacks, and develop new capabilities that address the specifics of APT attacks. By studying public APT cases and the offerings of the security industry, we presented this broad perspective on APT, which should establish common ground within the security community and provide guidance for further defensive research.

Acknowledgements. We want to thank the anonymous reviewers for the valuable comments. This research is partially funded by the Research Fund KU Leuven, iMinds, IWT, and by the EU FP7 projects WebSand, NESSoS and STREWS. With the financial support from the Prevention of and Fight against Crime Programme of the European Union (B-CCENTRE).

References

1. Alperovitch, D.: Revealed: Operation Shady RAT (2011)
2. Bejtlich, R.: What Is APT and What Does It Want (2010),
   http://taosecurity.blogspot.be/2010/01/
   what-is-apt-and-what-does-it-want.html

3. Bennett, J.T., et al.: Poison Ivy: Assessing Damage and Extracting Intelligence (2013)
4. Giura, P., Wang, W.: Using large scale distributed computing to unveil advanced persistent threats. SCIENCE 1(3) (2013)
5. Gragido, W.: Lions at the Watering Hole – The "VOHO" Affair (2012), http://blogs.rsa.com/lions-at-the-watering-hole-the-voho-affair/
6. Haq, T., Khalid, Y.: Internet Explorer 8 Exploit Found in Watering Hole Campaign Targeting Chinese Dissidents (2013)
7. Hutchins, E.M., et al.: Intelligence-Driven Computer Network Defense Informed by Analysis of Adversary Campaigns and Intrusion Kill Chains. In: Proceedings of the 6th International Conference on Information Warfare and Security (2013)
8. ISACA. Advanced Persistent Threat Awareness (2013)
9. Kaspersky. The Icefog APT: A Tale of Cloak and Three Daggers (2013)
10. Kindlund, D., et al.: Operation SnowMan: DeputyDog Actor Compromises US Veterans of Foreign Wars Website (2014)
11. FireEye Labs. Fireeye advanced threat report 2013 (2014)
12. McAfee Labs. Protecting Your Critical Assets: Lessons Learned from "Operation Aurora" (2010)
13. Liu, S.-T., Chen, Y.-M., Lin, S.-J.: A novel search engine to uncover potential victims for APT investigations. In: Hsu, C.-H., Li, X., Shi, X., Zheng, R. (eds.) NPC 2013. LNCS, vol. 8147, pp. 405–416. Springer, Heidelberg (2013)
14. Mandiant. The Advanced Persistent Threat (2010)
15. Mandiant. APT1: Exposing One of China's Cyber Espionage Unit (2013)
16. Information Warfare Monitor and Shadowserver Foundation. Shadows in the Cloud: Investigating Cyber Espionage 2.0 (2010)
17. NIST. Managing Information Security Risk: Organization, Mission, and Information System View. SP 800-39 (2011)
18. O'Gorman, G., McDonald, G.: The Elderwood Project (2012)
19. Zubair Rafique, M., et al.: Evolutionary algorithms for classification of malware families through different network behaviors. In: Proceedings of the Genetic and Evolutionary Computation Conference (2014)
20. Rivner, U.: Anatomy of an Attack (2011), https://blogs.rsa.com/anatomy-of-an-attack/
21. Schmid, M., et al.: Protecting data from malicious software. In: Proceedings of the 18th Annual Computer Security Applications Conference, IEEE (2002)
22. Singh, A., Bu, Z.: Hot Knives Through Butter: Evading File-based Sandboxes (2014)
23. Symantec. Advanced Persistent Threats: A Symantec Perspective (2011)
24. Tankard, C.: Advanced Persistent Threats and how to monitor and deter them. Network security 2011(8), 16–19 (2011)
25. Thomson, G.: APTs: a poorly understood challenge. Network Security 2011(11), 9–11 (2011)
26. Thonnard, O., Bilge, L., O'Gorman, G., Kiernan, S., Lee, M.: Industrial espionage and targeted attacks: Understanding the characteristics of an escalating threat. In: Balzarotti, D., Stolfo, S.J., Cova, M. (eds.) RAID 2012. LNCS, vol. 7462, pp. 64–85. Springer, Heidelberg (2012)
27. TrendLabs. Spear-Phishing Email: Most Favored APT Attack Bait (2012)
28. Villeneuve, N., Bennett, J.T.: XtremeRAT: Nuisance or Threat (2014)
29. Villeneuve, N., et al.: Operation Ke3chang: Targeted Attacks Against Ministries of Foreign Affairs (2013)

Dynamic Parameter Reconnaissance for Stealthy DoS Attack within Cloud Systems

Suaad Alarifi[2,3] and Stephen Wolthusen[1,2]

[1] Norwegian Information Security Laboratory,
Department of Computer Science,
Gjøvik University College, Norway
[2] Information Security Group,
Department of Mathematics,
Royal Holloway, University of London, UK
[3] King Abdulaziz University, Jeddah, Saudi Arabia
{s.alarifi,stephen.wolthusen}@rhul.ac.uk

Abstract. Public IaaS cloud environments are vulnerable to misbehaving applications and virtual machines. Moreover, cloud service availability, reliability, and ultimately reputation is specifically at risk from Denial of Service forms as it is based on resource over-commitment.

In this paper, we describe a stealthy randomised probing strategy to learn thresholds used in the process of taking migration decisions in the cloud (i.e. reverse engineering of migration algorithms). These discovered thresholds are used to design a more efficient, harder to detect, and robust cloud DoS attack family. A sequence of tests is designed to extract and reveal these thresholds; these are performed by coordinating stealthily increased resource consumption among attackers whilst observing cloud management reactions to the increased demand. We can learn the required parameters by repeating the tests, observing the cloud reactions, and analysing the observations statistically. Revealing these hidden parameters is a security breach by itself; furthermore, they can be used to design a hard-to-detect DoS attack by stressing the host resources using a precise amount of workload to trigger migration. We design a formal model for migration decision processes, create a dynamic algorithm to extract the required hidden parameters, and demonstrate the utility with a specimen DoS attack.

Keywords: CIDoS, IaaS security, Cloud Computing Security, Migration Security in the Cloud.

1 Introduction

Attacks specific to cloud infrastructure have recently gained attention [1,2]. Most of this earlier work targeted availability which affects reliability and might cause Service Level Agreement breaches.

High availability is critical in the cloud and it is a main concern for enterprises moving to cloud. There is competition between providers for high availability; they publish annually service outage status reports, where SLA only

B. De Decker and A. Zúquete (Eds.): CMS 2014, LNCS 8735, pp. 73–85, 2014.
© IFIP International Federation for Information Processing 2014

specify minimum availability requirements. In this paper, we design a stealthy randomising testing strategy to learn thresholds that are used in the process of taking migration decisions (i.e. reverse engineering of migration algorithms). We perform a series of tests to reveal these thresholds; these tests are based on a cloud specific DoS attack called Cloud-Internal Denial of Service (CIDoS) described earlier [3] together with statistical analysis. The attack mis-uses *migration* and *over-commitment* features, which are essential to cloud systems as permits elasticity, allowing virtual machines (VMs) to expand. Cloud systems rely on resource sharing to reduce cost by maximising utilisation of cloud hosts. If one of the VMs in the highly utilised host decides to expand, some of the co-resident VMs may be migrated to provide space for expansion. Moreover, as stated in [4] *"the host is oversubscribed; that is, if all the VMs request their maximum allowed CPU performance, the total CPU demand will exceed the capacity of the CPU"*; this is what we call misusing *over-commitment* and it is most harmful when there is *rapid* coordination between a group of malicious VMs.

In CIDoS, m co-resident VMs increase their workload to reach a threshold (time and strength) to trigger migration. In [3], these thresholds were assumed known to the attackers while in reality they are hidden and discovering them requires designing a new attack which we describe in this paper. We perform tests to reveal some of the cloud migration parameters that are used by migration algorithms. We design a formal model for migration decision process then create a dynamic algorithm to extract the required parameters. The mechanisms to extract these thresholds are adapts to dynamic changes in cloud algorithms. Revealing parameters is hence a security threat by itself; moreover, these can be used by malicious VMs to accurately generate the needed workload to repeated trigger migration resulting in *thrashing*. It is vital that the generated workload is no more than required to avoid detection and make the attack live longer. Conversely, attackers may also use the revealed parameters to avoid being migrated as we will see later. The rest of the paper is structured as follows. CIDoS attack is explained in section 2. Section 3 is the threat model while the literature review is in section 4. The attack is discussed in section 5; analysis and discussion are shown in section 6. Finally, section 7 covers conclusion and future work.

2   Attack Mechanism Outline

In the CIDoS family of attacks, attackers are assumed to be co-resident VMs; these VMs w.l.o.g. coordinate their consumption of host resources following a pattern distributed by the attack leader. The pattern is designed so that the total of the attackers' resource consumption plus the regular consumption will break a threshold causing migration for some of the VMs to balance the load in the over-utilised host. The migration process is targeted as it has a relatively high cost for the cloud operator (network, host utilisation, and ultimately energy), and may affect availability and reliability, also threatening SLA breaches. VMs can be migrated either *live* or *offline*, but both migration methods are expensive, particularly where service dependencies exist. Online migration implies migrating even the memory while it is running and in use and offline migration implies turning the VM off, disrupting services.

If attackers successfully force the cloud to enter a continuous state of migration, the whole service will have difficulty functioning. Furthermore, more dramatic orders might be issued such as turning *on* a new host or evacuate a host and turn it *off* to save energy which cost more than regular migration.

To prepare for the attack, there should be m malicious co-resident VMs; achieving co-residency is popular topic in cloud attacks; many techniques are suggested in [1,3] to attain co-residency or increase its possibility i.e. by misusing the placement algorithm (VMs distribution algorithm) or by using brute force strategy (create large number of VMs in the same area and terminate not co-resident ones).

After achieving co-residency, the attack leader has to create a covert channel to communicate and coordinate the attack among malicious VMs. Covert channels are usually used in cloud attacks, see [1,2]. Then the leader checks the capacity of the covert channel; if the covert channel is too narrow, the attack will be converted to a brute force scenario. In brute force, the leader only distributes the signal "attack now" to all participants and they in turn increase their consumptions as a response to the attacking order then the host might not be able to cope with the stress and there will be a wave of migration. This scenario is easy to detect and block by security defences in the cloud; regular host based intrusion detection system, HIDS, that is anomaly based can detect the sudden change in behaviour with high accuracy. Brute force scenario is not practically strong but it is a solution for very narrow covert channels.

If the covert channel is wide enough (over a threshold based on i.e. the amount of data need to be sent, the value of m and the available time to coordinate the attack), the leader will check the available number of co-resident malicious VMs (m); if m is *just over* the required number of VMs to form the attack ($m >= T_1$), then apply scenario 2. If m is *far over* T_1 (over another bigger threshold T_2, $m >= T_2 > T_1$) then go to scenario 1. T_1 and T_2 are safe thresholds that are calculated based on the host specifications, high specifications (i.e. number of processors and their speeds) means bigger T_1 and T_2 values [3].

Scenario 1: Attack Pattern Random Sampling

In this scenario, there is no scarcity of co-resident malicious VMs, therefore, there is no need for a neat distribution of the workload between attackers. Attackers will benefit from abundance to make it a more robust attack. Each malicious VM decides locally its part of the attack (the strength and timing of the workload waves). These choices are not completely random but they rely on two factors; first the peaks should be around specific points distributed by the leader but where exactly? and how strong they are? are decided locally. Second, the workload pattern of each of the attackers should be as close as possible to its previous workload (history) to avoid being caught by anomaly based HIDS.

So each VM decides locally but they are following the same plan distributed by the leader and the sum of the workloads should trigger migration by breaking the severity threshold T_s which is also distributed by the leader. The calculation of T_s will be discussed later in the paper.

Scenario 2: Spread-Spectrum Attack Distribution

Because of the shortage of participants in this scenario, the leader should design the attack neatly and each participant should know *exactly* where and how strong is the peaks that he/she should create. The leader predicts the normal workload pattern of the host for the next short interval of time and also predicts the attack pattern (the amount of workload need to be added to the predicted workload to break the severity threshold T_s); The leader also has to calculate the value of T_s and distribute it among attackers, see figure 1; the highlighted area in the figure will be divided into units and distributed among attackers; the distribution is by using spread-spectrum technique, see [3] for details.

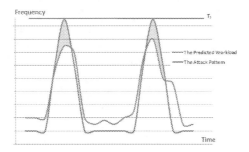

Fig. 1. Qualitative illustration of spread-spectrum attack [3]

The attack is coordinated by a protocol designed specifically for this task. The protocol establishes a secure communication channel among attackers using Group Key Agreement protocol. It also synchronises time among VMs with the consideration of Packet Delay Variation, tolerates failures, hides the identity of attackers, authenticates participants, and resists number of attacks i.e. reply attack, see [3] for details.

3   Threat Model

The primary motivation is designing a stealthy testing strategy to reveal migration algorithms parameters which can be used to improve CIDoS attack, make it more harmful and harder to detect. We succeed if we can extract these parameters and calculate their reliability. We target large-scale public cloud.

In the attack there are: the attack leader (i.e. the last to arrive malicious VM), other co-resident malicious VMs, the cloud host where malicious VMs live together with other innocent VMs, and a cloud management node where hosts management algorithms are run.

In our model we have the following assumptions; first, we assume that migration feature is *enabled* in the cloud service (some providers disable migration support for security and performance reasons but as we said earlier it is a *main* feature of the cloud). Second, we assume that the attack leader can monitor the host workload to be able to predict the workload pattern for future short interval of time and to be able to build an anomaly host based intrusion detection system (we will see its need later in the paper). This assumption is realistic because the host workload can be monitored by gathering observations from the environment or performing tests and measure the respond time of the host; furthermore, techniques from [2,5] can also be used to monitor the workload. Third, we assume that virtual servers have relatively steady workload pattern (mixing services in one VM is against best practice especially that the cost model is pay-for-use [3]). Furthermore, for simplicity we assume cloud hosts are homogeneous (same specifications), however, if this is not the case the attack still work but instead of discovering the host specifications only once for the whole cloud, attackers should perform this task once per host.

The attack propagation mechanism is not discussed here; several of them are described in [3].

4   Literature Review

There are number of cloud DoS attacks in the literature such as in [3,6], however, to the best of our knowledge, the proposed attack is new and heavily based on the understanding of migration management algorithms. One of the main challenges we had that migration policies and algorithms used by today's cloud service providers are not publicly revealed; however, many research papers are investigating them.

VM migration is the process of transferring a whole VM (including the running memory) from host to another for various reasons which are: to save energy thus reduce cost by evacuating and turning *off* (or sleep mode) low utilised hosts, for fault tolerance when dealing with faulty or malicious VMs, for maintenance reasons, and to reduce the load in over-utilised host thus avoid SLA violation.

Migration has high cost and should be used with caution; it introduces many challenges in security and performance i.e. minimising migration time to avoid consuming the network. In [7] they found because of live migration, applications performance degraded by 10%. VMs also have to be secured during migration.

Migration Mechanisms: Nodes management servers are responsible of managing migration depending on different factors such as utilisation and power-consumption. Status reports have to be collected from each host periodically to show its general status. The data from these reports are the inputs for a collection of migration algorithms. Many different algorithms are used in the cloud; we will discuss some of the most popular ones which are: overload detection, VM selection, and VM placement algorithms.

Beloglazov *et al.* in [4] proposed algorithms based on dynamic measurements generated by statistically analysing historical data. They also proposed four methods to detect overloaded hosts which are Median Absolute Deviation (specify the value of upper utilisation based on CPU utilisation deviation strength), Interquartile Range, Local Regression, and Robust Local Regression. For VMs selection they proposed three polices: migrate VMs with the minimum migration time calculated based on memory usage and NT bandwidth, random selection based on uniformly distributed discrete random variable, migrate VMs with the highest CPU utilisation correlation with other VMs calculated using multiple correlation coefficient. For VMs placement problem, they sorted VMs based on their CPU utilisations and allocated them to hosts that provide the minimum cost in term of power consumption using Best Fit Decreasing algorithm.

Another research, [8], also used dynamic utilisation thresholds to detect hosts overloading. The dynamic thresholds were calculated based on workload history (statistical analysis); Bala *et al.* measured the statistical dispersion using Median Absolute Deviation. For VM selection, *multipath correlation coefficient* had been used to describe relationship between measurements; these measurements were grouped in different level, each level affect the subsequent ones. The machine with the minimum expected workload and has the least influence on others is migrated (VMs with zero inter-correlation factors can be migrated). This policy has reduced the migration time and the number of migrations needed.

Overload Detection: Upper utilisation threshold can be set to decide if the host is overloaded or not; however, as stated in [4] "fixed utilization thresholds are not efficient for IaaS environments with mixed workloads that exhibit nonstationary resource usage patterns"; they suggested dynamic thresholds. Prediction algorithms are also needed to create these dynamic thresholds; for prediction, different techniques are used such as statistical analysis or machines learning algorithms [4, 9].

VM Selection Algorithm: Many policies are applied such as migrate the minimum number of VMs, the least active VM, a VM randomly, or the VM with the highest correlation [4, 10]. Discovering the used policy can help revealing the required parameters and improve the CIDoS as we will see later.

Placement Algorithm: The new location can be chosen based on different factors [4]; the most popular ones are to reduce power consumption and utilisation reasons (i.e. the minimum utilised host).

5   Estimating Cloud Migration Parameters

Attackers aim to extract some of the main parameters used by migration algorithms and use them to build more efficient and harder to detect DoS attack. Because of the power saving policy, the number of running hosts is dynamic and, as a consequence, the used thresholds are dynamics and the process of extracting parameters has to be dynamic too. Furthermore, we need to discover these thresholds as fast as possible because of the dynamicity of the environment. We also need to extract the required thresholds, measure their reliability, reduce the probability of accidental errors, consider the noise, consider not changing the host behaviour heavily to avoid affecting prediction algorithms, and measure the success of the attack. We dealt with this problem as a regular statistical experiment.

Extract the Required Parameters: This task is accomplished by reverse engineering the algorithms responsible for migration decisions. We start by designing a formal model of migration decision process.

Migration Decision Process: For the shortage of space we consider overloaded host detection migration policy..The host management node collects status reports periodically from all hosts. Data from status reports and other data from the environment are the inputs of the algorithms. Then an algorithm runs to decide whether the host under examination is over-loaded or predicted to be overload (to prevent over-utilisation before it occurs). The output of the algorithm is *zero* (if the host is not over-loaded) or *one* (if the host is over-loaded). If the output is *one* the management node will run VM selection algorithm to decide the best candidate VMs for migration. Then VMs placement algorithm will run to choose the best candidate destination hosts for VMs under migration. Lastly, VMs will be migrated either online or offline. The inputs of the over-load detection algorithm are: -the general overall status of all hosts in the same availability zone, -the specifications of the host under examination, -history, current and predicted CPU utilisations, -history, current and predicted memory utilisations, -history, current and predicted network traffic rate to and from the host, -possible errors, -time, and -hidden unknown variables.

We target large-scale public cloud; usually the effects of change on the general overall hosts status are not dramatic so it can be represented by a constant value (i.e. the effect on migration decision when having 1000 or 1003 hosts *on* is too low). We assumed that the hosts are homogeneous, therefore, the effect of host specifications can be constant value too. The error can be reduced by replicating the test many times and use hypothesis testing to decide whether to accept the revealed parameters or not (as we will see later). For simplicity, we only consider history, current and predicted CPU utilisations and time.

There are many methods for CPU utilisations prediction most of them are based on the history of the host; Multivariate Linear Regression model, MLR, can be used to perform the prediction as in [9]. History of CPU utilisations are partitioned into intervals and analysed to measure "how closely prediction matches observed utilization across the utilisation spectrum" [9].

Algorithm 1 is for over-loaded host detection; the algorithm notations are: $x_{history}$, $x_{current}$, and $x_{predicted}$ are CPU utilisation history, current, and prediction, -$x_{current}$ is the current CPU utilisation, -x_{time} is the time, -α is the constant value, -upperU is the dynamic upper utilisation threshold f $(\alpha + \beta_1 x_{current} + \beta_2 x_{history} + \beta_3 x_{time})$, -mig is a Boolean variable which is set to '1' if a migration required, and -if the current or predicted CPU utilisation is over upperU, migration is required.

Algorithm 1. Over-loaded Host Detection

Input: α, x_{time}, $x_{history}$, $x_{current}$, $x_{predicted}$ **Output:** mig
mig = 0
upperU = UpperThreshold(α, x_{time}, $x_{history}$, $x_{current}$)
if $x_{current}$ or $x_{predicted} \geq$ upperU **then**
    mig = 1
end if
Return mig

Cloud Migration Parameter Estimation: We developed an algorithm to extract the required parameters, see algorithm 2. First, the attack leader specifies the range of the test (the minimum, maximum CPU utilisation and time) that might cause migration (this is the *test range*). Then the leader designs a series of all possible test phases, portions them into chunks, and gathers them into a list called *chunksList*; each item in the list is called *chunk* and it has two variables, $x_{current}$ and x_{time}. The inputs of the algorithm are *chunksList* and $Bprofile_{normal}$ which is the profile of the host normal behaviour before the attack. The algorithm then tests the chunks in the list one by one until finding parameters that cause migration. *CIDoS.run* is a function with two arguments (CPU utilisation and time) to run a phase of CIDoS attack (the whole attack that has been described in 2). This function is responsible of coordinating malicious VMs resource consumption to stress the host and cause migration. It attacks using the time and strength passed to it in the variables *chunk.$x_{current}$* and *chunk.x_{time}*.

To be able to measure the success of the attack (does the tested parameters cause migration or not?), we create a new behaviour profile (for after attack) using the function *updateProfile* and calculate the distance between the old normal behaviour profile and the new normal behaviour profile using the function *compare(profile1, profile2)*. The function *updateProfile* is a regular anomaly based IDS to detect anomalies in the workload pattern of the host i.e. Hidden Markov Model based IDS (more details are shown later in the section). The behaviour profile is updated using fresh data (newly collected data from the current workload). The result of comparison between profiles is in the variable *SuspicionValue*; if *SuspicionValue* is greater than the threshold *simThreshold* that means the host behaviour has changed (probably because of migration) so initially accept the tested parameters and replicate the test *replicationNum* number of times to increase reliability and reduce the effect of accidental errors. *successCounter* is the number of successful replications, if it is greater than or equal to a threshold *successThreshold* then accept the tested parameters as reliable and exit the algorithm. The function *wait()* is to create a gap of time between test phases to avoid affecting the prediction algorithms.

If a VM has been migrated in the middle of the tests for another non malicious reason, this will not affect the reliability of the test because it will be discovered in the replications, as we said replications are to increase reliability and decrease the effect of accidental errors. The attacker need m malicious VMs to attack with, the value of m can be calculated depending on the host specifications. The stronger the host the more malicious VMs are needed to attack.

Algorithm 2. Dynamic attack permitting cloud migration hidden parameter estimation

```
1:  Input: chunksList, Bprofile_normal  Output: x_current, x_time
2:  for chunk in chunksList do
3:      wait()
4:      CIDoS.run(chunk.x_current, chunk.x_time)
5:      Bprofile_current = updateProfile ()
6:      SuspicionValue = compare (Bprofile_current, Bprofile_normal)
7:      if SuspicionValue > simThreshold then
8:          successCounter = 0
9:          for i = 0 → replicationNum do
10:             x_current1 = increment x_current
11:             wait()
12:             Bprofile_normal = updateProfile()
13:             CIDoS.run(chunk.x_current1, chunk.x_time)
14:             Bprofile_current = updateProfile()
15:             SuspicionValue = compare (Bprofile_current, Bprofile_normal)
16:             if SuspicionValue < simThreshold then
17:                 successCounter = successCounter + 1
18:             end if
19:         end for
20:         if successCounter ≥ successThreshold then
21:             Return x_current, x_time
22:         end if
23:     end if
24: end for
```

The time complexity of the algorithm depends on how many tests are needed, the size of the gap between tests and how many replicates should we make to increase the reliability of the result. The smaller *test range*, the less number of tests are needed. Furthermore, if we distribute the tests among different hosts we can perform them on parallel and the gap of time will be less or there will be no need for gap at all, however, the communication between attackers through the network increases the possibility of being caught by network based IDS.

How to Check Migration: The leader checks migration (measure the success of the attack) by building normal behaviour profiles for the host workload before and after each phase of the test; if there a deviation in the workload (anomaly detected in the terms of HIDS), that means it is highly probable that a migration has happened. If there is no deviation (no anomaly detected), that means the current test phase has failed and another phase should be performed using different $x_{current}$ or x_{time} values.

How to Build Normal Profiles: We assumed that the attack leader can monitor the host workload so it can create a normal behaviour profile for the host (host based anomaly detection system). The host based anomaly detection system detects any significant change in host behaviour. We first have to build a detection system; different algorithms can be used to build the system some are based on machine learning techniques such as Hidden Markov Model and others are based on statistical learning techniques such as regression [11]. These algorithms are used to model the workload of the host (create the normal behaviour profile of host workload). To obtain the required data for building the model, the attack leader can gather observations from the host by i.e. calculating host respond time or use side channel to collect data. Then, the host normal behaviour profile can be used to detect any deviations from normal workload pattern. The attack leader can calculate the *Suspicion Value* by comparing the normal profile to the current profile; to compare the two profiles different techniques can be used such as Kullback Leibler distance metric. If *Suspicion Value* is high, alert for anomaly. To decide, if the *Suspicion Value* is high or not, the leader has to specify another threshold to perform this task, *simThreshold*. This threshold is calculated based on the available resources to attack and the required degree of assurance attackers need.

If an anomaly has been detected this might mean a migration has happened; as we said earlier we use *Experiment Replication* (in statistical terms) to increase reliability and reduces the effect of noises generated by errors.

Interactive Hypothesis Testing by the Attacker: We replicate the experiment number of times to obtain statistically significant results. The attack leader has to:

- specify the number of replicates needed, *replicationNum*,
- specify the acceptable level of reliability, *successThreshold*,
- count the number of successful replications, *successCounter*, then
- run an interactive statistical hypothesis testing algorithm to decide whether to accept and distribute the tested values of $x_{current}$ and x_{time} as reliable or not.

The attack leader can form the hypothesis testing in many different ways, for example:

1. The null hypothesis H_0: SuspicionValue $= 0$
   H_1: SuspicionValue $\neq 0$ (one sided hypothesis)
   SuspicionValue variable is equal to *zero* if there is no change in the host behaviour (no migration) and is equal to *one* if there a change in the host behaviour (possible migration).
2. Assume H_0 is true
3. The null hypothesis distribution is computed by the number of permutations which is equal to *replicationNum* (it should be *replicationNum*+1 however because successCounter ≥ 1 so there will be at least one successful experiment)
4. Specify the significant level α.
   The values of the signification level is calculated based on the cost of committing a Type I error (accept and distribute inaccurate $x_{current}$ and x_{time}) and a Type II error (reject an accurate $x_{current}$ and x_{time}). The cost can be calculated depending on different factors i.e. the available resources.
5. The leader calculates the *successThreshold* based on α
6. Compute the t-test statistic
7. Then a decision rule is formed based on the threshold to decide whether to reject the H_0 (accept the tested values as reliable thus distribute them and use them for attacking) or to not reject H_0 (not accept the tested values and go to the next test phase)

8. Collect samples by running the experiment *replicationNum* number of times (experiment replications) and count the number of success and number or fail.
9. Draw a conclusion whether to reject or not reject H_0.

Although the test is replicated number of times to obtain statistically significant results, there is still a possibility for Type I and II errors. Type I error is rejecting a true null hypothesis, however, after the rejection the leader will try higher $x_{current}$ and x_{time} values which will trigger the attack using slightly higher values than required. Type II error is accepting a false null hypothesis; the attacker might attack using not enough time and strength and this might make the attack fail and also increase the possibility of being caught by security defences in the cloud. Therefore, when selecting the *successThreshold* value, the leader should consider the available security defences and balance the two errors.

Attacking Using the Revealed Parameter: After accepting the values of $x_{current}$ and x_{time}, the CIDoS attack can be formed based on them. The value of T_s (the severity threshold to be broken by the attackers) is $x_{current}$ and the duration of the attack is x_{time}. As described in section 2, in *scenario 1* the leader will broadcast the value of T_s while in *scenario 2* the leader will distribute the units each malicious VM has to cover and these units are calculated by the leader depending on the value of T_s.

Without knowing migration parameters accurately, attackers have to increase the workload to put the host in an over-utilised state; while by using relatively accurate parameters, attackers can trigger migration without over-utilising the host but with making the cloud management algorithms predict that the host will be in an over-utilised state then migrate some of the VMs to avoid future SLA violation (so the current workload will not break the thresholds but the predicted workload will do). This will make the attack harder to detect and also attackers will need less resources to attack with and the parameters can be broadcasted to all CIDoS VMs even in other hosts. This will increase the damage heavily especially that usually migration policies are the same for all cloud hosts.

Also by having a predicted workload that is over the threshold but very close to it by using accurate parameters, the cloud might migrate only one VM from the host (not large number of VMs which is the case if the workload is far over the threshold), migrating one VM increases the lifetime of the attack because other malicious co-resident VMs can increase their workload to cover the loss of one VM and continue with the attack. This is valid especially in *scenario 1* where large number of malicious VMs (far over required) are available. The attackers can keep covering the lost gradually until there are no enough malicious VMs to attack with or there are no other non-malicious VMs in the host; the leader can know this information if, for a series of migrations, only malicious VMs are being migrated. The leader can also know that if the only existed host workload is the collection of malicious VMs workloads. If the leader found out that this host is only occupied by malicious VMs, he/she can either reduce the workload to the minimum to allow for new arrivals or terminate most of the malicious VMs to activate the policy of save energy by migrating all VMs in that host then turn it *off* which is a bigger damage than regular migration especially if the host has to be turned *on* again after short time; it will consume the cloud resources and make the cloud management machine takes decisions based on false reasons. What is more, causing a migration for only one VM will also make the attack harder to detect because migrating large number of VMs in the same time might raise suspicion and lead to further investigations.

6   Analysis and Discussion

If this attack is coordinated between hosts (not only one host) the cloud management node will make a series of false resources consuming decisions which might saturate the network; the cloud management might also start *turning on* more hosts to cope with the fake increased demand. Moreover, if the attacker discovers the VM selection algorithm, he/she can avoid being migrated by for instance intensely using the memory which will make the cost of migrating the attacker VM high thus avoid being selected by the VM selection algorithm for migration. This is just an example, but how to escape migration depends on the used selection algorithm, however, the number of used algorithms is relatively small which ease the attacker task of discovering them. By avoiding migration, the attack will live longer because the group of malicious VMs that form the attack will stay together for long time and constantly attack the same host.

7   Conclusions and Future Work

In this paper we introduced a technique to reverse engineer the cloud migration algorithms, overload detection algorithm and save energy algorithm, to reveal hidden parameters and thresholds. Then these parameters are used to improve the CIDoS attack. We also designed a formal model for migration decision process and then an algorithm has been developed to extract the parameters from the model. We used anomaly based HIDS to measure the success of the attack. The reliability of the extracted values is calculated using an interactive statistical hypothesis testing. These values can be used to attack the host and also can be distributed to other malicious VMs in different hosts.

Based on the theoretical analysis reported in this paper, on-going and future work seeks to validate results experimentally and to refine both the precision and speed of parameter estimation, including by modulating the use of main memory.

References

1. Ristenpart, T., Tromer, E., Shacham, H., Savage, S.: Hey, you, get off of my cloud: exploring information leakage in third-party compute clouds. In: Proceedings of the 16th ACM Conference on Computer and Communications Security, CCS 2009, pp. 199–212. ACM, New York (2009)

2. Zhang, Y., Juels, A., Oprea, A., Reiter, M.: Homealone: Co-residency detection in the cloud via side-channel analysis. In: 2011 IEEE Symposium on Security and Privacy (SP), pp. 313–328 (2011)
3. Alarifi, S., Wolthusen, S.D.: Robust coordination of cloud-internal denial of service attacks. In: Third International Conference on Cloud and Green Computing (CGC), pp. 135–142 (2013)
4. Beloglazov, A., Buyya, R.: Optimal online deterministic algorithms and adaptive heuristics for energy and performance efficient dynamic consolidation of virtual machines in cloud data centers. Concurr. Comput.: Pract. Exper. 24(13), 1397–1420 (2012)
5. Bates, A., Mood, B., Pletcher, J., Pruse, H., Valafar, M., Butler, K.: Detecting co-residency with active traffic analysis techniques. In: Proceedings of the 2012 ACM Workshop on Cloud Computing Security Workshop, CCSW 2012, pp. 1–12. ACM, New York (2012)
6. Varadarajan, V., Kooburat, T., Farley, B., Ristenpart, T., Swift, M.M.: Resource-freeing attacks: Improve your cloud performance (at your neighbor's expense). In: Proceedings of the 2012 ACM Conference on Computer and Communications Security, CCS 2012, pp. 281–292. ACM, New York (2012)
7. Voorsluys, W., Broberg, J., Venugopal, S., Buyya, R.: Cost of virtual machine live migration in clouds: A performance evaluation. In: Jaatun, M.G., Zhao, G., Rong, C. (eds.) Cloud Computing. LNCS, vol. 5931, pp. 254–265. Springer, Heidelberg (2009)
8. Bala, A., Chana, I.: Vm migration approach for autonomic fault tolerance in cloud computing. In: Int'l Conf. Grid and Cloud Computing and Applications, GCA 2013 (2013)
9. Davis, I.J., Hemmati, H., Holt, R.C., Godfrey, M.W., Neuse, D.M., Mankovskii, S.: Regression-based utilization prediction algorithms: An empirical investigation. In: Proceedings of the 2013 Conference of the Center for Advanced Studies on Collaborative Research, CASCON 2013, pp. 106–120. IBM Corp, Riverton (2013)
10. Singh, A., Kinger, S.: Virtual machine migration policies in clouds. International Journal of Science and Research (IJSR) 2, 364–367 (2013)
11. Cherkasova, L., Ozonat, K.M., Mi, N., Symons, J., Smirni, E.: Anomaly? application change? or workload change? towards automated detection of application performance anomaly and change. In: DSN, pp. 452–461. IEEE Computer Society (2008)

Touchpad Input for Continuous Biometric Authentication

Alexander Chan[1], Tzipora Halevi[2], and Nasir Memon[2]

[1] Hunter College High School, New York, NY, USA
[2] New York University Polytechnic School of Engineering, Brooklyn, NY, USA

Abstract. Authentication is a process which is used for access control in computer security. However, common existing methods of authentication, which are based on authentication during the login stage, are insecure due to the lack of authentication after the initial instance. Ideally, authentication should be continuous and should not interfere with a user's normal behavior as to not create an inconvenience for the user. Behaviometric identification, for example, verifies a user's identity based on his behavior, both continuously and without interruption. This work shows that it is possible, with great accuracy, to identify different users based on their touchpad behaviors. While linear classifiers proved ineffective at classifying touchpad behavior, kernel density estimation and decision tree classification each proved capable of classifying data sets with over 90% accuracy.

Keywords: behavior, biometrics, behaviometrics, touchpad.

1 Introduction

In the context of digital security, authentication is a method of verifying identity. Authentication typically functions as a gatekeeper, granting certain users access to resources restricted to others. A web administrator, for example, a trusted user maintaining a website, can grant other users privileges and shut down the website. In order to grant the administrator access to such privileges while excluding all others, the administrator must verify his identity via authentication.

Authentication is dependent on three factors, which can be combined to increase security: ownership, knowledge, and inherence [2]. Ownership refers to a physical token that a user has, such as a credit card or a passport. Knowledge refers to something a user knows, such as a password. Inherence refers to features inherent to the user, or physical characteristics and behavior, for example, a fingerprint or typing rhythm.

In addition to these three factors of authentication, there are two main types of authentication, static and continuous. Static authentication methods verify a user's identity only once, at the first moment of access [1]. Once authenticated statically, however, any new user can subsequently obtain access to the original user's data simply by using the same device. Vulnerabilities such as these suggest

B. De Decker and A. Zúquete (Eds.): CMS 2014, LNCS 8735, pp. 86–91, 2014.

that static authentication is inadequate for many situations in which security is a priority.

Continuous authentication minimizes this vulnerability. Unlike static methods, continuous authentications *continuously* verify a user's identity during session use, even long after the initial verification [1]. The simplest method for continuous authentication is repeated prompting for authentication (e.g. a password). However, this method is certain to inconvenience the user in proportion to the frequency of prompting or the level of security. Behaviometric identifiers, on the other hand, which monitor a user's behavior and authenticate the user by means of that behavior, solve this problem.

In this study we assess the usefulness of a touchpad, an input device found on many laptops, as a tool for behaviometric identification. It is found that the ability to authenticate a user based on touchpad data is achieved. Section 2 discusses related works, and our approach is presented in Section 3. Section 4 states our experimental results, and we conclude in Section 5.

2   Related Work

Behavioral biometrics have been widely explored with many different identifiers, including eye movements and pointing devices (mice) [4][5]. These authentication processes use pattern recognition. Gamboa et al. developed a preliminary biometric authentication system using two types of density estimation, multi-modal non-parametric estimation and unimodal parametric estimation [4]. It was shown that there was no difference in the Equal Error Rate (EER), or the rate at which the false acceptance and rejection rates are equal, between the two algorithms. In addition, it was discovered that as the time the user used the pointing device to train the algorithm increased, the EER decreased.

In addition to the aforementioned examples of biometric identifiers, there have been numerous studies exploring touch sensors as a behavioral biometric, most commonly touchscreens [3][6][9][11]. Some of these studies focus on the act of drawing a "lock pattern" [1]. It was shown that each participant drew the lock pattern differently, and users could be differentiated. However, it was also shown that in order to obtain a low EER of 2%, at least 250 keystrokes were required. This time taken to train and build a classification model can be an inconvenience to users. Another disadvantage of authentication method is that it is static. It only analyzes initial login behavior.

Similar to this is biometric authentication using touch gestures on multi-touch devices. Sae-Bae et al. showed that touch gestures can uniquely identify users [9][10]. However, this study, like the one by Angulo et al., focused solely on static authentication.

Touch gestures as a means of continuous identification was explored by Frank et al. and Roy et al. [3][7]. Frank et al. analyzed smartphone scrolling behavior, classifying thirty different variables via k-nearest neighbor and support vector machine. Roy et al. used a Hidden Markov Model on mobile systems, improving on previous studies as to ease updating of trained classifiers, and as only the user of the device needs to provide training data. We expand on this approach by testing touchpad behavior, and comparing multiple algorithms to identify the most accurate and efficient one.

3   Data Collection

Data was collected exclusively from the built-in Multi-touch trackpad of a Mac-Book Air. The "MacBook Multitouch"[1] program was used to collect raw gesture data from each user's touchpad behavior for 15 minutes. Each participant "surfed the web."

Data from six different participants were collected. The participants were unaware that their behavior was being recorded, and so the program recorded their normal behavior. The data collected was stored in separate plain text log files. The structure of this raw data included a timestamp, an identifier for each individual finger, the finger size, the finger angle, the major and minor axis of the finger, the position, velocity and pressure of the finger, two relative position measures, and two different states. "States" refer to notable events such as lifting a finger or stopping finger movement. The relative position values indicated how far a finger was from the center or the edge of the touchpad.

A MATLAB script was written to format the raw data into a comma-separated value file. This file contained the same values as the raw data, except that data associated with distinct fingers was placed into distinct lists. Only the first 10,000 values were used from each file, and five participant's data were combined into a larger file. The data of the sixth participant was unable to be read by the software used, and was therefore omitted from the data analysis. This combined file also included new data values, the results of calculations performed on the original raw data. These calculations included the finger area, equal to the product of the major and minor axis; finger location, equal to the product of the x position and y position; absolute velocity $(v_x^2 + v_y^2)$; and the velocity angle $(\arctan \frac{v_x}{v_y})$.

The combined data file incorporated 12 features for each finger for five fingers, plus a value for the number of fingers on the touchpad at that instance, for a total of 61 features. Each individual participant's data was assigned a class name, a requirement for data set classification. Waikato Environment for Knowledge Analysis (WEKA) was used for data classification, a process in which algorithms build models based on training data to be able to predict the classification of future data points.

Six algorithms were tested in this work:

1. Simple logistic regression
2. Naive Bayes
3. Bayes network
4. J48
5. Random forest
6. k-nearest neighbor

---

[1] http://www.steike.com/code/multitouch/

Simple logistics, naive Bayes, and Bayes network are linear type classifiers. J48 and random forest both use decision trees as the primary classification technique. k-nearest neighbor, a kernel density estimation type classifier, was tested four different times, each time with a different k value.

For each trial, the model was built using a 10 fold cross validation. The data was partitioned into 10 sections. For each class, nine sections, or 9000 values, were used as training data, and the remaining section (1000 values) were used as test data. This was repeated ten times, such that each section was used as test data.

4   Results

The classification accuracy (identification rate), kappa statistic and relative absolute error were calculated using the number of correct classified instances by each classifier. The accuracy (identification rate) is simply the number of correctly classified instances over the total number of instances, in this case, 50,000. The kappa statistic takes into account chance agreement, and so is generally a more accurate indicator of how well a classifier performs than is the sample accuracy. The relative absolute error normalizes the total absolute error.

These values are listed in Table 1 for each classification algorithm.

Table 1. Performance accuracy of different algorithms

Classification Algorithm	Classification Accuracy	Kappa Statistic (κ)	Relative Absolute Error
Simple logistic regression	65.47%	0.5684	62.07%
Naive Bayes	29.65%	0.1207	87.53%
Bayes network	70.88%	0.6360	36.92%
1-nearest neighbor	95.13%	0.9391	6.10%
2-nearest neighbor	94.28%	0.9285	7.16%
3-nearest neighbor	94.14%	0.9267	8.14%
4-nearest neighbor	93.72%	0.9215	9.04%
Random forest	96.37%	0.9546	15.39%
J48	94.12%	0.9265	8.39%

Both the simple logistic regression and naive Bayes algorithms had a low sample accuracy when tested against the data set. Random Forest, J48, and k-nearest neighbor all performed well. The kappa statistic showed lower accuracy values for all classification algorithms, with a large reduction in accuracy for the naive Bayes, simple logistic regression, and Bayes network classifier. The relative absolute error values for the three poorest classifiers, simple logistic regression, naive Bayes, and Bayes network, were higher than the error rates for the other classifiers. Interestingly, the random forest classifier, although it had the highest sample accuracy and kappa statistic, also had a higher error rate than other similarly performing classifiers.

The k-nearest neighbor algorithm shows an interesting trend, namely, as the value of k increases, the sample accuracy and kappa statistic decrease, while the relative absolute error increases.

Confusion matrices were also generated for each algorithm. We have selected one confusion matrix representing each type of classification in Table 2-4.

Table 2. Naive Bayes

a	b	c	d	e	
205	444	269	2522	6560	a
44	365	132	4012	5447	b
62	75	1376	4847	3640	c
0	0	36	4040	5924	d
0	0	20	1140	8840	e

Table 3. k-nearest neighbor, $k = 1$

a	b	c	d	e	
9524	54	83	128	211	a
25	9790	83	45	57	b
160	145	9187	233	275	c
121	34	146	9348	351	d
117	24	32	111	9716	e

Table 4. Random forest

a	b	c	d	e	
9509	31	172	119	169	a
29	9821	100	35	15	b
119	75	9574	141	91	c
120	17	193	9551	119	d
59	13	80	119	9729	e

"a", "b", "c", "d", and "e" represent the different classes, or the users that generated test data. The top row represents the predicted class, and the side row represents the actual class. In the naive Bayes matrix, the majority of values were classified as either class "d" or class "e". Both k-nearest neighbor and random forest algorithms classified most values correctly.

5   Discussions and Conclusions

The low sample accuracy of the simple logistic regression and naive Bayes algorithms suggests that linear classification algorithms are not optimal methods to classify a data set of this nature. Since linear classification algorithms fail the data is not linear, which conclusion is in accord with that of other behavioral biometric studies [1]. Linear algorithms also took the longest time to generate a model based on test data.

The non-linear classifiers (decision tree and kernel density estimation) have a high sample accuracy and κ (both $> 90\%$). Random forest classification produced the highest sample accuracy, but it does not have the lowest relative absolute error, and it is not the fastest algorithm. k-NN (with $k = 1$) resulted in the lowest error rate.

It was reported by Angulo et al. that random forest classification resulted in the lowest error rate of the algorithms tested, and that performance was constant when testing various lock patterns [1]. Our study confirms these findings, as the different patterns tested can be compared to the wide ranges of behavior of a user on a touchpad. The various lock patterns that participants drew on the touchscreen can be compared to various touchpad gestures such as dragging a finger, two-finger scroll, and tapping. Random forest was also found to be the most accurate algorithm.

In a k-NN classification, the optimal value for k is 1. This is most likely due to other instances being too far away from the query point, expanding the nearest neighbors region, and thus lowering overall accuracy.

The confusion matrices reveal that the naive Bayes classifier predicted the majority of instances as either class "d" or class "e". This can be explained by looking at trends in the raw data. These two participants did not use more than 2 fingers at a time. Therefore, for the values of the other three fingers, zero was used as a placeholder. This made the model skew its predictions towards these two classes, and therefore most values were classified as either "d" or "e". One way to fix this problem is to ignore zero values, which may increase the accuracy of the naive Bayes classifier.

Future work includes using only one user's training data, similar to that described by Roy et al.. The classified data can also be modified to consist of entire strokes or gestures, rather than individual timestamps.

References

1. Angulo, J., Wästlund, E.: Exploring Touch-screen Biometrics for User Identification on Smart Phones. Privacy and Identity Management for Life 375, 130–143 (2012)
2. Campi, A.: How strong is strong user authentication? ISACA Journal 5, 42–45 (2012)
3. Frank, M., Biedert, R., Ma, E., Martinovic, I., Song, D.: Touchalytics: On the applicability of touchscreen input as a behavioral biometric for continuous authentication. IEEE Transactions on Information Forensics & Security 8(1), 136–148 (2012), doi:10.1109/TIFS.2012.2225048
4. Gamboa, H., Fred, A.: A Behavioural Biometric System Based on Human Computer Interaction. In: Proc. SPIE, vol. 5404 (2004)
5. Juhola, M., Zhang, Y., Rasku, J.: Biometric verification of a subject through eye movements. Computers in Biology and Medicine 43, 42–50 (2013)
6. Kurkovsky, S., Syta, E.: Approaches and issues in location-aware continuous authentication. Computational Science and Engineering, 279–283 (2010), doi:10.1109/CSE.2010.42
7. Roy, A., Halevi, T., Memon, N.: An HMM-Based Behavior Modeling Approach for Continuous Mobile Authentication
8. Sae-Bae, N., Memon, N.: Online Signature Verification on Mobile Devices. 2014 IEEE Transactions on Information Forensics and Security 9(6), 933–947 (2014), doi:10.1109/TIFS
9. Sae-Bae, N., Ahmed, K., Isbister, K., Memon, N.: Biometric-Rich Gestures: A Novel Approach to Authentication on Multitouch Devices. In: Conference on Human Factors in Computing Systems (2012)
10. Sae-Bae, N., Memon, N., Isbister, K.: Investigating Multi-touch Gestures as a Novel Biometric Modality. In: 2012 IEEE Fifth International Conference on Biometrics: Theory, Applications and Systems, BTAS (2012)
11. Saevanee, H., Bhatarakosol, P.: User Authentication using Combination of Behavioral Biometrics over the Touchpad acting like Touch screen of Mobile Device. Computer and Electrical Engineering, 82–86 (2008), doi:10.1109/ICCEE.2008.157

A Federated Cloud Identity Broker-Model for Enhanced Privacy via Proxy Re-Encryption

Bernd Zwattendorfer, Daniel Slamanig*, Klaus Stranacher,
and Felix Hörandner

Institute for Applied Information Processing and Communications (IAIK),
Graz University of Technology (TUG), Inffeldgasse 16a, 8010 Graz, Austria
{bernd.zwattendorfer,daniel.slamanig,klaus.stranacher}@iaik.tugraz.at
felix.hoerandner@student.tugraz.at

Abstract. Reliable and secure user identification and authentication are key enablers for regulating access to protected online services. Since cloud computing gains more and more importance, identification and authentication in and across clouds play an increasing role in this domain too. Currently, existing web identity management models are often just mapped to the cloud domain. Besides, within recent years several cloud identity management models such as the *cloud identity broker-model* have emerged. In the aforementioned model, an identity broker in the cloud acts as hub between various service and identity providers. While this seems to be a promising approach for adopting identity management in cloud computing, still some problems can be identified. A notable issue is the dependency of users and service providers on the same central broker for identification and authentication processes. Additionally, letting an identity broker store or process sensitive data such as identity information in the cloud brings up new issues, in particular with respect to user's privacy. To overcome these problems, we propose a new cloud identity management model based on the federation between different cloud identity brokers. Thereby, users and service providers can select their favorite cloud identity broker without being dependent on one and the same broker. Moreover, it enhances user's privacy by the use of appropriate cryptographic mechanisms and in particular proxy re-encryption. Besides introducing the model we also provide a proof of concept implementation thereof.

Keywords: cloud computing, identity management, cloud identity, cloud identity broker, federated cloud identity broker, privacy, proxy re-encryption.

1 Introduction

In security-sensitive areas of applications such as e-Government identity management is a key issue. Over the time, several identity management systems

---

* Daniel Slamanig has been supported by the Austrian Research Promotion Agency (FFG) through project ARCHISTAR, grant agreement number 832145.

B. De Decker and A. Zúquete (Eds.): CMS 2014, LNCS 8735, pp. 92–103, 2014.

have already evolved [2]. The Security Assertion Markup Language (SAML), Shibboleth, OpenID, or WS-Federation are just a few popular examples. They all usually follow a similar architectural concept involving the stakeholders *user (U)*, *service provider (SP)*, and *identity provider (IdP)* [3]. Thereby, a user wants to access a protected resource at a service provider. To mitigate efforts for the service provider, the identification and authentication process is handled by the identity provider. After successful authentication, the identity provider transfers identity and user data to the service provider for access decision making.

Since cloud computing plays a steadily increasing role in the IT sector, secure identity management is equally important in the cloud domain. Identity management systems in the cloud can benefit from cloud advantages such as high scalability or cost savings, since no in-house infrastructure needs to be hosted and maintained. A couple of cloud identity management-systems have already evolved [7–9]. One example is the so-called *cloud identity broker-model*, where an identity broker in the cloud acts as hub between multiple service providers and identity providers [7]. The advantage of adopting the broker concept is that the identity broker hides the complexity of different identity providers from the service provider. Although the cloud identity-broker model is a promising model in the cloud domain, still some disadvantages can be found. One major drawback is that both users and service providers have to rely on one and the same cloud identity provider for identification and authentication. This heavily decreases user's and service provider's flexibility in choosing their cloud identity broker of choice. In addition, the *cloud identity broker-model* – when applied in a public cloud – lacks in privacy, because identity data are stored and processed in the cloud. However, privacy is one main issue with respect to cloud computing [15].

To eliminate these problems, we propose a new cloud identity management-model which, on the one hand, increases freedom of choice in terms of cloud identity broker selection and, on the other hand, preserves user's privacy with respect to the cloud identity broker and – whenever possible – to the identity provider. We address the first issue by applying a federation of cloud identity brokers and the second issue by incorporating appropriate cryptographic techniques.

2   Federated Cloud Identity Broker-Model

In this section we propose our new cloud identity management-model which federates cloud identity brokers. The general idea is that users encrypt their identity data using their public key of a proxy re-encryption scheme and these data can be re-encrypted to a service provider.

2.1   Cryptographic Preliminaries

Subsequently, we briefly discuss required cryptographic primitives and we denote a proxy re-encryption and signature key pair of A by $(\mathsf{sk}_A, \mathsf{pk}_A)$ and $(\mathsf{sk}'_A, \mathsf{pk}'_A)$ respectively. Concatenation of two bitstrings a and b denoted as $a\|b$ is assumed to be realized in a way such that all individual components are uniquely recoverable.

Digital Signatures: A digital signature scheme (DSS) is a triple $(\mathcal{K}, \mathcal{S}, \mathcal{V})$ of poly-time algorithms, whereas $\mathcal{K}$ is a probabilistic key generation algorithm that takes a security parameter κ and outputs a private and public key pair (sk, pk). The probabilistic signing algorithm $\mathcal{S}$ takes as input a message $M \in \{0,1\}^*$ and a private key sk, and outputs a signature σ. The verification algorithm $\mathcal{V}$ takes as input a signature σ, a message $M \in \{0,1\}^*$ and a public key pk, and outputs a single bit $b \in \{\texttt{true}, \texttt{false}\}$ indicating whether σ is a valid signature for M.

Proxy Re-Encryption: A unidirectional single-use proxy re-encryption (US-PRE) scheme allows a semi-trusted proxy given a re-encryption key to transform a message encrypted under the key of party A into another ciphertext to the same message encrypted for party B. The proxy thereby neither gets access to the plaintext nor the respective decryption keys and can only transform in one direction (from A to B) and one ciphertext can be transformed only once (no transitivity). A US-PRE is a tuple $(\mathcal{S}, \mathcal{K}, \mathcal{RK}, \mathcal{E}_\mathcal{R}, \mathcal{RE}, \mathcal{D}_\mathcal{R})$ of poly-time algorithms. The algorithm $\mathcal{S}$ runs a setup and produces system parameters params. $\mathcal{K}$ is a probabilistic key generation algorithm that takes a security parameter κ and outputs a private and public key pair $(\mathsf{sk}_i, \mathsf{pk}_i)$. The re-encryption key generation algorithm $\mathcal{RK}$ takes as input a private key sk_i and another public key pk_j, and outputs a re-encryption key $\mathsf{rk}_{i \to j}$. The probabilistic encryption algorithm $\mathcal{E}_\mathcal{R}$ gets a public key pk_i and a plaintext M, and outputs $c_i = \mathcal{E}_\mathcal{R}(\mathsf{pk}_i, M)$. The (probabilistic) re-encryption algorithm $\mathcal{RE}$ gets as input a ciphertext c_i under pk_i and a re-encryption key $\mathsf{rk}_{i \to j}$, and outputs a re-encrypted ciphertext $c_j = \mathcal{RE}(\mathsf{rk}_{i \to j}, c_i)$ for pk_j. The decryption algorithm $\mathcal{D}_\mathcal{R}$ takes private key sk_j and a ciphertext c_j, and outputs $M = \mathcal{D}_\mathcal{R}(\mathsf{sk}_j, c_j)$ or an error $\bot$. We base our implementation on the schemes of [1].

2.2 Model Architecture

The proposed new cloud identity management model relies on a federated approach. Thereby, dependency on one single cloud identity broker is removed by using multiple cloud identity brokers that are able to communicate with each other. Users and service providers can select their preferred cloud identity broker for authentication, thus both identity brokers can actually provide and support different functionality. The only prerequisite is that identity data transfer is possible between the individual cloud identity brokers. Figure 1 illustrates this *federated cloud identity broker-model*.

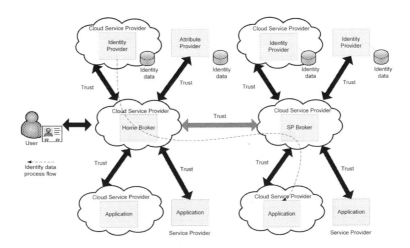

Fig. 1. Federated Cloud Identity Broker-Model

In the following, we briefly describe the components involved:

User: A user wants to access protected resources from a service provider. For identification and authentication, the user relies on her favorite cloud identity broker (user's home broker), which manages different identity providers and attribute providers the user is registered with.

Service Provider: A service provider offers various services to users and requires proper identification and authentication.

Identity Provider: The identity provider stores user's identity data. Furthermore, the identity provider is responsible for user identification and authentication.

Attribute Provider: The attribute provider stores additional attributes of the user's identity data. These additional attributes can be retrieved from the attribute provider during an authentication process.

Home Broker: The user's home broker constitutes the cloud identity broker the user is affiliated with. The user trusts this broker and has a contractual relationship with it. The home broker manages all identity providers and attribute providers, where the user is registered with.

Service Provider Broker: The service provider broker (SP broker) has an affiliation with the service provider the user wants to authenticate. The SP broker manages the communication with the user's home broker for the service provider.

2.3   Requirements

When designing this new *federated cloud identity broker-model*, we kept the following requirements in mind, which need to be fulfilled:

Individual Selection of the Cloud Identity Broker: Both users and service providers are able to individually select the cloud identity broker of their choice.

Trust: The service provider and identity provider are trusted, whereas the cloud provider which hosts and operates the identity broker, is assumed to be semi-trusted (*honest but curious*). This means, the identity broker works correctly, but might be interested in inspecting users' identity data. With our model we can also assume the identity providers to be semi-trusted.

Privacy: For our model we demand the support of the privacy characteristics *user-centricity* (the user always stays under full control on which data are disclosed to the service provider and cloud identity broker) and *selective disclosure* (the user is able to select the amount of data to disclose to the service provider and cloud identity broker). Furthermore, users' identity data should be treated confidential and users' privacy must be preserved with respect to all entities in the cloud.

Easy Integration into Existing Infrastructures: The new model should be easily integrable into existing infrastructures, meaning that service providers and identity providers can easily connect to the cloud identity broker through standardized and already existing interfaces.

3   Concrete Model and Proof of Concept

Subsequently, we provide details of the model by means of a proof of concept implementation. Thereby, we designed and developed one demo service provider, two cloud identity brokers (the user's home broker and the SP broker), one attribute provider, and additionally integrated two existing identity providers, i.e., Twitter and one self-hosted OpenID provider. Figure 2 illustrates the implemented architecture and its components, which will be described in detail in the next subsection.

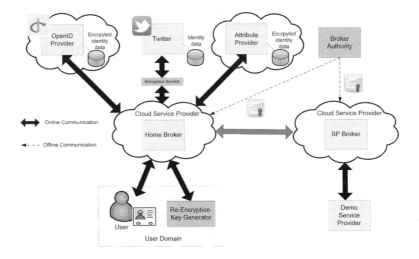

Fig. 2. Implementation Architecture of the Federated Cloud Identity Broker-Model

In order to meet the previously defined requirements, three additional components need to be introduced. These new as well as the other components will be described in detail in the next subsection.

3.1   Components

In this section we give implementation details on the individual components.

Demo Service Provider: The demo service provider has actually no particular functionality, it just requires proper user identification and authentication. To minimize the amount of data transferred and to respect user's privacy, the service provider is able to request only specific attributes from the user for service provisioning. In addition, the service provider can request a certain level of quality for the identity and the authentication process. This form of quality assurance is modeled as authentication levels, similar to the ones proposed by the NIST [16], STORK [10], or ISO/IEC [12].

SP Broker: The SP broker has been selected by the service provider and thus they share a contractual relationship. The SP broker communicates with the user's home broker and forwards the authentication request to it. Additionally, the SP broker offers a user interface where the user can provide location information of her home broker.

Home Broker: The location of the user's home broker is identified via a user-specific URL, which points to this broker. The URL format is similar to the one used by the OpenID protocol. The user-customized URL is not persistent and can be changed by the user anytime. Before being able to use the functionality of the home broker, the user has to register with it. The home broker holds metadata for the user which include the identity providers the user is able to use and is registered with, and which attribute providers can be connected. The home broker communicates with the identity providers for user identification and authentication and with the attribute providers for attribute transfer. During the authentication process, the home broker presents the user an identity provider selection page and the requested attributes from the service provider. Thereby, the user can select the identity source the requested attributes should be retrieved from. If data are retrieved from different identity data sources (e.g., from an identity provider and an attribute provider), the home broker does a mapping to a common (semantic) format.

Broker Authority: The broker authority is responsible for managing the trust relationships between cloud identity brokers. For that, it issues certificates for signature public keys of the individual brokers. The respective signing keys are used to sign messages exchanged between brokers, ensure an authentic communication channel, and thus verify the trust relationships. Note that this is merely a virtual entity and any (set of) mutually trusted certification authorities will be sufficient in practice.

Twitter: In our scenario, we use Twitter as an identity provider. When registering, Twitter stores a couple of user attributes such as the user's full name or language.

OpenID Provider: In this implementation we set up our own OpenID provider. The reason is that we want to ensure confidentiality of user's attributes with respect to the identity provider and the two brokers. To achieve this, the user encrypts her attributes under the user's public key of a proxy re-encryption scheme before storing them at the OpenID provider. At this stage, only the user is able to decrypt the attributes again. The sole attribute, which is visible in plaintext to the OpenID provider, is the user's OpenID identifier. A similar approach is discussed in [14], however, in this paper data are not encrypted by the user but by a host organization.

Attribute Provider: For the attribute provider we use the same approach as for the OpenID provider. Hence, the user stores her identity data at the attribute provider in encrypted format only. The only attribute the attribute provider is able to inspect in plaintext is an identifier to link the encrypted attributes to a specific user. At the attribute provider, no explicit user authentication is required.

Re-Encryption-Key Generator: The re-encryption-key generator is an entity that runs directly in the user's domain to avoid any private key transfer to another party. In our implementation, the user allows her identity data, which are encrypted for her and stored at the identity/attribute provider, to be re-encrypted by the home broker for a service provider. This way, the identity data remains always confidential even if routed through the identity brokers residing in the cloud. The functionality of the re-encryption-key generator is computing the re-encryption $rk_{U \rightarrow SP}$ by taking the private key of the user sk_U and the public key of the service provider pk_{SP}.

Encryption Service: The encryption service enables the encryption of data coming from an identity provider such as Twitter, which does not support storage of encrypted attributes, by the user. Hence, identity data stays always confidential before transmission to the cloud identity brokers.

3.2   Communication Interfaces

We now briefly describe the used communication protocols and how they were implemented. We thereby describe the interfaces and protocols, respectively, between two entities at a time. All communication interfaces are secured using SSL/TLS for transport security, hence this fact will not be mentioned again explicitly in the individual descriptions.

Service Provider ↔ SP Broker: Actually, arbitrary identity and authentication protocols can be used for this communication channel. Nevertheless, in our implementation we relied on an amended version of the SAML AuthnRequest/Response Protocol [5] using the SAML HTTP-POST Binding [4]. In particular, amendments are the inclusion of requested attributes as well as the requested authentication level in the SAML authentication request. In fact, the amended protocol is similar to the STORK protocol [11], which will play an important role in identification and authentication processes across Europe in the near future[1]. Trust is established by means of signature certificates. However, there is no explicit trust framework required, trust can be negotiated bilaterally.

SP Broker ↔ home Broker: Again, for this communication path we rely on the amended SAML protocol. Exchanged messages are also digitally signed (certificates are signed by the trusted broker authority). This ensures that only by the authority authorized brokers are able to trust and communicate with each other.

Home Broker ↔ Twitter: For retrieving identity data from Twitter we used the OAuth 1.0 protocol. However, the communication path is intercepted by the trusted encryption service that allows users to encrypt their identity data before presenting it to the home broker.

---

[1] There are only minor differences between our used SAML protocol and the STORK protocol. Differences mainly target the format and semantic of transferred attributes, as e.g., single encrypted attributes are not supported within STORK.

Home Broker ↔ OpenID Provider: For this communication channel we implemented the OpenID 2.0 interface. This is somewhat related to the work in [14].

Home Broker ↔ Attribute Provider: For simplicity, in our proof of concept implementation we use a customized web service interface. The request message includes requested attributes and an identifier of the user, the response then simply returns the corresponding encrypted attributes.

Home Broker ↔ re-encryption-key Generator: Communication is based on the SAML AttributeQuery/Response Protocol [5]. The attribute query thereby includes the public key of the service provider pk_{SP}. By calling the local re-encryption-key generator with the users private key sk_U the user obtains the re-encryption key $rk_{U \to SP}$, which is wrapped in the response. In our implementation we use a non-interactive, unidirectional, and single-use proxy re-encryption scheme of [1].

Broker Authority ↔ SP Broker/Home Broker: The exchange of certificates between the broker authority and the brokers is actually an offline process. Exchange is carried out using appropriate organizational mechanisms.

3.3 Process Flows

Subsequently, we present the secure identification and authentication process using the implementation of our proposed *federated cloud identity broker-model*. Identification and authentication is explained by contacting the OpenID and the attribute provider.

Setup: The following setup is required before running an authentication process:

– We assume the user trusts the service provider, Twitter, the encryption service, and the re-encryption-key generator (latter runs in the user's domain). In contrast to that, we assume the cloud identity brokers (SP broker and home broker), the OpenID provider, and the attribute provider semi-trusted (*honest but curious*), meaning that they work correctly but might be interested in inspecting user's data.

– The broker authority has certified the trustworthiness of the two brokers by certifying the signature public keys and thus verifying the trust relationship between the brokers. We denote the respective signature key pairs as $(sk'_{SP-Broker}, pk'_{SP-Broker})$ and $(sk'_{Home-Broker}, pk'_{Home-Broker})$. These keys are used for signing the SAML messages exchanged between the two brokers.

– A bilateral trust relationship has been negotiated between the service provider and the SP broker. To enforce this trust relationship on technical level, certified signature public keys have been exchanged. We denote these signing key pairs of the SP (sk'_{SP}, pk'_{SP}) and assume that the SP broker uses $(sk'_{SP-Broker}, pk'_{SP-Broker})$. These keys are used for signing the exchanged SAML messages between SP and SP Broker. In addition, the service provider holds a proxy re-encryption key pair (sk_{SP}, pk_{SP}).

- A bilateral trust relationship exists between the user's home broker and the individual identity providers. The establishment of this trust relationship is protocol dependent, however, both channels (between home broker and Twitter and between home broker and the OpenID provider) are authentic.
- The user possesses a proxy re-encryption key pair (sk_U, pk_U) and has already stored personal attributes in encrypted format at the OpenID provider and the attribute provider. We denote a set of user encrypted attributes as $c_{U_i} = (c_{U_1}, \ldots, c_{U_m})$ and the corresponding plaintext attributes as $a_i = (a_1, \ldots, a_m)$.
- The user has a contractual relationship with the home broker, has registered in her profile the identity/attribute providers she wants to use, and has stored appropriate authentication credentials for the attribute provider. Additionally, the user holds a unique personal identifier (uniqueID) to be identifiable at the home broker.

Authentication Process:

1. A user wants to access a protected resource from the service provider.
2. Since the service provider requires authentication, it forwards the user to its affiliated SP broker. This SAML authentication request includes the set of attributes (req_attr), which should be provided during the authentication process, the requested authentication level (req_auth_level), and the public encryption key pk_{SP} of the service provider. The request is signed by the service provider resulting in signature $\sigma_{SP} = \mathcal{S}(sk'_{SP}, req\_attr \| req\_auth\_level \| pk_{SP})$
3. First, the broker verifies σ_{SP}. Furthermore, the SP broker asks the user to provide location information of her home broker. The user enters a URL, which is a composition of a uniqueID of the user at the home broker and the home broker's domain (e.g., https://user.home-broker.com).
4. The SP broker again creates a signature $\sigma_{SP-Broker} = \mathcal{S}(sk'_{SP-Broker}, req\_attr \| req\_auth\_level \| pk_{SP} \| uniqueID)$ and forwards the authentication request of the SP to the user's home broker (using the SAML protocol).
5. The home broker verifies $\sigma_{SP-Broker}$. Based on the uniqueID, the user is identified at the home broker. The home broker presents the user a web page, which shows the requested attributes req_attr of the service provider. Additionally, the user can select at which identity provider she wants to authenticate (only those identity providers are shown, which were registered by the user and which support the requested authentication level req_auth_level). Furthermore, the user can select for every individual attribute if it should be retrieved from the identity provider – if providable – or from an affiliated attribute provider. In our example we assume that the user selects the OpenID provider as an identity provider and that additional attributes should be retrieved from the attribute provider.
6. Based on the user's OpenID identifier the user is redirected to the OpenID provider.
7. The user authenticates at the OpenID provider using appropriate credentials.

8. The attributes, which have been selected for retrieval from the OpenID provider, are returned to the home broker in encrypted fashion. We assume the user encrypted attributes $(c_{U_1}, \ldots, c_{U_j})$ to be returned.

9. Since in our scenario only a subset of the requested attributes can be retrieved from the OpenID provider, additional attributes are fetched from the attribute provider. Communication and retrieval is based on a pre-negotiated access token as used in OAuth, which is shared between the home broker and the attribute provider, to identify the user at the attribute provider and allow the broker access to the user's data.

10. The remaining attributes $(c_{U_k}, \ldots, c_{U_m})$ are returned to the home broker in encrypted format.

11. Now all requested attributes $(c_{U_1}, \ldots, c_{U_m})$ are located at the home broker, but they are still encrypted for the user. To make these attributes readable for the SP, re-encryption needs to be applied. A re-encryption key generation request is sent by the home broker to the local re-encryption key generator, which includes the public key of the service provider $\mathsf{pk_{SP}}$. The user additionally has to provide the key generator access to her private key $\mathsf{sk_U}$.

12. The re-encryption key generator computes the re-encryption key from the service provider's public and the user's private key and returns the re-encryption key $\mathsf{rk_{U \to SP}} = \mathcal{RK}(\mathsf{sk_U}, \mathsf{pk_{SP}})$ to the home broker.

13. The home broker re-encrypts all collected attributes for the service provider resulting in $(c_{SP_1} \ldots, c_{SP_m})$ by running $c_{SP_i} = \mathcal{RE}(\mathsf{rk_{U \to SP}}, c_{U_i})$ for all $1 \le i \le m$. Additionally, it wraps the re-encrypted attributes and the actual authentication level $\mathsf{auth\_level}$ into a SAML assertion and computes a signature $\sigma_{Home-Broker} = \mathcal{S}(\mathsf{sk'_{Home-Broker}}, c_{SP_1} \| \ldots \| c_{SP_m} \| \mathsf{auth\_level})$.

14. The SAML assertion is returned within the authentication response to the SP broker. The SP broker verifies $\sigma_{Home-Broker}$, computes a signature $\sigma_{SP-Broker} = \mathcal{S}(\mathsf{sk'_{SP-Broker}}, c_{SP_1} \| \ldots \| c_{SP_m} \| \mathsf{auth\_level})$ and forwards the authentication response to the service provider.

15. The service provider verifies the received response by verifying $\sigma_{SP-Broker}$ and obtains the decrypted attributes $(a_1 \ldots, a_m)$ by running $a_i = \mathcal{D}_\mathcal{R}(\mathsf{sk_{SP}}, c_{SP_i})$ for all $1 \le i \le m$.

16. Based on the decrypted identity and attribute data $(a_1 \ldots, a_m)$ and the $\mathsf{auth\_level}$ the service provider is able to provide the desired protected resources to the user.

In contrast to the above description, Twitter does not allow to store encrypted data. However, we still are able to achieve privacy when using Twitter. In this case, identity data needs to be encrypted by the user before being transferred from Twitter to the home broker.

Recurring Authentications: Most of the time, running through the complete authentication process described before might be cumbersome for the user. Therefore, our implementation is able to remember some selections the user did in her first authentication process, if the user wants so. For instance, in a recurring authentication process the steps 3 and 4 (indicating the home broker) can be omitted, because the SP broker is able to remember user's choice during her first authentication. In addition, step 9 (providing authentication credentials to the identity provider) can be skipped if single sign-on (SSO) [6] is supported by the selected identity provider. Also the key generation steps 13-15 are not necessary, as the re-encryption key for a particular service provider can be stored for re-use in the user's profile at the home broker. Avoiding as many user interactions as possible definitely increases usability of our solution.

4   Evaluation and Discussion

In this section we evaluate our model and implemented solution regarding the requirements specified in Section 2.3.

Individual Selection of the Cloud Identity Broker: Both, the user and the service provider are able to select the cloud identity broker of their choice. The service provider just needs to establish a trust relationship with the broker and implement the communication interface it offers. In addition, the user can contract another broker and registers her desired identity and attribute providers. The user is identified by the broker by a uniqueID.

Trust: Trust between two broker is grounded through the broker authority. The pairwise trust relationships between service provider and SP broker, and between home broker and identity provider depend on bilateral agreements. There is no direct trust relationship between service provider and identity provider because the brokers act as intermediary. Hence, trust is brokered between service provider and identity provider.

Privacy: The requirement of user-centricity is achieved because individual attributes can be stored encrypted for the user only at an identity provider or attribute provider. If this is not possible (e.g., with Twitter), a trusted encryption service can be used as intermediary to encrypt identity data before transmitting it to the cloud identity broker. Only the user is in control to decrypt the data or to generate re-encryption keys. We support selective disclosure because the user is able to select the attributes she wants to transfer at the home broker (i.e. the service provider only gets the attributes which it has requested and the user gave consent for). In addition, confidentiality of user attributes with respect to the cloud identity broker is achieved through proxy re-encryption.

Easy Integration into Existing Infrastructures: The complete model can be easily adopted by service providers. Service providers just need to establish a contractual and trust relationship with their desired SP broker. Furthermore, they just need to implement one specific interface to the SP broker and not many interfaces to different identity providers as required in traditional settings. Implementation efforts can be reduced by providing appropriate software libraries. Additional identity providers or attribute providers can be easily integrated by home brokers. The brokers just need to implement their communication protocols offered by the identity providers or attribute providers.

5   Conclusions and Future Work

In our proof of concept implementation we showed that federating identity brokers provides greater flexibility to users in identity/attribute provider selection. However, such a brokered trust relationship might bring up liability discussions, in particular, if identity providers are grounded by national law.

Besides setting up a more sophisticated and complex network of cloud identity brokers, future work will include the integration of additional providers such as Facebook, Google, or even national eID solutions (e.g., based on ideas related to [17]). Moreover, the integration of the STORK framework [13] could boost the number of (high quality) identity providers supported. A possible approach, how this could be realized, has been discussed in [18].

References

1. Ateniese, G., Fu, K., Green, M., Hohenberger, S.: Improved proxy re-encryption schemes with appl. to secure distributed storage. ACM Trans. Inf. Syst. Secur. 9(1), 1–30 (2006)
2. Bauer, M., Meints, M., Hansen, M.: D3.1: Structured Overview on Prototypes and Concepts of Identity Management System. FIDIS (2005)
3. Bertino, E., Takahashi, K.: Identity Management: Concepts, Technologies, and Systems. Artech House (2011)
4. Cantor, S., Hirsch, F., Kemp, J., Philpott, R., Maler, E.: Bindings for the OASIS Security Assertion Markup Language (SAML) V2.0. OASIS (2009)
5. Cantor, S., Kemp, J., Philpott, R., Maler, E.: Assertions and Protocols for the OASIS Security Assertion Markup Language (SAML) V2.0. OASIS (2009)
6. De Clercq, J.: Single sign-on architectures. In: Davida, G.I., Frankel, Y., Rees, O. (eds.) InfraSec 2002. LNCS, vol. 2437, pp. 40–58. Springer, Heidelberg (2002)
7. Cloud Security Alliance: Security Guidance for Critical Areas of Focus in Cloud Computing V3.0. Csa (2011)
8. Gopalakrishnan, A.: Cloud Computing Identity Management. SETLabs Briefings 7(7), 45–55 (2009)
9. Goulding, J.T.: Identity and access management for the cloud: CA Technologies strategy and vision. Tech. Rep. May, CA Technologies (2010)
10. Hulsebosch, B., Lenzini, G., Eertink, H.: STORK D2.3 - Quality authenticator scheme. Tech. rep., STORK (March 2009)
11. Alcalde-Morano, J., et al.: STORK D5.8.3b Interface Specification. STORK (2011)
12. JTC1/SC27: ISO/IEC DIS 29115 - Information technology – Security techniques – Entity authentication assurance framework (2013)
13. Leitold, H., Zwattendorfer, B.: STORK: Architecture, Implementation and Pilots. In: ISSE, pp. 131–142 (2010)
14. Nuñez, D., Agudo, I., Lopez, J.: Integrating OpenID with Proxy Re-Encryption to enhance privacy in cloud-based identity services. In: CloudCom, pp. 241–248 (2012)
15. Pearson, S., Benameur, A.: Privacy, Security and Trust Issues Arising from Cloud Computing. In: IEEE CloudCom, pp. 693–702 (November 2010)
16. Burr, W.E., et al.: SP 800-63-1. Elec.Authentication Guideline (2011)
17. Zwattendorfer, B., Slamanig, D.: On Privacy-Preserving Ways to Porting the Austrian eID System to the Public Cloud. In: Janczewski, L.J., Wolfe, H.B., Shenoi, S. (eds.) SEC 2013. IFIP AICT, vol. 405, pp. 300–314. Springer, Heidelberg (2013)
18. Zwattendorfer, B., Slamanig, D.: Privacy-preserving realization of the stork framework in the public cloud. In: SECRYPT, pp. 419–426 (2013)

D–Shuffle for Prêt à Voter

Dalia Khader

daliakhader@googlemail.com

Abstract. Prêt à Voter is an end–to–end verifiable voting scheme, that uses paper based ballot forms that are turned into encrypted receipts. The scheme was designed to be flexible, secure and to offer voters a familiar and easy voting experience. Secrecy of the vote in Prêt à Voter relies on encoding the vote using a randomized candidate list in the ballots. In a few variants of Prêt à Voter a verifiable shuffle was used in the ballot generation phase in order to randomize the candidates. Verifiable shuffles are cryptographic primitives that re–encrypt and permute a list of ciphertexts. They provide proofs of correctness of the shuffle and preserve secrecy of the permutation. This paper proposes a new verifiable shuffle "D–Shuffle" that is efficient. We provide a security proof for the D–Shuffle. Furthermore, we show that using the D–shuffle for generating ballots in Prêt à Voter scheme ensures its security against: "Authority Knowledge Attack" and "Chain of Custody Attack".

Keywords: E-voting, Verifiable Shuffle, Zero knowledge proofs.

1 Introduction

A shuffle is a permutation and re-randomization of a set of ciphertexts. Shuffling itself is relatively easy; the challenge is to provide a proof of correctness of a shuffle that anyone can verify without revealing the permutation. A mix-net is a series of chained servers each of which applies a shuffle to some input ciphertexts, before passing the output to the next server. Mix-nets were used widely in e-voting schemes. The main motivation in using them is to submit encrypted votes into a mix-net where every mix-server shuffles the votes. The output of the mix-net is then decrypted providing anonymity to the voters. Using verifiable shuffles prevents mix-servers from cheating.

In this paper we focus on one of the well known end-to-end verifiable schemes: Prêt à Voter . The Prêt à Voter approach to verifiable voting, randomizing candidate order on ballot to encode votes, was first proposed by Ryan in [16]. Since then several papers were introduced to add extra interesting properties to the original scheme [16, 18, 21]. Verifiable shuffles were used in Prêt à Voter either to mix the encrypted receipts before publishing them on a public bulletin board, and/or to randomize the candidates on the ballot. The shuffle we propose in this paper is focused on the latter case.

B. De Decker and A. Zúquete (Eds.): CMS 2014, LNCS 8735, pp. 104–117, 2014.
© IFIP International Federation for Information Processing 2014

1.1 Prêt à Voter Overview

In "Prêt à Voter " ballots are given to voters via a confidential channel. The ballot has a left hand side (LHS) with a randomly permuted list of candidates, and a right hand side (RHS) which carries an encryption of the order of the candidates in the LHS, usually referred to as *the onion* for historical reasons. Each ballot has a unique serial number (which could be a hash of the onion), (SN), for administrative purposes such as searching for the ballot on the bulletin board, etc (See Figure 3, Original scheme).

The voting takes place in the polling station. In the booth, the voter places a mark next to the name of the candidate she wants to vote for. She separates the RHS from LHS, shreds the LHS and takes the RHS to an official who scans and sends it to the tallying authority. A signed copy of the RHS is given to the voter to keep. The onions are used in the tabulation to interpret the voter's mark on the scanned RHS, enabling the tallying authorities to count the votes. The voter can verify that her vote has been received by checking the onion, serial number and choice of index, against the published results on the bulletin board.

The details of the procedure of tabulation, randomization of ballots, tallying, distributing the ballots, etc, varies in the different versions of Prêt à Voter [16, 18, 21]. On a conceptual level the procedure is the same. Random auditing of the ballots is used in all versions of Prêt à Voter to ensure the well-formedness of ballot forms. The auditing procedure involves decrypting onions on selected ballot forms and checking that they correspond to the LHS order. Given that the authorities responsible of creating the ballots can not predict which ballots will be chosen for auditing, it is hard to cheat without a high possibility of getting caught.

1.2 Motivation and Contribution

The Victorian State elections [5, 4, 3] considered developing the first state government-level universally verifiable public e-voting system in the world, based on Prêt à Voter . The proposed mechanism of constructing the ballot was adopted from [21] and is based on using a verifiable shuffle to permute the candidates on the ballot. The proof of shuffle is used as proof of well formness of the ballot. The scheme in [21] had two vulnerabilities:

– Authority knowledge attack: All ballots are generated by one authority. Therefore this authority is trusted to maintain both privacy and receipt-freeness. Generating the ballots in a distributed fashion is desirable, because it ensures that no one but the voter ever learns the candidate ordering. However, there are three major obstacles preventing from that in [21]:
  • Proving the ballot is well-formed in the distributed fashion.
  • Printing the ballot without the printer(s) learning the order.
  • Ensuring robustness so that the scheme can be run even in the presence of some dishonest election officials.

- Chain of Custody: The ballot secrecy in Prêt à Voter relies on the fact that no one can know the order of the candidates unless they own the decryption key of the onion. However, the ballot form LHS contains the candidate order as plaintext. This means that the chain of custody between the ballot generation and until the ballot reaches the voter should be trusted. Ryan and Peacock have discussed an alternative approach [17] referred to as Print–on–Demand. The idea is to print ballot forms at the point they are needed. The ballot will have two onions–the LHS one which can be decrypted in the polling station, and RHS one which can be decrypted by the Prêt à Voter tellers as in the original scheme.

The verifiable shuffle needs to be efficient to cope with the number of ballots generated and verified in the election time. In this paper we propose an efficient and secure verifiable shuffle for that purpose referred to as the D–shuffle (it uses disjunctive proofs for verifying the shuffle hence the name). The D–shuffle can also provide a distributed way of creating the ballot and can provide parallel shuffling that enables Print–on–Demand with minimum computational cost.

2   The Design of the Verifiable D–Shuffle

In the design of the D–Shuffle we require an encryption scheme with Homomorphism and Re-encryption properties. Assume we have an encryption scheme $E = (KeyGen, Enc, Dec)$. Let the key pair generated be (pk, sk). Let r_1, r_2 be the randomization factors used in encrypting. Let M, M_1, M_2 be plaintext messages. The properties we require in this paper are:

- Homomorphism: Multiplying two ciphertexts results with a third ciphertext such that: $Enc(pk, M_1, r_1).Enc(pk, M_2, r_2) = Enc(pk, M_1 + M_2, r_1 + r_2)$;
- Re-encryption: An encryption $CT = Enc(pk, M, r_1)$ can be re-encrypted such that $ReEnc(CT, r_2) = Enc(pk, M, r_1 + r_2)$.

The general idea behind our shuffle is derived from Theorem 1. We explain the Theorem using Definition 1 and prove it as follows;

Definition 1. *Sequence* $M = (m_1, \ldots, m_n)$ *is a super–increasing sequence if every element of the sequence is positive integers and is greater than the sum of all previous elements in the sequence (i.e.* $m_k > \sum_{i=1}^{k-1} m_i$ *).*

Theorem 1. *Let* $M = (m_1, \ldots, m_n)$ *be a super–increasing sequence and* $S = \sum_{i=1}^{n} m_i$. *If* $X = (x_1, \ldots, x_n)$ *is a solution of*

$$S = \sum_{i=1}^{n} x_i$$

such that $\forall j \in \{1, \ldots, n\} : x_j \in M$, *then* $(x_1, \ldots, x_n)$ *is a permutation of* M.

Proof. Recall the subset sum problem: a sequence of integers M and an integer S, find any non-empty subset X that sums to S. This problem is proven to have either one unique solution or none [11] over super-increasing sequences. Given Theorem 1 assumes the existence of the subset $X \subseteq M$ and assumes that $S = \sum_{i=1}^{n} x_n$ then by the uniqueness property X is a permutation of M.

2.1 Intuition Behind the Design

We explain the intuition behind our design of the D–Shuffle using Theorem 1. The general idea is to assume all elements of Theorem 1 are encrypted and we prove the theorem holds using zero knowledge proofs. Let M be a super–increasing sequence that is encrypted and fed to the D–Shuffle as input. Assume the output is the encrypted version of $X = (x_1, \ldots, x_n)$. According to Theorem 1 the output is a permutation if the following two conditions hold:

1. **The Belonging Condition:** $\forall j \in \{1, \ldots, n\} : x_j \in M$.
   In the D–Shuffle this is equivalent to saying "All output ciphertexts belong to the list of all input ciphertexts". We require the disjunctive re-encryption proof shown in Figure 1.
2. **The Summation Condition:** $S = \sum_{i=1}^{n} m_i = \sum_{i=1}^{n} x_k$.
   In the D–Shuffle this is equivalent to saying that the homomorphic summation of the input ciphertexts and the homomorphic summation of the output ciphertexts are encryptions of the same plaintext value (i.e. the output sum is just a re–encryption of the input sum). We require the re-encryption proof shown in Figure 2.

Statement: Given the ciphertext $\hat{c}_j$ and list of ciphertexts $\{c_1, \ldots, c_n\}$ prove the knowledge of r such that the following is true: $[\hat{c}_j = ReEnc(c_i, r)] \wedge [c_i \in \{c_1, \ldots, c_n\}]$
Creating the proof:
$\pi_j = DRE.Proof(\{c_1, \ldots, c_n\}, \hat{c}_j, pk, r)$
Verifying:
$\{0,1\} = DRE.Verify(\{c_1, \ldots, c_n\}, \hat{c}_j, pk, \pi_j)$

Fig. 1. Disjunctive Re-Encryption (DRE)

Statement: Given two ciphertexts $c, \hat{c}$ prove knowledge of r such that: $\hat{c} = ReEnc(c, r)$
Creating the proof: $\pi = RE.Proof(c, \hat{c}, r)$
Verifying: $\{0,1\} = RE.Verify(c, \hat{c}, \pi)$

Fig. 2. Re-Encryption Zero Knowledge Proof (RE)

2.2 The Construction of the D–Shuffle

Let the plaintext we intend to encrypt and shuffle be the super–increasing sequence $M = (m_1, \ldots, m_n)$. We start with creating a list $\{c_1, \ldots, c_n\}$ such that

$c_k = Enc(pk, m_k, 1)$. Note that we can verify correctness of the encryption easily since the randomization is 1.

The Shuffling Procedure:

1. Choose $r_1 \ldots r_n$ random values.
2. Create the output list $\{\grave{c}_1, \ldots, \grave{c}_n\}$ of ciphertexts by re–encrypting and permuting such that $\grave{c}_j = ReEnc(c_k, r_k)$ for some $c_k \in \{c_1, \ldots, c_n\}$.
3. Create $\pi_j = DRE.Proof(\{c_1, \ldots, c_n\}, \grave{c}_j, pk, r)$.
4. Let $S = \sum_{k=1}^{n} m_k$ and $R = \sum_{k=1}^{n} r_k$.
5. Let $C = Enc(pk, S, n+1) = \prod_{k=1}^{n} c_k$. Note that the randomization factor equals $n+1$ since the randomization factors of the c_k is all equal to 1.
6. Let $\grave{C} = \prod_{k=1}^{n} \grave{c}_k = Enc(pk, S, n+1+R) = ReEnc(C, R)$.
7. Create Re-Encryption Zero Knowledge Proof $\bar{\pi} = RE.Proof(C, \grave{C}, R)$.

One can have a mix–net where each mix–server i runs the D–shuffle on the output of the server $i-1$.

Verifying the Shuffle:

1. Compute from the input ciphertexts $C = \prod_{k=1}^{n} c_k$.
2. Compute from the output ciphertexts $\grave{C} = \prod_{k=1}^{n} \grave{c}_k$.
3. For all j s.t. $j \in \{1, \ldots, n\}$; Check $DRE.Verify(\{c_1, \ldots, c_n\}, \grave{c}_j, pk, \pi_j) = 1$.
4. Check $RE.Verify(C, \grave{C}, \bar{\pi}) = 1$.

2.3   Security of the D–Shuffle

There are three properties that a verifiable shuffle should achieve: secrecy of the permutation, soundness of the proofs, and correctness of the proofs.

– Correctness of the verification of the shuffle implies that an honest prover (shuffler) has to be able to create the re-encryption and zero knowledge proofs such that they verify correctly. This is achieved by assuming correctness of the zero knowledge proofs used in Figure 1 and Figure 2.
– Soundness of the verification of shuffle implies that no dishonest prover (shuffler) can produce a proof of shuffle that verifies correctly. This is guaranteed with the soundness of the proofs and the uniqueness property in Theorem 1.
– Secrecy of the permutation depends on two security notions, the zero knowledge property of the proofs and on the security of the encryption scheme (see appendix, IND-V-CPA,IND-V-CCA1, or IND-V-CCA2).

2.4   On Instantiations of the D–Shuffle

The D–Shuffle requires homomorphic properties to verify the sums. Exponential ElGamal and Paillier were heavily used for voting applications for their homomorphic properties. In the Victorian State elections [5, 4, 3] the suggestion was to use Exponential ElGamal. In this paper we focus on having general constructions of the D–shuffle and Prêt à Voter . Recent security analysis showed that using IND–CCA2 encryptions for creating ballots [1, 2, 9] is sufficient to guarantee secrecy of vote. If we require both homomorphic properties and IND–CCA2 security then we can use Naor–Yung encryptions [1, 2, 9] or Cramer–Shoup encryption [13, 20]. The two mentioned encryption schemes have an extractable part of the cipher that is homomorphic.

2.5   On the Efficiency of D–Shuffle

The main advantage of the D–Shuffle is the fact that it is non–interactive. The first non-interactive verifiable shuffle was proposed in [7], however, the proofs were extremely large $15n + 120$, where n is the number of ciphertexts being shuffled. In a more recent result by Lipmaa and Zhang [12], the size of the proof dropped to $6n + 11$. In the D–shuffle assuming we use ElGamal Exponential, the disjunctive zero knowledge proof for an ElGamal encryption is $2n$ and the zero knowledge proof of Re-Encryption for ElGamal is two more elements, causing the total to drop to $2n + 2$. Jakobsson et al [8] proposed a technique for making mix nets robust and efficient, called randomized partial checking. The general idea is to ask each server to reveal a pseudo-randomly selected subset of its input/output relations, therefore providing strong evidence of correctness. The secrecy of the permutation also gets compromised using such a technique to a certain level [10]. The D–shuffle allows the verifier to choose the balance between "correctness proofs vs efficiency" as they require without compromising secrecy. The verifier can choose randomly the number of disjunctive proofs he would like to obtain since the proofs are independent and given the disjunctive proofs do not reveal any input/output relations, the permutation remains secret.

3   The D-Shuffle Used for Prêt à Voter

The ceremony of the voting, tabulation and verification of the vote remain unchanged as described in §1.1. Each candidate is presented in a code m_i such that the set $(m_1, \ldots, m_n)$ is super–increasing and is publicly announced. The onion contains an encrypted list of the different candidates i.e. a permutation of $\{\mathsf{Enc}(pk, m_1, r_1), \mathsf{Enc}(pk, m_2, r_2), \ldots, \mathsf{Enc}(pk, m_k, r_k)\}$ that corresponds to the order of the candidates on the LHS.

The ballot creation uses the D–Shuffle such that each mix–server i verifies the zero knowledge proofs of server $i - 1$, shuffles the outputs of $i - 1$ and publishes the new zero knowledge proofs on a bulletin board. The initial ciphertexts input to mix–net, i.e. server $i = 1$, is $\{\mathsf{Enc}(pk, m_1, 1), \ldots, \mathsf{Enc}(pk, m_k, 1)\}$ which is verifiable by everyone since the randomization factors are 1 and the candidate codes is public information. The final list of ciphertexts is printed as the onion on the ballot. The auditing of the ballot and checking its well formness can be done in three ways depending on level:

- Extreme Auditing: Verifying all the zero knowledge proofs on the bulletin board. This can be done by any entity that has the means and computational powers. Partial checking of the proofs can be applied here.
- Basic Auditing: Checking the onion on the ballots against the Serial Number SN on the bulletin board. This can be by any entity that is willing to act as an observer to the elections and no computational power or cryptographic knowledge is required.
- Voter Auditing: Decrypting the RHS and checking it against the LHS. This is the traditional Prêt à Voter technique used by the voters to audit the ballots if they want too.

Among the three techniques, the voter auditing technique is the most user friendly for the voters. However, ballots used for auditing using that technique should not be used for voting. This can be enforced because the only way to audit is to ask the authorities with the decryption key to reveal the candidates order in the onion and at that point the SN is flagged as unusable for election.

Multi-authority Ballot Generation. Each mix-server in the mix-net can be considered an independent authority such that the values that correspond to the ciphertexts published on the final ballot are unknown to any of them. Therefore the privacy and receipt-freeness can not be broken by any of the mix-servers or any number of them. To break privacy and receipt-freeness all mix-servers have to collude. This partially solves "Authority knowledge attack":

- Proving the ballot is well-formed in the distributed fashion. Each mix-server publishes enough zero knowledge proofs to verify that the shuffling is correct and honest. Therefore the final printed ballot is proven well formed given all the proofs published verify correctly.
- Ensuring robustness so that the scheme can be run even in the presence of some dishonest election officials. This is done using the three auditing techniques mentioned earlier.

Print–On–Demand vs Preprinted Ballots. In Prêt à Voter secrecy of the ballot relies on the assumption that the LHS was not revealed to any entity other than the voter. This means that the chain of custody between the creation of a ballot form and its use in a polling station needs to be trusted. Alternatively, the ballot can be printed in the polling station at the time of the vote [19]. This is what is referred to as print–on–demand scenario. The ballot given to the voter will have two onions one that can be decrypted in the booth in private and printed out to resemble the LHS and the other is the traditional Prêt à Voter onion existing on the RHS (See Figure 3) which is decrypted in the tallying

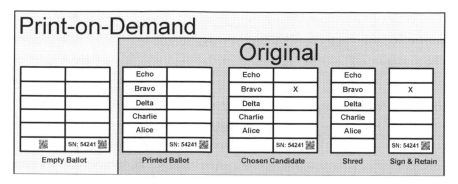

Fig. 3. Prêt à Voter : The Ceremony

Statement: Given the pair of ciphertext $(c\grave{1}_{,j}, c\grave{2}_{,j})$ and list of pair of ciphertexts $\{(c_{1,1}, c_{2,1}), \dots, (c_{1,n}, c_{2,n})\}$ prove the knowledge of r_1, r_2 such that the following is true: $[c\grave{1}_{,j} = ReEnc(c_{1,i}, r_1)] \wedge [c\grave{2}_{,j} = ReEnc(c_{2,i}, r_2)] \wedge [(c_{1,i}, c_{2,i}) \in \{(c_{1,1}, c_{2,1}), \dots, (c_{1,n}, c_{2,n})\}]$
Creating the proof:
$\pi_j = DDRE.Proof(\{(c_{1,1}, c_{2,1}), \dots, (c_{1,n}, c_{2,n})\}, (c\grave{1}_{,j}, c\grave{2}_{,j}), pk, r_1, r_2)$
Verifying:
$\{0, 1\} = DDRE.Verify(\{(c_{1,1}, c_{2,1}), \dots, (c_{1,n}, c_{2,n})\}, (c\grave{1}_{,j}, c\grave{2}_{,j}), pk, \pi_j)$

Fig. 4. Disjunctive Double Re-Encryption

phase. This avoids the chain of custody issues. Ballot forms can be audited in the same way as previously, by printing the RHS first, and then checking that it matches the LHS. The voting experience with the exception of printing the LHS remains the same too. To achieve print–on–demand one can provide a double ciphertext disjunctive zero knowledge proof as shown in the Figure 4 in place of the disjunctive proofs used earlier.

The print-on-demand solves the remaining two problems:

– Chain of Custody: The ballots are generated such that parallel shuffling takes place and no mix server knows the final order. The ballot generated does not contain any plaintext and the LHS is encrypted from the point the ballot is generated and until it reaches the polling station.
– Authority knowledge attack regarding printers: The double ciphered mix-net can be implemented such that we have multiple printers in the booth. Assume we have three printers in each booth, then we can replace the key pair(pk_L, sk_L) with (pk_{p1}, sk_{p1}), (pk_{p2}, sk_{p2}) and (pk_{p3}, sk_{p3}). Each printer outputs part of the LHS and none of the printers will fully know the ballot.

4   Conclusion

We propose a new verifiable shuffle referred to as the D–Shuffle. The new shuffle is efficient, sound, complete, and ofcourse reserves the secrecy of the permutation. The D–shuffle when used for creating ballots in a Prêt à Voter scheme, it prevents "Authority Knowledge Attack" and "Chain of Custody Attack".

References

1. Bernhard, D., Cortier, V., Pereira, O., Smyth, B., Warinschi, B.: Adapting helios for provable ballot privacy. In: Atluri, V., Diaz, C. (eds.) ESORICS 2011. LNCS, vol. 6879, pp. 335–354. Springer, Heidelberg (2011)
2. Bernhard, D., Pereira, O., Warinschi, B.: How not to prove yourself: Pitfalls of the fiat-shamir heuristic and applications to helios. In: Wang, X., Sako, K. (eds.) ASIACRYPT 2012. LNCS, vol. 7658, pp. 626–643. Springer, Heidelberg (2012)
3. Buckland, R., Wen, R.: The future of e-voting in australia. IEEE Security & Privacy 10(5), 25–32 (2012)
4. Burton, C., Culnane, C., Heather, J., Peacock, T., Ryan, P.Y.A., Schneider, S., Srinivasan, S., Teague, V., Wen, R., Xia, Z.: A supervised verifiable voting protocol for the victorian electoral commission. In: E-Voting 2012, pp. 81–94.
5. Burton, C., Culnane, C., Heather, J., Peacock, T., Ryan, P.Y.A., Schneider, S., Srinivasan, S., Teague, V., Wen, R., Xia, Z.: Using prêt à voter in victorian state elections. In: EVT/WOTE 2012. USENIX (2012)
6. Chaum, D., Pedersen, T.P.: Wallet Databases with Observers. In: Brickell, E.F. (ed.) CRYPTO 1992. LNCS, vol. 740, pp. 89–105. Springer, Heidelberg (1993)
7. Groth, J., Lu, S.: A non-interactive shuffle with pairing based verifiability. In: Kurosawa, K. (ed.) ASIACRYPT 2007. LNCS, vol. 4833, pp. 51–67. Springer, Heidelberg (2007)
8. Jakobsson, M., Juels, A., Rivest, R.: Making mix nets robust for electronic voting by randomized partial checking. In: EVT/WOTE, pp. 339–353. USENIX (2002)
9. Khader, D., Ryan, P.Y.A.: Receipt freeness of prêt à voter provably secure. IACR Cryptology ePrint Archive, page 594 (2011)
10. Khazaei, S., Wikström, D.: Randomized partial checking revisited. In: Dawson, E. (ed.) CT-RSA 2013. LNCS, vol. 7779, pp. 115–128. Springer, Heidelberg (2013)
11. Koblitz: A course in number theory and cryptography, pp. 112–114. Springer (1987)
12. Lipmaa, H., Zhang, B.: A more efficient computationally sound non-interactive zero-knowledge shuffle argument. In: Visconti, I., De Prisco, R. (eds.) SCN 2012. LNCS, vol. 7485, pp. 477–502. Springer, Heidelberg (2012)
13. Loftus, J., May, A., Smart, N.P., Vercauteren, F.: On cca-secure somewhat homomorphic encryption. In: Miri, A., Vaudenay, S. (eds.) SAC 2011. LNCS, vol. 7118, pp. 55–72. Springer, Heidelberg (2012)
14. Hirt, M., Sako, K.: Efficient Receipt-Free Voting Based on Homomorphic Encryption. In: Preneel, B. (ed.) EUROCRYPT 2000. LNCS, vol. 1807, pp. 539–556. Springer, Heidelberg (2000)
15. Pedersen, T.P.: A Threshold Cryptosystem without a Trusted Party. In: Davies, D.W. (ed.) EUROCRYPT 1991. LNCS, vol. 547, pp. 522–526. Springer, Heidelberg (1991)
16. Ryan, P.Y.A.: A variant of the chaum voter-verifiable scheme. In: Issues in the theory of security, WITS, pp. 81–88. ACM (2005)

17. Ryan, P.Y.A., Peacock, T.: Threat analysis of cryptographic election schemes, CS-TR:971 NCL (2006)
18. Ryan, Z.P.Y.A., Bismark, D., Heather, J., Schneider, S., Xia: Prêt à voter: a voter-verifiable voting system. Trans. Info. For. Sec. 4, 662–673 (2009)
19. Ryan, P.Y.A., Peacock, T.: Prêt à voter: a systems perspective. CS.TR.929, NCL (2005)
20. Wikström, D.: A universally composable mix-net. In: Naor, M. (ed.) TCC 2004. LNCS, vol. 2951, pp. 317–335. Springer, Heidelberg (2004)
21. Xia, Z., Culnane, C., Heather, J., Jonker, H., Ryan, P.Y.A., Schneider, S., Srinivasan, S.: Versatile Prêt à Voter: Handling Multiple Election Methods with a Unified Interface. In: Gong, G., Gupta, K.C. (eds.) INDOCRYPT 2010. LNCS, vol. 6498, pp. 98–114. Springer, Heidelberg (2010)

A   Secrecy of the D–Shuffle

We recall the definition of IND-CCA2, given a public-key encryption scheme that consists of the three algorithms (KeyGen, Enc, Dec).

Definition 2. *A public-key encryption scheme achieves IND-CCA2 security if any polynomial time attacker only has negligible advantage in the attack game, shown in Fig. 5. Note that the advantage is defined to be $|\Pr[b' = b] - \frac{1}{2}|$.*

---

1. *Setup.* The challenger takes the security parameter λ as input, and runs KeyGen to generate (pk, sk).
2. *Phase 1.* The attacker is given pk and can issue a polynomial number of decryption queries with any input: Given C, the challenger returns $\mathsf{Dec}(C, sk)$. At some point, the attacker chooses M_0, M_1 of equal length and sends them to the challenger for a challenge.
3. *Challenge.* The challenger selects $b \in_R \{0,1\}$ and returns $C_b = \mathsf{Enc}(M_b, pk)$ as the challenge.
4. *Phase 2.* The attacker can issue a polynomial number of decryption oracle queries with any input except for C_b.
5. *Guess*: At some point the attacker terminates Phase 2 by outputting a guess b' for b.

Fig. 5. IND-CCA2 Game

In Definition 2, if we remove *Phase 2* in the attack game then it becomes the definition for IND-CCA1. Furthermore, if we completely disallow the attacker to access the decryption oracle then it becomes the standard IND-CPA security.

A.1   Indistinguishable Vectors of Ciphertexts

To facilitate our security analysis of the D–Shuffle, we proposed a different security model (i.e. IND-V-CCA2 security) for public key encryption schemes. We show that this new security model is equivalent to the standard IND-CCA2.

1. *Setup.* The challenger takes the security parameter λ as input, and runs KeyGen to generate (pk, sk).
2. *Phase 1.* The attacker is given pk and can issue a polynomial number of decryption queries with any input: Given C, the challenger returns $\mathsf{Dec}(C, sk)$. At some point, the attacker chooses a list $M_1, \ldots, M_n$ of equal length and two permutation P_0, P_1 and sends them to the challenger for a challenge.
3. *Challenge.* The challenger computes $\forall k \in \{1, \ldots, n\}; C_k = \mathsf{Enc}(M_k, pk)$. The challenger computes them according to P_0, P_1 such that:
   $\{\grave{C}_1, \ldots, \grave{C}_n\} = P_0(\{C_1, \ldots, C_n\})$
   $\{\tilde{C}_1, \ldots, \tilde{C}_n\} = P_1(\{C_1, \ldots, C_n\})$.
   The challenger sets $E_0 = (\{\grave{C}_1, \ldots, \grave{C}_n\}, \{\tilde{C}_1, \ldots, \tilde{C}_n\})$ and $E_1 = (\{\tilde{C}_1, \ldots, \tilde{C}_n\}, \{\grave{C}_1, \ldots, \grave{C}_n\})$. The challenger randomly chooses $b \in \{0, 1\}$, and sends E_b to adversary.
4. *Phase 2.* The attacker can issue a polynomial number of decryption oracle queries with any input except for $C \notin E_b$.
5. *Guess*: At some point the attacker terminates Phase 2 by outputting a guess b' for b.

Fig. 6. IND-V-CCA2 Game

1. *Setup.* The challenger takes the security parameter λ as input, and runs KeyGen to generate (pk, sk). He gives the public parameters to $\mathcal{A}$ who forwards them to $\mathcal{A}^\dagger$
2. *Phase 1.* Every time $\mathcal{A}$ queries the decryption oracle from $\mathcal{A}^\dagger$, $\mathcal{A}^\dagger$ queries the decryption oracle from the challenger. The response of the challenger is forwarded to $\mathcal{A}$.
3. *Challenge.* The $\mathcal{A}^\dagger$ sends $M_0, \ldots, M_n$ together with two permutations (P_0, P_1), to $\mathcal{A}$. $\mathcal{A}$ computes the ciphertexts $C_1, \ldots, C_n$ such that $C_i = Enc(M_i, pk)$. The $\mathcal{A}$ forwards M_0, M_1 to the challenger. The challenger selects $b \in_R \{0, 1\}$ and returns $C_b = \mathsf{Enc}(M_b, pk)$ as the challenge. $\mathcal{A}$ assigns $C_0 = C_b$ and then permutes: $\{\grave{C}_1, \ldots, \grave{C}_n\} = P_0(\{C_1, \ldots, C_n\})$; $\{\tilde{C}_1, \ldots, \tilde{C}_n\} = P_1(\{C_1, \ldots, C_n\})$; $\mathcal{A}$ sets: $E_0 = (\{\grave{C}_1, \ldots, \grave{C}_n\}, \{\tilde{C}_1, \ldots, \tilde{C}_n\})$; $E_1 = (\{\tilde{C}_1, \ldots, \tilde{C}_n\}, \{\grave{C}_1, \ldots, \grave{C}_n\})$; Finally he flips a coin d and sends E_d to $\mathcal{A}$
4. *Phase 2.* Querying the decryption oracle is constraint to not sending the ciphertexts of the challenge.
5. *Guess*: $\mathcal{A}^\dagger$ returns a guess $\grave{d}$. If $\grave{d} = d$, the adversary $\mathcal{A}$ guesses $\grave{b} = 0$ else flip a coin to decide on $\grave{b}$

Fig. 7. IND-V-CCA2 versus IND-CCA2

Definition 3. *A public-key encryption scheme achieves IND-V-CCA2 security if any polynomial time attacker only has negligible advantage in the attack game, shown in Fig. 6.*

In the model in Figure 6, if we remove *Phase 2* in the attack game then it becomes the definition for IND-V-CCA1 (equivalent to IND-CCA1). Furthermore, if we completely disallow the attacker to access the decryption oracle then it becomes the standard IND-V-CPA (equivalent to IND-CPA) security.

We proof the following theorem:

Theorem 2. *If there exist an Adversary $\mathcal{A}^\dagger$ that breaks the IND-V-CCA2 then their exist an Adversary $\mathcal{A}$ that can break the IND-CCA2 (See Figure 7)*

Note that if $b = 1$ the simulation is unfaithful, however the probability of guessing the right $\hat{b}$ remains. Adding up the probability of winning when $b = 0$ leads to $\frac{\epsilon}{4} + \frac{1}{4}$ and probability of winning when $b = 1$ is $\frac{1}{4}$. Advantage of winning is: $Adv_{IND-CCA2}(k) = |Pr[\mathcal{A}\ winning] - \frac{1}{2}| = \frac{\epsilon}{4}$. This advantage is non-negligible when ϵ is non-negligible.

A.2 On the Secrecy of the D–Shuffle Permutation

The two properties of correctness and soundness derive directly from the Zero Knowledge proofs. In this section we elaborate more on the secrecy of the permutation. Imagine their exist an adversary $\mathcal{A}$ that can guess the permutation of the verifiable D–Shuffle. This adversary can be used as a subroutine for $\mathcal{A}^\dagger$ for breaking the IND-V-(CPA,CCA1,CCA2) as follows:

- In the challenge, the adversary $\mathcal{A}^\dagger$ chooses $M_1, \ldots, M_n$, P_0, and P_1 sends them to $\mathcal{C}$.
- He receives back E_b back. Note that E_b has two permuted lists.
- $\mathcal{A}^\dagger$ chooses the first list and simulates the zero knowledge proofs.
- $\mathcal{A}^\dagger$ sends the list and the simulated proofs to $\mathcal{A}$.
- $\mathcal{A}$ should return either P_0 or P_1. If P_0 is returned then $\mathcal{A}^\dagger$ answers back his guess as $\hat{b} = 0$ otherwise $\hat{b} = 1$

Furthermore, the same adversary $\mathcal{A}$ can be used as a sub–routine for $\mathcal{A}^\ddagger$ to break the zero knowledge properties as follows:

- $\mathcal{A}^\ddagger$ encrypts a list of $M_1 \ldots, M_n$ to obtain $c_1, \ldots, c_n$,
- It permutes them to $\grave{c}_1, \ldots, \grave{c}_n$.
- It queries the zero knowledge oracle for the disjunctive proofs of each cipher.
- Computes the Zero knowledge of the sum as done in Figure 2.
- Sends the proofs together with $\grave{c}_1, \ldots, \grave{c}_n$ to $\mathcal{A}$.
- If the proofs are real then $\mathcal{A}$ should return back the expected permutation, otherwise $\mathcal{A}$ gives a guess which is unlikely to be the permutation (probability is $n!$) and implies the zero knowledge proofs were a simulation only.

B Non-interactive Zero knowledge proofs

Equality between discrete logs: Proving knowledge of the discrete logarithm x to bases $f, g \in \mathbb{Z}_p^*$, given h, k where $h \equiv f^x \bmod p$ and $k \equiv g^x \bmod p$ [15, 6].

Sign. Given f, g, x, select a random nonce $w \in_R \mathbb{Z}_q^*$. Compute Witnesses $f' = f^w \bmod p$ and $g' = g^w \bmod p$, Challenge $c = \mathcal{H}(f', g') \bmod q$ and Response $s = w + c \cdot x \bmod q$. Output signature as (f', g', s)

Verify. Given f, g, h, k and signature (f', g', s, c), check $f^s \equiv f' \cdot h^c \pmod{p}$ and $g^s \equiv g' \cdot k^c \pmod{p}$, where $c = \mathcal{H}(f', g') \bmod q$.

A valid proof asserts $\log_f h = \log_g k$; that is, there exists x, such that $h \equiv f^x \bmod p$ and $k \equiv g^x \bmod p$.

Re-Encryption proofs for Exponential ElGamal Imagine you have two Exponential ElGamal ciphertexts for the key-pairs$(y = g^x, x)$:

1. $c = (u_1, v_1) = (g^{r_1}, y^{r_1} g^m)$,
2. $\grave{c} = (u_2, v_2) = (g^{r_1+r_2}, y^{r_1+r_2} g^m)$.

In other words $\grave{c} = ReEnc(c, r_2)$. A zero knowledge proof of Re-Encryption is simply done by the prover providing a zero knowledge proof of the equality between discrete logs between u_2/u_1 and v_2/v_1 to the bases g, y respectively.

Disjunctive Re-encryption Proof for Exponential ElGamal Let $h = g^y$. Given $(u_i, v_i) = (g^x g^\zeta, h^x \cdot h^\zeta \cdot g^m)$ is a re-encryption of $(u, v) = (g^x, h^x \cdot g^m)$ for a random $\zeta \in \mathbb{Z}_p^*$. Prove that (u_i, v_i) belongs to the list $\{(u_1, v_1), \ldots, (u_n, v_n)\}$ [14].

Sign. Select random values $d_1, \ldots, d_n, r_1, \ldots, r_n \in \mathbb{Z}_p^*$. Compute $a_t = (\frac{u_t}{u})^{d_t} g^{r_t}$, $b_t = (\frac{v_t}{v})^{d_t} h^{r_t}$ where $t \in \{1, \ldots, i-1, i+1, \ldots, n\}$. Choose randomly a nounce $\omega \in \mathbb{Z}_p^*$. Let $a_i = g^\omega$ and $b_i = h^\omega$. Compute challenge $c = \mathcal{H}(E||a_1|| \ldots ||a_n||b_1|| \ldots ||b_n)$ where $E = (u||v||u_1||v_1|| \ldots ||u_n||v_n)$. Compute $d_i = c - \sum_{t=1.t \neq i}^{n} d_y$. Compute $r_i = \omega - \zeta d_i$ then Witnesses $d_1, \ldots, d_n$, Challenge c and Response $r_1, \ldots, r_n$. Output signature of knowledge (r_t, d_t) where $t \in [1, n]$

Verify. Let $E1 = (\frac{u_1}{u})^{d_1} g^{r_1}|| \ldots ||(\frac{u_n}{u})^{d_n} g^{r_n}$. Let $E2 = (\frac{v_1}{v})^{d_1} g^{r_1}|| \ldots ||(\frac{v_n}{v})^{d_n} g^{r_n}$. Check $\sum_{t=1}^{n} d_t = \mathcal{H}(E||E1||E2)$

A valid proof asserts that $(u_i, v_i) \in \{(u_1, v_1), \ldots, (u_n, v_n)\}$.

Disjunctive Double Re-Encryption Proofs for Exponential ElGamal Given the following:

- Let $h = g^y$. Let $(CT, \bar{CT})$ be a pair of ElGamal Encryption for the same message m.
- Let $CT_i = (u_i, v_i) = (g^{x_1} g^{\zeta_1}, h^{x_1} \cdot h^{\zeta_1} \cdot g^m)$ be a re-encryption of $(u, v) = (g^{x_1}, h^{x_1} \cdot g^m)$ for a random $\zeta_1 \in \mathbb{Z}_p^*$.
- Let $\bar{CT}_i = (\bar{u}_i, \bar{v}_i) = (g^{x_2} g^{\zeta_2}, h^{x_2} \cdot h^{\zeta_2} \cdot g^m)$ be a re-encryption of $(\bar{u}, \bar{v}) = (g^{x_2}, h^{x_2} \cdot g^m)$ for a random $\zeta_2 \in \mathbb{Z}_p^*$.

Prove that $(CT_i, \bar{CT}_i)$ belongs to the list $\{(CT_1, \bar{CT}_1), \ldots, (CT_n, \bar{CT}_n)\}$.

Sign. Select random values $d_1, \ldots, d_n, r_1, \ldots, r_n, R_1, \ldots, R_n \in \mathbb{Z}_p^*$.
For $t \in \{1, \ldots, i-1, i+1, \ldots, n\}$, compute:
$\alpha_t = (\frac{u_t \cdot v_t}{u \cdot v})^{d_t} (g \cdot h)^{r_t}$ and $\beta_t = (\frac{\bar{u}_t \cdot \bar{v}_t}{\bar{u} \cdot \bar{v}})^{d_t} (g \cdot h)^{R_t}$ and

$$\delta_t = (\frac{u_t \cdot v_t \cdot v}{\bar{u}_t \cdot \bar{v}_t \cdot u})^{d_t}(g \cdot h)^{R_t - r_t}$$

Choose randomly the nounces $\omega_1, \omega_2 \in \mathbb{Z}_p^*$. Let $\alpha_i = (g \cdot h)^{\omega_1}$ and $\beta_i = (g \cdot h)^{\omega_2}$, and $\delta_i = \dfrac{\beta_i}{\alpha_i}$.

Compute challenge $c = \mathcal{H}(E||\alpha_1|| \ldots ||\alpha_n||\beta_1|| \ldots ||\beta_n||\delta_1|| \ldots ||\delta_n)$ where $E = (u||v||u_1||v_1|| \ldots ||u_n||v_n)$. Let $d_i = c - \sum_{t=1, t \neq i}^{n} d_y$, $r_i = \omega_1 - \zeta_1 d_i$, and $R_i = \omega_2 - \zeta_2 d_i$. Witnesses is $d_1, \ldots, d_n$, Challenge is c and Response is $r_1, \ldots, r_n$, $R_1, \ldots, R_n$.

Output signature of knowledge (r_t, d_t, R_t) where $t \in [1, n]$

Verify. Let $E_1 = ((\frac{u_1 \cdot v_1}{u \cdot v})^{d_1}(g \cdot h)^{r_1}|| \ldots ||(\frac{u_n \cdot v_n}{u \cdot v})^{d_n}(g \cdot h)^{r_n})$. Let $E_2 = ((\frac{\bar{u}_1 \cdot \bar{v}_1}{\bar{u} \cdot \bar{v}})^{d_1}(g \cdot h)^{R_1}|| \ldots ||(\frac{\bar{u}_n \cdot \bar{v}_n}{\bar{u} \cdot \bar{v}})^{d_n}(g \cdot h)^{R_n})$. Let $E_3 = ((\frac{u_1 \cdot v_1}{\bar{u}_1 \cdot \bar{v}_1}\frac{v}{u})^{d_1}(g \cdot h)^{R_1 - r_1}|| \ldots ||(\frac{u_n \cdot v_n}{\bar{u}_n \cdot \bar{v}_n}\frac{v}{u})^{d_n}(g \cdot h)^{R_n - r_n})$. Check $\sum_{t=1}^{n} d_t = \mathcal{H}(E||E_1||E_2||E_3)$.

If true accept the signature of knowledge otherwise reject it.

A valid proof asserts that $(u_i, v_i) \in \{(u_1, v_1), \ldots, (u_n, v_n)\}$.

An Approach to Information Security Policy Modeling for Enterprise Networks

Dmitry Chernyavskiy and Natalia Miloslavskaya

Information Security of Banking Systems Department
National Research Nuclear University MEPhI (Moscow Engineering Physics Institute)
31 Kashirskoe shosse, 115409, Moscow, Russia
D.S.CH@mail.ru, NGMiloslavskaya@mephi.ru

Abstract. Network security management is one of the most topical concerns of information security (IS) in modern enterprises. Due to great variety and increasing complexity of network security systems (NSSs) there is a challenge to manage them in accordance with IS policies. Incorrect configurations of NSSs lead to outages and appearance of vulnerabilities in networks. Moreover, policy management is a time and resource consuming process, which takes significant amount of manual work. The paper discusses issues of policy management process in its application for NSSs and describes a policy model aimed to facilitate the process by means of specification of IS policies independently on platforms of NSSs, selection of the most effective NSSs aligned with the policies, and implementation of the policies in configurations of the NSSs.

Keywords: Information Security Policy, Policy Management Process, Network Security System, Finite Automaton, Algebra.

1 Introduction

Network security in most enterprises relies on such network security systems (NSSs) as firewalls and intrusion detection/prevention systems (IDS/IPS) [1]. However, management of NSSs faces challenges tied with time-consuming manual processes, lack of visibility in information security (IS) policies and configuration errors, which lead to network outages and appearance of vulnerabilities [2]. For instance, a policy (hereafter "policy" means "IS policy") for Check Point or Cisco firewalls may consist of thousands of rules and such complexity of policies is the main cause of configuration errors [3,4].

Thus, on the one hand, increasing number of NSSs and their increasing functionality allow to counter more threats and reduce IS risks as a result. On the other hand, complexity of NSSs' management leads to new risks and time-consuming processes, which reduce overall efficiency of NSSs utilization. Therefore, policy management process for NSSs needs simplification in order to reduce probability of errors and efforts on time-consuming tasks.

A formal approach to policy modeling presented in the paper is aimed to facilitate the process by means of specification of policies independently on platforms of NSSs,

B. De Decker and A. Zúquete (Eds.): CMS 2014, LNCS 8735, pp. 118–127, 2014.

selection of the most effective NSSs, and translation of the specified policies into configurations of the NSSs. The contributions of the paper are (a) a policy model for NSSs based on a finite automaton representation of an NSS, (b) an approach to classification of NSSs and selection of the most effective NSS, and (c) a policy algebra based on the model.

The paper is organized as follows. Section 2 overviews policy management process for NSSs and discusses related work on policy modeling. Basic notions of the policy model for NSSs and the approach for selection of the most effective NSS are presented in Section 3. Section 4 introduces the policy algebra for NSSs. Finally, Section 5 concludes the paper.

2   Related Work

Models of policy management process are presented in [5,6,7,8]. All the models consider policy management as iterative process and include similar operations. The most detailed description of policy management process is presented in [5] and from the standpoint of NSSs management the following operations of the process are important. During Policy Assessment step a request for initial policy creation or update of the existing one is evaluated in order to identify policy conflicts and effects. The requested change should be made in the framework of existing IS maintenance system (ISMS includes IS management system and security tools and measures). Identification of IS threats for assets and a list of appropriate options of NSSs that counter the threats, payroll and non-payroll cost of the options as well as determination of options priority are included in Risk Assessment step. Creation of new policies or update of existing ones proceeds during Policy Development step. Requirements for ISMS are derived upon Requirements Definition step in order to assure that it is aligned with new policies. In the course of Controls Definition step the requirements to ISMS are transformed into a selection of the best options of NSSs and requirements to them. Upon Controls Implementation step the NSSs are installed and configured in accordance with the policies. Compliance and audit checks carried out during Monitor Operations step in order to ensure that ISMS functions in alignment with the policies. Review Trends and Manage Events step includes identification of events and trends (internal and external in relation to an enterprise) that may indicate a need to make changes in the policies. Further, during the step possible changes are evaluated against any appropriate criteria in order to make sure that the changes are essential and escalated to the beginning of the process [5]. In addition, if during Policy Assessment, Risk Assessment or Policy Development steps it is identified that some policies are not needed any more, then they must be retired [7]. Note that policy management process is iterative due to continuous changes in technologies, business environment and legal requirements [8].

Thus, in the scope of the process there are the following significant groups of tasks: (a) development and update of policies, (b) selection of the best options of NSSs that are in line with the policies, (c) translation of the policies into configurations of the selected NSSs, and (d) detection and resolution of conflicts in the policies. Formal policy models can be applied to the process in order to automate the tasks and as a result reduce time-consuming efforts and probability of errors. Policy modeling approaches are extensively discussed in literature, some of them are presented in [9,10,11,12,13].

The modeling method [9] is based on four independent atomic functionalities (end-flow, channel, transform, and filter functionalities) and a formal language that allows specification and validation of policies for the functionalities. However, such functionalities as logging and alerting are not presented in the model. The model also lacks means for selection of the best options of functionalities.

An access-control language based on XML syntax and Organization-Based Access Control (OrBAC) model, which is an extension of Role-Based Access Control (RBAC), is given in [11] and intended to specify firewall policies. While OrBAC supports definition of obligation policies and contexts, the language, however, does not include these capabilities and deals only with authorization policies. Another limitation is consideration only of IP addresses, protocols and ports as filtering parameters in the policies, which does not allow specification of more sophisticated filtering policies that inspect other parameters of network packets.

Another method based on OrBAC is described in [11]. The method supports definition of different contexts and obligations within relevant contexts. However, when a policy cannot be implemented by the existing security architecture, the method does not provide means to select appropriate security functionalities for the policy.

An approach [12, 13] provides specification of OrBAC policies and contexts as well as derivation of configurations for security functionalities. It also allows selection of the best options of functionalities in terms of their cost. For this purpose the approach introduces a notion of "closely equivalent" functionalities but lacks any formal criterion to identify such functionalities.

A formal framework presented in [14] provides means for synthesizing secure network configurations. The framework utilizes a network topology, security requirements and business constraints such as usability and budget limits as inputs in order to derive a cost-effective placement of NSSs in the topology. The framework uses policy requirements only as inputs, but does not include capabilities for specification of policies and their translation into configurations of NSSs. Functionalities of NSSs within the framework are considered as "primitive isolation patterns", which can be composed into "composite isolation patterns"; however, a formal classification criterion of the functionalities is not presented.

Hence, the considered approaches either do not support specification of all types of policies for NSSs or do not provide means for selection of the best options of NSSs.

3   A Policy Model

A system is called an *NSS* if it is intended to directly or indirectly secure information transferable through an enterprise's network. Assume that function of an NSS is to form any output in accordance with a policy by means of processing of network traffic that comes to its input. In the general case an output of an NSS is network traffic or messages such as log entries and alerts that sent to other systems or IS administrator's console.

Let P be a set of all possible policies that NSSs can implement. Actually, P consists of sequences of symbols that form commands for different NSSs. If any NSS uses GUI instead of CLI, its policy can be expressed as a text string. For instance, the first rule of Check Point firewall policy shown on Fig. 1 can be written as *"N=1 Source=Any Destination=Web-Server Service=Any ..."* or in any other way that reflects semantics of the rule. Also, the set P includes the empty sequence ε. Let T be a set of network traffic, where $t \in T$ is a network packet (i.e., a sequence of bits), or the empty sequence ε, which means absence of traffic. Consider an NSS as a finite automaton:

$$F =< T \times P, S, T \times M, \delta, f >,$$

where $T \times P$ is an input alphabet, S is a finite set of internal states of the NSS, $T \times M$ is an output alphabet, $\delta : T \times P \times S \to S$ is a state-transformation function and $f : T \times P \times S \to T \times M$ is an output function, M is a set of output messages, which also includes ε (similar to the case of the set T). An NSS functions in discrete time τ and transforms an input traffic $t(\tau) \in T$ into an output traffic $t'(\tau) \in T$ in accordance with a policy $p(\tau) \in P$. An NSS changes its internal state $s(\tau) \in S$ into state $s(\tau + 1) \in S$ while it functions (Fig. 2). The set S can include such parameters as time, number and sequence of packets in a session and other parameters essential to model stateful analysis of network traffic. Such NSS as a stateless packet filter can be considered as an NSS with one state, i.e., $|S| = 1$.

NO	SOURCE	DESTINATION	VPN	SERVICE	ACTION	TRACK	INSTALL ON	TIME	COMMENT
1	★ Any	Web-Server	★ Any Traffic TCP http	accept	— None	Corporate-gw	★ Any	Allow connections to corporate web server
2	Internal-net	SQL-Server	★ Any Traffic TCP MS-SQL	accept	— None	Corporate-gw	★ Any	Allow connections from internal network to corporate database server
3	Admin-subnet	Management	★ Any Traffic TCP CPMI	accept	— None	Corporate-gw	★ Any	Allow connections from administrator's network to Check Point management server
4	★ Any	★ Any	★ Any Traffic	★ Any	drop	— None	Corporate-gw	★ Any	Drop all other traffic

Fig. 1. An example of Check Point firewall policy

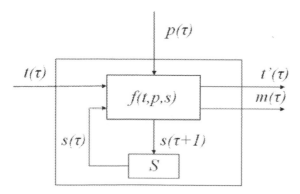

Fig. 2. A finite automaton model of an NSS

Assume that every policy $p \in P$ is represented as a triple of the following finite vectors:

- $\vec{x} = (x_1, x_2, \ldots)$ is an input vector, describing an input traffic of an NSS, where $x_i \in X_i$, while X_i is a set of parameters of any homogenous nature (for instance, X_i can be a set of IP addresses, protocols, port numbers or any other attribute of network traffic);
- $\vec{y} = (y_1, y_2, \ldots)$ is an output vector, describing an output traffic and/or messages generated by an NSS, were $y_i \in Y_i$ while Y_i is a set of parameters of output network traffic of any homogenous nature (similar to the case of the input vector) or a set of parameters of the messages;
- $\vec{z} = (z_1, z_2, \ldots)$ is a state vector, describing an internal state of an NSS. For instance, $z_i \in Z_i$ can be a system time of an NSS.

Any policy $p \in P$ is said to be *definite* if the triple of the policy consists of explicitly defined parameters (concrete protocols, IP addresses, ports, messages, etc.). Any policy that consists of parameters expressed in general view without concretization of elements of corresponding sets (IP address, protocol or port in general, etc.) it is called a *generalized* policy. Note that all policies from the set P are definite policies, since only definite policies are implementable by NSSs. By P_{gen} denote a set of generalized policies. For instance, vector $\vec{x} = (192.168.1.1, TCP, 80)$ belongs to a definite policy, while $\vec{x}_{gen} = (Source\ IP, Protocol, Port)$ is the vector of corresponding generalized policy, where Source IP is the set of source IP addresses, Protocol is the set of protocols, Port number is the set of ports. For any generalized policy $p_{gen} \in P_{gen}$ there is a corresponding subset P' of definite policies from the set P, this subset is denoted by $Def(p_{gen})$. Let P_{sub} be the set of subsets of P, then $Def(p_{gen})$ is the injective map $Def: P_{gen} \to P_{sub}$.

The input, output, and state vectors of any generalized policy p are denoted by $X(p)$, $Y(p)$, and $Z(p)$, respectively. Let $\leq$ be the partial order relation on P_{gen} such that $p \leq p'$ if and only if all parameters of the vectors of the generalized policy p are included in the respective vectors of the generalized policy p':

$$p \leq p' \leftrightarrow X(p) \subseteq X(p'), Y(p) \subseteq Y(p'), Z(p) \subseteq Z(p').$$

Let $\mathcal{F}$ be a set of all existing NSSs. The fact that an NSS $F \in \mathcal{F}$ is capable to implement a policy $p \in P$ or a subset of policies $P' \subseteq P$, i.e., p or P' is included to definitional domain of the state-transformation function δ and the output function f of F, is denoted by $F(p)$ and $F(P')$ in the case of a policy and a subset of policies respectively. Any $F \in \mathcal{F}$ is defined on the entire set T and in the general case on some subset $P' \subseteq P$, where P' can be expressed as the finite union:

$$P' = Def(p_{gen1}) \cup Def(p_{gen2}) \cup \ldots \cup Def(p_{genk}).$$

An NSS $F(Def(p_{gen})) \in \mathcal{F}$ is said to be *simple* if there does not exist an NSS $F' \in \mathcal{F}$ that implements any policy with excluded parameters:

$$F(Def(p_{gen})) \in \mathcal{F}_s \leftrightarrow \nexists\, F'(Def(p'_{gen})) \in \mathcal{F}: p'_{gen} \leq p_{gen} \wedge p'_{gen} \neq p_{gen},$$

where $\mathcal{F}_s$ is the set of simple NSSs. In other words, if exclusion of any subset of parameters from a policy leads to meaningless policy that cannot be implemented by any NSS, then the NSS is simple. Let $P_s = \{p_{gen} \in P_{gen} : \exists F(Def(p_{gen})) \in \mathcal{F}_s\}$ be the set of generalized policies that corresponding definite policies can be implemented by simple NSSs. If an NSS is not simple, it is called *composite*. Simple NSSs can be combined parallel or sequentially with the purpose of constructing a composite NSS.

For example, when considering Check Point firewall policy (Fig. 1) and network address translation (NAT) policy (Fig. 3), the NSSs can be decomposed to simple NSSs that implement single rules. Fig. 4 shows an example of the composite NSS that implements mentioned firewall and NAT policies. Note that the latter rule of the firewall policy in Fig. 1 is not presented in Fig.4 because each simple NSS F_{fw} blocks by default any traffic that does not match its policy (i.e., it outputs the empty sequence ε). In contrast with firewall policies, NAT policy accepts any traffic by default, therefore an additional simple NSS F_{nat} with the default policy (which accepts all traffic that does not match the other NAT rules) is introduced into the model in Fig. 4. Note also that state blocks S (shown in Fig. 2) of each simple NSS are not depicted in Fig. 4 for the sake of compactness.

Two simple NSSs $F_1(Def(p_{gen1}))$, $F_2(Def(p_{gen2})) \in \mathcal{F}_s$ are called *equivalent* if and only if they produce equal outputs for equal inputs while implementing policies:

$$F_1\left(Def\left(p_{gen1}\right)\right) \cong F_2\left(Def\left(p_{gen2}\right)\right) \leftrightarrow$$

$$\forall p_1 \in Def\left(p_{gen1}\right) \exists p_2 \in Def\left(p_{gen2}\right) : f_1^*(t, p_1, s_1) = f_2^*(t, p_2, s_2) \forall t \in T^* \wedge$$

$$\forall p_2 \in Def\left(p_{gen2}\right) \exists p_1 \in Def\left(p_{gen1}\right) : f_2^*(t, p_2, s_2) = f_1^*(t, p_1, s_1) \forall t \in T^*$$

where s_1 and s_2 are initial states of F_1 and F_2 respectively, T^* is a set of finite sequences of network packets, f_1^* and f_2^* are extensions of f_1 and f_2 to T^*.

By this equivalence relation the set of simple NSSs partitioned to equivalence classes. All simple NSSs inside any equivalence class produce equal outputs while implementing respective policies and processing network traffic. However, their policies from the syntax point of view can be different.

In order to demonstrate the equivalence of NSSs consider Check Point and Cisco firewalls along with the following policy: *"Hosts from the network 192.168.1.0/24 are allowed to establish connections to 80 TCP-port on server 10.1.1.10. Connection attempts must be logged"*. Note that the policy consists of two parts: authorization (allows connections to the server) and obligation (requires logging of connection attempts). Each of two selected NSSs are able to implement the policy. It can be represented in Check Point as shown in Fig. 5. In order to implement the policy in Cisco it is necessary to add one rule to an access-list (for instance, access-list 101):

```
access-list 101 permit tcp 192.168.1.0 255.255.255.0 host
10.1.1.10 eq 80 log
```

NO	ORIGINAL PACKET			TRANSLATED PACKET			INSTALL ON	COMMENT
	SOURCE	DESTINATION	SERVICE	SOURCE	DESTINATION	SERVICE		
1	Web-Server	★ Any	★ Any	Web-Server	= Original	= Original	Corporate-gw	Automatic rule (see the network object data).
2	★ Any	Web-Server	★ Any	= Original	Web-Server	= Original	Corporate-gw	Automatic rule (see the network object data).

Fig. 3. An example of Check Point NAT policy

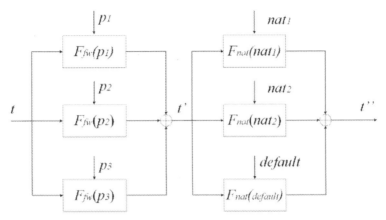

Fig. 4. A composition of simple NSSs

NO	SOURCE	DESTINATION	VPN	SERVICE	ACTION	TRACK	INSTALL ON	TIME	COMMENT
1	Network-192.168.1.0_24	Server-10.1.1.10	★ Any Traffic	TCP http	accept	Log	Corporate-gw	★ Any	

Fig. 5. Check Point firewall policy

The input vectors of generalized policies for Check Point and Cisco are equal: (Source Address, Destination Address, Protocol, Destination Port). Note that the field "service" in Check Point policy (Fig. 5) implies protocol and destination port. Output traffic is the same as an input and it is expressed with keywords *accept* and *permit* in the case of Check Point and Cisco respectively. In addition, a log message must be generated that is expressed with keyword *log* in both cases. Thus, the output vectors are equal for both NSSs: (Accept, Log). State vectors of Check Point and Cisco policies are (VPN, Time, Comment) and (Access-list Number) respectively. However, the parameters of Check Point's state vector are not initialized and consequently do not affect the policy. Access-list number of Cisco is not essential in this case either. Semantics of these two rules are equal and hence the NSSs are equivalent. Undoubtedly, Check Point and Cisco firewalls are not equivalent in general, but abstractions of them (i.e., simple NSSs) that implement the considered policies are equivalent.

The approach to classification of NSSs consists of the following high-level steps:

- decomposition of an NSS to simple NSSs;
- sorting out the triple of vectors of the generalized policy for each simple NSS;
- search for an equivalence class for each simple NSS:

— if there exists a class such that a simple NSS is equivalent to, then it must be added to the class;
— if there is no appropriate equivalence class for a simple NSS, then it forms its own class.

The classification facilitates evaluation of an NSS $F \in \mathcal{F}$ by means of assigning the following rating R_F:

$$R_F = \sum_i W_{F_i} I_{F_i}^F,$$

where $W_{F_i} > 0$ is a weight of a simple NSS F_i (for instance, the number of IS threats that the NSS counters), which can be calculated by an expert evaluation, and $I_{F_i}^F \in \{0,1\}$ is an indicator that shows whether an NSS F is included into equivalence class F_i.

The classification of NSSs built in terms of the described equivalence helps to find NSSs with required functions. For instance, if it is necessary to use functions F_a, F_b, and F_c in some node of an enterprise's network in order to implement particular policy, then an NSS that is simultaneously included in equivalence classes F_a, F_b, and F_c can be selected for this purpose. If there are more than one NSS with required functions then the most effective solution among them is the one that has maximum rating-cost ratio:

$$\frac{R_F}{C_F} \rightarrow max,$$

where C_F is sum of payroll and non-payroll cost of an NSS F. In addition, if there does not exist an NSS that is included in all required classes, then combinations of NSSs that cover the classes can be considered taking into account cumulative rating-cost ratio for each appropriate combination:

$$\sum_j \frac{R_{F^j}}{C_{F^j}} \rightarrow max$$

where $j \in \{j_1, j_2, \dots, j_k\}$, $\{F^{j_1}, F^{j_2}, \dots, F^{j_k}\}$ is the set of NSSs in the combination.

4   A Policy Algebra

All NSSs inside any equivalence class produce equal outputs while implementing policies. However, in the general case their policies from the syntax point of view are different. As can be seen from the above examples, Check Point does not use CLI and it is not possible to compare its policy with the analogue in Cisco from the syntax point of view; however, the policies have equal semantics. Thus, in the general case there are multiple policies that describe the same simple NSS inside an equivalence class. In order to reduce redundancy of policies for NSSs the set of simple policies P_s needs to be substituted for a set of simple unified policies P_u and $|P_u|$ must be minimal. Consequently, only one generalized policy needs to be assigned for every single equivalence class. In other words, if the set $\mathcal{F}_s$ consists of N classes then it is required to have N generalized policies in order to specify policies for all NSSs.

Let $\Omega = \{S, \Phi, \sigma\}$ be a many-sorted signature, where $S = \{s_t, s_m, s_1, s_2, \ldots, s_l\}$ is a set of sorts while s_t and s_m are sorts of network traffic and messages respectively, $\Phi = \{+, \varphi_1, \ldots, \varphi_N\}$ is a set of functional symbols, $\sigma(\varphi_i) = < s_t, s_{i1}, \ldots, s_{ik}, s_m, s_t >$ is a sort function that defines sorts of arguments $s_t, s_{i1}, s_{i2}, \ldots, s_{ik}$ and sorts of values s_m, s_t for every functional symbol $\varphi_i \in \Phi$. In addition, suppose that $\sigma(+) = < s_t, s_t, s_t >$, i.e., function "+" has two arguments of the sort of network traffic and a value of the same sort (two examples of the function are shown in Fig. 4).

Let $V = V_{s_t} \cup V_{s_m} \cup V_{s_1} \cup \ldots \cup V_{s_l}$ be a set of variables, where V_{s_i} is a set of variables of a certain sort $s_i \in S$. Suppose that Θ is the set of Ω-terms that is recursively defined as follows:

- any variable V_{s_i} is a Ω-term θ_{s_i} of the sort s_i;
- any finite expression $\varphi_i(\theta_{s_t}, \theta_{s_{i1}}, \theta_{s_{i2}}, \ldots, \theta_{s_{ik}}, \theta_{s_m}, \theta_{s_t})$ such that $\sigma(\varphi_i) = < s_t, s_{i1}, s_{i2}, \ldots, s_{ik}, s_m, s_t >$ is a Ω-term of the sort s_t, where $\theta_{s_t}, \theta_{s_m}$, and $\theta_{s_{ij}}$ are any variables of corresponding sorts s_t, s_m, and s_{ij}.

Suppose that any $s_i \in S$ is a name of a certain parameter of generalized policy, any $\varphi_i \in \Phi$ is a designation of a certain equivalence class of NSSs, then $\varphi_i(\theta_{s_t}, \theta_{s_{i1}}, \theta_{s_{i2}}, \ldots, \theta_{s_{ik}}, \theta_{s_m}, \theta_{s_t})$ is a representation of the output function of an NSS from equivalence class designated by φ_i that includes representation of respective simple policy. By construction, Θ includes representations of all generalized policies for simple and composite NSSs. For instance, the NSS shown in Fig. 4 can be represented as follows:

$$\begin{cases} F_{fw}(t, p_1, s) + F_{fw}(t, p_2, s) + F_{fw}(t, p_3, s) = t' \\ F_{nat}(t', nat_1, s) + F_{nat}(t', nat_2, s) + F_{nat}(t', default, s) = t'' \end{cases}$$

where F_{fw} and F_{nat} are designations of equivalence classes; $p_i, nat_j, default$, and s are collections of parameters of respective policies and states (parameters of policies consist of input, output and state vectors). Note that notations $+(\theta_{s_t}, \theta_{s_t})$ and $\theta_{s_t} + \theta_{s_t}$ are equivalent.

Let (A, I) be a many-sorted algebra, where A is a carrier set of the algebra and I is an interpretation of the signature Ω. For every sort $s_i \in S$ the interpretation associates a subset $A_{s_i} \subseteq A$ and for every functional symbol $\varphi_i \in \Phi$ it associates the function $f_i : A_{s_t} \times A_{s_{i1}} \times A_{s_{i2}} \times A_{s_{ik}} \to A_{s_m} \times A_{s_t}$ that defines the output function of an NSS of the respective equivalence class F_i. Thus, the algebra models all definite policies for simple NSSs of each equivalence class as well as definite policies for composite NSSs.

In order to translate the policies into the native policy formats of concrete NSSs' platforms described many-sorted algebra can be represented as a formal language with a generative grammar $G = (\mathcal{T}, \mathcal{N}, \mathcal{S}, R)$, where $\mathcal{T}$ is a terminal vocabulary that reflects carrier set A, $\mathcal{N}$ is a non-terminal vocabulary that includes terms, $\mathcal{S} \in \mathcal{N}$ is a starting non-terminal symbol of every policy, and R is a set productions. Representation of the policies in the form of a formal language allows application of the existing parsing algorithms.

5   Conclusion

The approach to policy modeling presented in the paper is based on finite automaton model of an NSS. Decomposition of an NSS to simple NSSs and their classification facilitates composition of policies and selection of the most effective NSSs aligned with them. Policies are considered independently on platforms of NSSs and can be specified identically for equivalent NSSs. Application of translation methods for unified policies allows implementation of policies in concrete NSSs platforms.

The future challenge for the approach is development of derivation method from RBAC policies into described NSSs policies and building of conflict resolution methods. Construction of an algorithm for classification of NSSs is also a future work.

References

1. 2014 Cyberthreat Defense Report North America & Europe, CyberEdge Group (2014)
2. The State of Network Security 2013: Attitudes and Opinions, AlgoSec (2013)
3. Chappell, M.J., D'Arcy, J., Striegel, A.: An Analysis of Firewall Rulebase (Mis) Management Practices. Journal of Information System Security Association (ISSA) 7, 12–18 (2009)
4. Wool, A.: Trends in Firewall Configuration Errors: Measuring the Holes in Swiss Cheese. IEEE Internet Computing 14(4), 58–65 (2010)
5. Rees, J., Bandyopadhyay, S., Stafford, E.H.: PFIRES: a Policy Framework for Information Security. Communications of the ACM 46(7), 101–106 (2003)
6. Wahsheh, L.A., Alves-Foss, J.: Security Policy Development: Towards a Life-Cycle and Logic-Based Verification Model. American Journal of Applied Sciences 5(9), 1117–1126 (2008)
7. Knapp, K.J., Morris Jr., R.F., Marshall, T.E., Byrd, T.A.: Information security policy: An Organizational-level Process Model. Computers & Security 28(7), 493–508 (2009)
8. Tuyikeze, T., Potts, D.: An Information Security Policy Development Life Cycle. In: South African Information Security Multi-Conference, pp. 165–176 (2010)
9. Laborde, R., Kamel, M., Barrera, F., Benzekri, A.: Implementation of a Formal Security Policy Refinement Process in WBEM Architecture. In: 4th Latin American Network Operations and Management Symposium, pp. 65–76 (2005)
10. Cuppens, F., Cuppens-Boulahia, N., Sans, T., Miège, A.: A Formal Approach to Specify and Deploy a Network Security Policy. In: Dimitrakos, T., Martinelli, F. (eds.) Workshop FAST. IFIP AICT, vol. 173, pp. 203–218. Springer, Boston (2005)
11. Preda, S., Cuppens-Boulahia, N., Cuppens, F., Garcia-Alfaro, J., Toutain, L.: Model-Driven Security Policy Deployment: Property Oriented Approach. In: Massacci, F., Wallach, D., Zannone, N. (eds.) ESSoS 2010. LNCS, vol. 5965, pp. 123–139. Springer, Heidelberg (2010)
12. Preda, S., Cuppens-Boulahia, N., Cuppens, F., Touting, L.: Architecture-Aware Adaptive Deployment of Contextual Security Policies. In: 5th International Conference on Availability, Reliability and Security, pp. 87–95 (2010)
13. Garcia-Alfaro, J., Cuppens, F., Cuppens-Boulahia, N., Preda, S.: MIRAGE: A Management Tool for the Analysis and Deployment of Network Security Policies. In: Garcia-Alfaro, J., Navarro-Arribas, G., Cavalli, A., Leneutre, J. (eds.) DPM 2010 and SETOP 2010. LNCS, vol. 6514, pp. 203–215. Springer, Heidelberg (2011)
14. Rahman, M.A., Al-Shaer, E.: A Formal Framework for Network Security Design Synthesis. In: 33rd International Conference on Distributed Computing Systems, pp. 560–570 (2013)

Part III

Extended Abstracts

Introduction to Attribute Based Searchable Encryption

Dalia Khader

daliakhader@googlemail.com

Abstract. An Attribute Based Searchable Encryption Scheme (ABSE) is a public key encryption with keyword search (PEKS) where each user owns a set of attributes, and the senders decide on a policy. The policy is a function of these attributes expressed as a predicate and determines, among the users of the system, who is eligible to decrypt and search the ciphertext. Only members who own sufficient attributes to satisfy that policy can send the server a valid search query. In our work we introduce the concept of a secure ABSE by defining the functionalities and the relevant security notions.

Keywords: PEKS, Attribute Based Encryption, Public Key Cryptography.

1 Introduction

Searchable encryption (SE) is an encryption scheme that supports keyword based retrieval of documents. The main challenge of SE is to allow third parties to search the ciphertexts without giving them decrypting capabilities. This has been an active research area for more than a decade. Song et al. [5] proposed the first scheme that enables searchability in symmetric encryption while Boneh et al. [2] introduced a scheme for public key encryption with keyword search (PEKS).

Searchable encryption schemes assume that the user sending the search query owns the decryption key and that the sender has to know the identity of the user querying the data in order to encrypt using the corresponding encryption key. This raises the question, what if the encrypted data is shared between several receivers and is kept in a remote shared storage that is not trusted for confidentiality?

Attribute-Based Encryption (ABE) [4] addresses this problem. An ABE is a scheme in which each user is identified by a set of attributes, and some function of those attributes, the policy, is used to decide on decryption capabilities. The two types of ABE schemes are: key-policy and ciphertext-policy [3, 1].

This paper defines a new primitive attribute based searchable encryption (ABSE). In ABSE senders decide on a policy that determines user's eligibility not only for decrypting but also for searching the data. Unlike existing proposals in the literature [6], ours is based on a hybrid system of key and cipher policy which gives more flexibility, a strong security, and allows for multi-authorities.

2 Formal Definition of ABSE

To define an ABSE we introduce the five entities involved: a central authority $\mathcal{TTP}$ who sets up the system, a server $\mathcal{S}$ where all encrypted data is uploaded to. An encryptor

B. De Decker and A. Zúquete (Eds.): CMS 2014, LNCS 8735, pp. 131–135, 2014.

$\mathcal{E}$ who uploads the data and sets the policy. The querier $\mathcal{Q}$ who wants to search the server and download documents. Many attribute authorities $\mathcal{AT}$ each responsible of a set of attributes and that give out private keys to users owning these attributes.

Definition 1. *An Attribute Based Searchable Encryption Scheme consists of the following probabilistic polynomial time algorithms:* **ABSE** $:= \bigl(TSetup,\ AddUser,$ $ASetup,\ AttG,\ PrdG,\ PrdVK,\ PrdQT,\ ABSE,\ TrpG,\ TEST\bigr)$

TSetup(k) $\rightarrow$ **(PP, UMK)** : Run by $\mathcal{TTP}$ to set up the system. Takes a security parameter k and outputs public parameters PP and a user master key UMK which is kept secret.

AddUser(PP, UMK) $\rightarrow$ **(RK$_i$, SK$_i$)** : Run by $\mathcal{TTP}$ every time a user registers with the system. It outputs a registration key RK_i that will be used to register with attribute authorities and servers. It outputs SK_i that is secret to the user and will be used in creating trapdoors.

ASetup(PP) $\rightarrow$ **(AMK$_j$, APK$_j$)** : Run by $\mathcal{AT}$ to set up the attribute authority. It outputs an attribute master key AMK_j which is secret to $\mathcal{AT}$ and is used to create attribute private keys when users register. It also outputs an attribute public key APK_j which is used in building the policies and is public to all.

AttG(RK$_i$, AMK$_j$) $\rightarrow$ **ASK$_{i,j}$** : Run by $\mathcal{AT}$ to register a user i, and outputs an attribute private key $ASK_{i,j}$ that will be used in proving possession of attribute j.

PrdG(Ψ, $\mathcal{AP}$) $\rightarrow$ **(ST$_\Psi$, IT$_\Psi$)** : Given a predicate Ψ and a list of attribute public keys $\mathcal{AP} = \{APK_j\}_{j=1}^m$, the algorithm generates a searching token ST_Ψ that will be used in creating trapdoors and an indexing token IT_Ψ used for creating searchable ciphertext.

PrdVK(Ψ) $\rightarrow$ **VT$_\Psi$** : Run by $\mathcal{S}$. For each predicate in the system the server creates a verification token VT_Ψ that is kept secret to the server.

PrdQT(Ψ, VT$_\Psi$, RK$_i$, $\mathcal{AP}$) $\rightarrow$ **QT$_{i,\Psi}$** : Run by the $\mathcal{S}$. Given a predicate verification token VT_Ψ and a registration key RK_i, the server outputs a query token $QT_{i,\Psi}$ that allows the user i to search for keywords encrypted under the predicate Ψ.

ABSE(W, Ψ, IT$_\Psi$) $\rightarrow$ **E$_{\Psi,w}$** : Run by $\mathcal{E}$. For a keyword W and under token IT_Ψ create a searchable ciphertext $E_{\Psi,W}$.

TrpG(W, Ψ, QT$_{i,\Psi}$, ST$_\Psi$, SK$_i$, $\mathcal{AS}_i$) $\rightarrow$ **T$_{\Psi,w}$** : Run by $\mathcal{Q}$. Given a keyword, a query token, a searching token, a user secret key and a set of user private attribute keys $\mathcal{AS}_i = \{ASK_{i,j}\}_{j=1}^m$, output a trapdoor $T_{\Psi,W}$.

TEST(E$_{\Psi,w}$, T$_{\Psi,w}$, VT$_\Psi$, RK$_i$) $\rightarrow$ **{0, 1}** : Run by the $\mathcal{S}$. Given a searchable ciphertext, a trapdoor, a verification token and a registration key output 1 if the user satisfies the predicate and if the keyword is found, otherwise output 0.

On the Security of ABSE The security notions of an ABSE are: correctness, security against Attribute Based Chosen Keyword Attack (ACKA) and security against Attributes Forgeability Attacks (AFA). We need three game models to define these notions (See Figures 1(a), 1(b), 1(c)) where the adversary is given access to certain oracles and a trace of the responses is recorded. Both are explained below.

CUL	Corrupted Users	HUL	Honest Users	CRK	Corrupted RK_i
CRK	Corrupted RK_i	HA	Honest $\mathcal{AT}$	CA	Corrupted $\mathcal{AT}$
$CASK$	Revealed $ASK_{i,j}$	$TrapL$	Queried trapdoors	$HASK$	Non-revealed $ASK_{i,j}$
$PredL$	List of (ST_Ψ, IT_Ψ)	$RQTL$	Revealed $QT_{i,\Psi}$	QTL	Non-revealed $QT_{i,\Psi}$
VTL	Non-revealed VT_Ψ	$RVTL$	Revealed VT_Ψ		

AddUsr : Adds user i to the system by running $AddUser$, and adding (RK_i, SK_i) to HUL.

UsrCpt : Corrupts user i by revealing (RK_i, SK_i) and adding them to CUL and CRK.

RKCpt : Partially corrupts user i by revealing registration key RK_i and adding it to CRK.

AddAtt : Adds an honest attribute authority j to the system by running $ASetup$, computing (APK_j, AMK_j) and publishing APK_j.

AMKCpt : Corrupts attribute authority j by revealing AMK_j and adding to CA.

AddASK : Runs $AttG$ to compute $ASK_{i,j}$, and adds it to $HASK$.

ASKCpt : Corrupts an attribute private key by revealing $ASK_{i,j}$ and adding it to $CASK$.

TrapO : The challenger generates a trapdoor for certain keyword W using a querying token $QT_{i,\Psi}$ and searchable token ST_Ψ on behalf of user i with set of attributes $\mathcal{AS}_i$. The list $TrapL$ is updated with all the information used as input and as output to the algorithm $TrpG$.

AddPred : Generates a searchable token and an indexing token (ST_Ψ, IT_Ψ) for predicate Ψ by running $PrdG$ and then updates the list $PredL$.

AddVT : Runs $PrdVK$ to obtain a verification token VT_Ψ and updates VTL.

RevealVT : Corrupting the verification token VT_Ψ by revealing it and $RVTL$ is updated.

AddQT : Generates a querying token $QT_{i,\Psi}$ by running $PrdQT$, then QTL is updated.

RevealQT : The querying token $QT_{i,\Psi}$ of user i and predicate Ψ is revealed to the adversary and the list $RQTL$ is updated.

Ch$_b$: Challenges the adversary to guess whether a trapdoor T_b ($b \in \{0,1\}$) was generated for keyword W_0 or W_1. The adversary chooses the predicate, the set of attributes and the user he would like to be challenged upon.

Correctness of ABSE. This property demands that if a searchable encryption $E_{\Psi,W}$ was produced correctly, i.e. using valid IT_Ψ and if a trapdoor $T_{\Psi,W}$ was introduced correctly using valid $QT_{i,\Psi}, ST_\Psi, SK_i, \mathcal{AS}_i$, then the $TEST$ algorithm should return 1 if the predicate is satisfied $\Psi(\mathcal{AS}_i) = 1$ and the keywords match $W = W'$, otherwise the $TEST$ algorithm should return 0. Figure 1(a) explains the details. Formally, the ABSE is said to be correct if for a security parameter k and all polynomial time adversaries $\mathcal{A}$ the following advantage is negligible: $\text{Adv}_{\mathcal{A}}^{corr}(k) = |Pr[\text{Exp}_{\mathcal{A}}^{corr}(k) = 1]|$

Attribute Based Chosen Keyword Attacks. We define security for an ABSE in the sense of semantic–security. The aim is to ensure that an encryption $ABSE$ does not reveal any information about keyword W except to a $\mathcal{Q}$ who satisfies the policy and can create trapdoors. We define the security against an active attackers $\mathcal{A}$ whose given access to a set of oracles shown in Figure 1(b). Let the advantage of winning the game be defined as follows: $\text{Adv}_{\mathcal{A}}^{ACKA}(k) = |Pr[\text{Exp}_{\mathcal{A}}^{ACKA_0}(k) = 1] - Pr[\text{Exp}_{\mathcal{A}}^{ACKA_1}(k) = 1]|$

An ABSE scheme is said to be secure against an ACKA if for a given security parameter k and all polynomial time adversary $\mathcal{A}$ the advantage $\text{Adv}_{\mathcal{A}}^{\text{ACKA}}(k)$ is negligible.

Attribute Forgeability Attack. This security notion captures forgeability of trapdoors where the adversary can produce a trapdoor without having the sufficient attribute set that satisfies the predicate Ψ. The adversary is given access to the oracles described in Figure 1(c). The challenge is to produce a pair of searchable encryption $E_{\psi'}^*$ and trapdoor $T_{\psi'}^*$ under predicate Ψ' such that the $TEST(E_{\psi'}^*, T_{\psi'}^*, VT_{\Psi'}, RK_i')$ outputs 1 for a given RK_i'. The definition includes coalition of attributes. Formally, an ABSE scheme is said to be secure against an AFA if for a security parameter k and all polynomial time adversaries $\mathcal{A}$ the following advantage is negligible: $\text{Adv}_{\mathcal{A}}^{\text{AFA}}(k) = |Pr[\text{Exp}_{\mathcal{A}}^{AFA}(k) = 1]|$

3   Conclusion

We define a new ABSE scheme and the security notions required. A working construction and security proofs are provided in a full version of this paper.

Experiment $\text{Exp}_{\mathcal{A}}^{\text{corr}}(k)$:

- $(PP, UMK) \leftarrow TSetup(k)$
- $HUL, HA, PredL, HASK, QTL, VTL = \phi$
- $(SK_i, RK_i, \mathcal{AS}_i, QT_{i,\Psi}, ST_{\Psi}, IT_{\Psi}) \leftarrow \mathcal{A}(PP : AddUsr(.), AddAtt(.), AddASK(.,.), AddPred(.,.), AddQT(.,.), AddVT(.))$
- If $[(SK_i, RK_i) \notin HUL] \vee [\exists j \in \Psi$ s.t. $(AMK_j, APK_j) \notin HA] \vee [\exists j \in \mathcal{AS}_i$ s.t. $(ASK_{i,j}) \notin HASK] \vee [VT_{\Psi} \notin VTL]$: Return 0
- $ABSE(W, IT_{\Psi}) \to E_{\Psi.W}; \quad TrpG(W', QT_{i,\Psi}, ST_{\Psi}, SK_i, \mathcal{AS}_i) \to T_{\Psi.W}$
- If $[[\Psi(\mathcal{AS}_i) \neq 1] \vee [W \neq W']] \wedge [TEST(E_{\Psi.W}, T_{\Psi.W}, VT_{\Psi}, RK_i) = 0]$: Return 1
- If $[[\Psi(\mathcal{AS}_i) = 1] \wedge [W = W']] \wedge [TEST(E_{\Psi.W}, T_{\Psi.W}, VT_{\Psi}, RK_i) = 1]$: Return 1
- Else Return 0

(a) Correctness Game Model

Experiment $\text{Exp}_{\mathcal{A}}^{\text{ACKA}}(k)$:

- $(PP, UMK) \leftarrow TSetup(k)$
- $CUL, HUL, CRK, HA, CA, CASK, HASK, TrapL, PredL, QTL, RQTL, RVTL, VTL = \phi$
- $\hat{b} \leftarrow \mathcal{A}(PP : UsrCpt(.), RKCpt(.), AMKCpt(.), ASKCpt(.,.), RevealQT(.,.), AddVT(.), RevealVT(.), TrapO(.,.,.,.,.), AddUsr(.), AddAtt(.), AddPred(.,.), AddQT(.,.), AddASK(.,.), Ch(.,.,.,.,.))$
- Return $\hat{b}$

(b) Security against ACKA

Experiment $\text{Exp}_{\mathcal{A}}^{\text{AFA}}(k)$:

- $(PP, UMK) \leftarrow TSetup(k)$
- $CUL, HUL, CRK, HA, CA, CASK, HASK, TrapL, PredL, QTL, RQTL, RVTL, VTL = \phi$
- $(T_{\psi'}^*, E_{\psi'}^*, \Psi', RK_i') \leftarrow \mathcal{A}(PP : UsrCpt(.), RKCpt(.), AMKCpt(.), ASKCpt(.,.), RevealQT(.,.), AddVT(.), RevealVT(.), TrapO(.,.,.,.,.), AddUsr(.), AddAtt(.), AddPred(.,.), AddQT(.,.), AddASK(.,.))$
- If $[TEST(E_{\psi'}^*, T_{\psi'}^*, VT_{\Psi'}, RK_i') = 0] \vee [\Psi' \subseteq CA] \vee [T_{\psi'}^* \in TrapL] \vee [[VT_{\Psi'} \in RVTL] \wedge [\forall j \in \Psi', j \in CASK \cup CA]] \vee [[VT_{\Psi'} \notin RVTL] \wedge [\exists i$ s.t $\forall j \in \mathcal{AS}_i, j \in CASK_i \cup CA$ and $RK_i' = RK_i]]$: Return 0.
- Else Return 1

(c) Security against AFA

References

1. Bethencourt, J., Sahai, A., Waters, B.: Ciphertext-policy attribute-based encryption. In: IEEE SSP 2007, pp. 321–334 (2007)
2. Boneh, D., Di Crescenzo, G., Ostrovsky, R., Persiano, G.: Public key encryption with keyword search. In: Cachin, C., Camenisch, J.L. (eds.) EUROCRYPT 2004. LNCS, vol. 3027, pp. 506–522. Springer, Heidelberg (2004)
3. Goyal, V., Pandey, O., Sahai, A., Waters, B.: Attribute-based encryption for fine-grained access control of encrypted data. In: ACM CCS 2006, pp. 89–98 (2006)
4. Sahai, A., Waters, B.: Fuzzy identity-based encryption. In: Cramer, R. (ed.) EUROCRYPT 2005. LNCS, vol. 3494, pp. 457–473. Springer, Heidelberg (2005)
5. Song, D.X., Wagner, D., Perrig, A.: Practical techniques for searches on encrypted data. In: SSP 2000. IEEE (2000)
6. Zheng, Q., Xu, S., Ateniese, G.: Vabks: Verifiable attribute-based keyword search over outsourced encrypted data. IACR ePrint

Risk Analysis of Physically Unclonable Functions

Andrea Kolberger[1], Ingrid Schaumüller-Bichl[1], and Martin Deutschmann[2]

[1] University of Applied Sciences Upper Austria, Austria
{andrea.kolberger, ingrid.schaumueller-bichl}@fh-hagenberg.at
[2] Technikon Forschungs- und Planungsgesellschaft mbH, Austria
codes@technikon.com

Abstract. Physically unclonable functions (PUFs) are an emerging technology that have been proposed as central building blocks in a variety of cryptographic application areas. Keys are not stored permanently anymore, but generated as needed using unique "fingerprints" that are inherent in each device. Since PUFs are "noisy" functions responses generated by a certain PUF instantiation are error-prone and therefore highly sophisticated error correction is required to reliably reconstruct the respective PUF response. To be aware of potential threats and vulnerabilities concerning PUF-based security schemes a risk analysis on different use cases was performed in order to gain requirements for the development and implementation of effective error correction methods as well as requirements regarding the whole operational life cycle of such tokens.

Keywords: Physically Unclonable Function (PUF), Risk Analysis, Vulnerabilities and Threats, Authentication, HW/SW Binding, Key Generation, Error Correction, Fuzzy Extractor, Cryptographic Applications.

1 Introduction

PUFs are inherently "noisy" which means that responses of a single PUF instantiation to one and the same challenge always slightly differ. Such responses cannot be directly used in cryptographic applications. Thus error correction processing is required in order to generate a reliable and stable PUF response. Also, the PUF's behaviour depends on environmental conditions like voltage supply, ambient temperature and ageing effects. All of these circumstances need to be taken into account when creating a PUF-based security scheme. Our risk analysis considers in addition to the error correction methods the whole operational life cycle of PUF-based security modules. We analysed different use cases and the related communication protocols. Considering the pre-operational phase (manufacturing, delivery, ...) as well as the usage of the token in the field we identified several threats and vulnerabilities due to either active attacks or the noisy, unstable behaviour of a PUF instantiation. The outcome of the analysis provided valuable input for defining requirements on the error correction mechanisms as well as requirements on the environment to ensure a reliable and secure usage of PUF-based devices. Furthermore the results formed the basis for the preparation of a Protection Profile for PUFs according to Common Criteria (CC) [1] that was presented at the IFIP SEC 2014 in Marrakech, Morocco [9].

B. De Decker and A. Zúquete (Eds.): CMS 2014, LNCS 8735, pp. 136–139, 2014.

2   Physically Unclonable Functions

A Physically Unclonable Function (PUF), i.e. a function embodied in a physical structure, contains random and unique information which originates from uncontrollable process variations during manufacturing in integrated circuits (IC). The basic idea is to use this "fingerprint" to serve as security anchor in various applications. The usage of PUFs enables the design of cryptographic applications without storing sensitive information such as keys in memory at all. For practical usability, PUFs should be easy to evaluate whereas they are considered unclonable because it is extremely difficult to make either a hardware clone, a mathematical model of the behaviour of the structure, or a software program that can compute the response to a challenge in a reasonable amount of time [4]. In [10] Maes and Verbauwhede present an extensive overview of PUFs and PUF-like proposals. One established technique are SRAM PUFs that make use of the fact that SRAM cells tend to have the same state after power up very consistently. Thus, a challenge consists of an address range and the response is the value of the respective SRAM cells after power up. Owing to time, temperature and voltage variations, some bits tend to flip [6]. Therefore so called fuzzy extractors are put in place, which take care that existing bit flips are corrected (e.g. by means of error correction codes). The basic principle of the so-called Arbiter PUFs [3] is to conduct a race on two paths on a chip. Therefore the challenges consist of a vector shaping the path of the "race" and an Arbiter circuit then decides, which path "won" the race, resulting in one bit response (0 or 1). Beside the noisy characteristic of PUFs, also ageing effects have to be taken into account, when developing PUF-based solutions. It is known that the response behaviour of a PUF instantiation is likely to slightly alter in the course of its lifespan. Therefore the noise levels would increase over time in the absence of anti-ageing protocols.

3   Risk Analysis

Performing the comprehensive risk analysis first different use cases were defined that cover a broad field of applications. Based on these use cases we identified several threats which were assessed in a further step. In doing so threats were not only considered as a malicious activity of an attacker. Even the PUF itself, because of its physical properties and noisy behaviour, might act in an undesired manner and therefore cause damage. The risk of the identified threats was calculated by the parameters "Risk Exposure" and "Impact". The ranges of these parameters were adapted to the specific terms of PUFs.

Use Cases. In the risk analysis we evaluated five different use cases. *One-Way Authentication* describes a very simple use case. PUF responses are used to authenticate the PUF-based token, but in this communication protocol no cryptographic actions are foreseen. Thus, a PUF-based token is accepted when the generated response is close enough to the reference response. As compared to *Mutual Authentication* [7], both entities in a protocol are authenticated using cryptographic algorithms to reliably generate and reconstruct unique responses. Use case *Secret Key Generation and Session Key Exchange* applies PUF responses as a key to encrypt the session key used for further communication. Both use cases *Key Zeroization* and *Hardware/Software Binding* are based on the usage of logically reconfigurable PUFs (LR-PUFs), i.e. the behaviour of a PUF instantiation can be changed by adding some state information [2,8].

Results of Risk Analysis. The results of the performed risk analysis and the assessment of threats and vulnerabilities were prioritised with respect to the calculated risk value in order to highlight the most important ones. The analysis showed that the usage of a weak fuzzy extractor and/or weak error correction as well as PUF failures cause the highest risks. This means that the fuzzy extractor as well as the error correction must not reveal any information regarding the PUF-individual response because helper data, generated by the fuzzy extractor, are public information. At the same time these methods have to ensure the reliable reconstruction of secrets/keys from an error-prone response even in case of ageing and variation of environmental conditions. Another security relevant function is the manipulation of state information used for LR-PUFs. State information is public too and it must not be changed by unauthorized entities. Some further risks concern the PUF's environment that cannot be treated by the PUF itself. Therefore requirements and assumptions on the (pre-)operational environment have to be defined considering the underlying PUF technology as well as the intended use case. For example each PUF-based token has to be enrolled with different, unpredictable and random challenges in order to prevent guessing of valid challenges. Further the exchange of the database (comprising challenge-response pairs) between the enrolment facility and the customer has to be performed in a secure way in order to ensure confidentiality and integrity. Also, the analysis showed that model building attacks strongly depend on the PUF type and thus must be discussed separately. Literature already provides numerous papers [5,11,12,13] that might be considered.

4   Conclusion and Outlook

The results of the risk analysis formed the basis for the preparation of the security problem definition (SPD) and the security solution definition (SSD) in our Protection Profile for PUFs. These parts include potential threats, assumptions that are made on the TOE's environment as well as organizational security policies (OSPs). In order to achieve the security objectives several security functional requirements were derived including some extended components considering PUF specific needs. In the ongoing project the defined requirements are implemented in a prototype comprising PUFs and realizing mutual authentication and key generation. As a next step the prototype will be evaluated against these requirements in order to prove that the identified threats are countered and the security objectives are achieved.

Acknowledgements. This work is co-financed by the Austrian Research Promotion Agency (FFG) in the FIT-IT line within the project CODES (835932): Algorithmic extraction and error correction codes for lightweight security anchors with reconfigurable PUFs. The project partners are Technikon Forschungs- und Planungsgesellschaft mbH, Alpen-Adria Universität Klagenfurt and University of Applied Sciences Upper Austria - Campus Hagenberg.

References

1. Common Criteria for Information Technology Security Evaluation, Part 1: Introduction and General Model. CCMB-2012-09-001, Version 3.1, Revision 4 (2012)
2. Eichhorn, I., Koeberl, P., van der Leest, V.: Logically reconfigurable PUFs: memory-based secure key storage. In Proceedings of the Sixth ACM Workshop on Scalable Trusted Computing, STC 2011, 59–64, New York, USA (2011)
3. Fruhashi, K., Shiozaki, M., Fukushima, A., Murayama, T., Fujino, T.: The arbiter-PUF with high uniqueness utilizing novel arbiter circuit with Delay-Time Measurement. In: IEEE International Symposium on Circuits and Systems (ISCAS), pp. 2325–2328 (2011)
4. Gassend, B., Clarke, D., van Dijk, M., Devadas, S.: Controlled Physical Random Functions. In: IEEE (ed.) Proceedings of the 18th Annual Computer Security Applications Conference (ACSAC 2002), USA (2002)
5. Gassend, B., Lim, D., Clarke, D., van Dijk, M., Devadas, S.: Identification and authentication of integrated circuits. Concurrency and Computation: Practice and Experience 16(11), 1077–1098 (2004)
6. Handschuh, H.: Hardware-Anchored Security Based on SRAM PUFs, Part 1. IEEE Security Privacy 10(3), 80–83 (2012)
7. Van Herrewege, A., Katzenbeisser, S., Maes, R., Peeters, R., Sadeghi, A.-R., Verbauwhede, I., Wachsmann, C.: Reverse fuzzy extractors: Enabling lightweight mutual authentication for PUF-enabled rFIDs. In: Keromytis, A.D. (ed.) FC 2012. LNCS, vol. 7397, pp. 374–389. Springer, Heidelberg (2012)
8. Katzenbeisser, S., Kocabas, U., van der Leest, V., Sadeghi, A.-R., Schrijen, G.-J., Schröder, H., Wachsmann, C.: Recyclable PUFs: Logically Reconfigurable PUFs (2007)
9. Kolberger, A., Schaumüller-Bichl, I., Brunner, V., Deutschmann, M.: Protection profile for PUF-based devices. In: Cuppens-Boulahia, N., Cuppens, F., Jajodia, S., Abou El Kalam, A., Sans, T. (eds.) SEC 2014. IFIP AICT, vol. 428, pp. 91–98. Springer, Heidelberg (2014)
10. Maes, R., Verbauwhede, I.: Physically Unclonable Functions: A Study on the State of the Art and Future Research Directions. In: Sadeghi, A.-R., Naccache, D. (eds.) Towards Hardware-Intrinsic Security, Information Security and Cryptography, pp. 3–37. Springer, Heidelberg (2010)
11. Majzoobi, M., Koushanfar, F., Potkonjak, M.: Testing Techniques for Hardware Security. In: IEEE International Test Conference, ITC 2008, pp. 1–10 (2008)
12. Rührmair, U., Sehnke, F., Sölter, J., Dror, G., Devadas, S., Schmidhuber, J.: Modeling attacks on physical unclonable functions. In: Proceedings of the 17th ACM Conference on Computer and Communications Security, CCS 2010, New York, NY, USA, pp. 237–249 (2010)
13. Sölter, J.: Cryptanalysis of Electrical PUFs via Machine Learning Algorithms. Master's thesis, Technische Universität München (2009)

Decentralized Bootstrap
for Social Overlay Networks

Rodolphe Marques[1] and André Zúquete[2]

[1] IT, University of Aveiro, Portugal
[2] DETI / IEETA, University of Aveiro, Portugal
{rodolphe.marques,andre.zuquete}@ua.pt

Abstract. In this paper we show how we can use social networks to bootstrap a social overlay network. This overlay network is different from others, in the sense that it enables participants to share services on a personal basis, unlike other overlay networks that provide a single service for all peers. Since the overlay network is not supposed to have central servers for managing a single service, its bootstrap and the direct communication among pairs of participants is challenging. However, the actual social networks, such as Twitter, Facebook and Google+ already provide an API that enables participants to exchange direct messages, which will be the basis of our bootstrap mechanism.

Keywords: Privacy, P2P interactions, social networks.

1 Introduction

Privacy is hard to achieve in centralized architectures [1], since one needs to trust in service providers to mediate all the information that we disclose while being out of the clients' control. On the other hand, more private communication channel in the Internet could be achieved if one could interact directly to the intended persons or entity, without central services.

The goal of our work is to provide human-to-human (H2H) private services using the Internet, as stated in [5]. We distinguish H2H from peer-to-peer (P2P) because, on the latter, peers are just participants (on particular protocols) that are alike and don't cooperate strictly on a one-to-one basis, while we want to provide means for clear, personal interactions, where persons can act differently.

H2H private services allow pairs of clearly identified persons to provide services to one another without service-oriented mediators. The set of services provided by each person involved in a H2H interaction can be different, there is no need to have reciprocity. Such service provisioning takes place over a Virtual Private Link (VPL, see Fig. 1). We don't see a VPL as a Virtual Private Network, since the former will enable only a controlled access to a set of (well-defined) services, while the latter usually provides an access to a network, where many (ill-defined) services may exist.

The VPLs used by all persons exploring our system will form an overlay network (of services). This overlay network is not oriented to a single service,

B. De Decker and A. Zúquete (Eds.): CMS 2014, LNCS 8735, pp. 140–143, 2014.

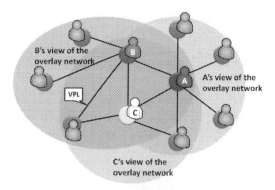

Fig. 1. Overview of the overlay network, formed by many different human-centric, H2H interactions on top of VPLs. Private interaction between A and B can start either because A invited B to join his (view of the) overlay network or vice-versa. A, B and C can provide services among themselves in a private way, without knowing the full extent of the entire overlay network (e.g., C may not know that A interacts with B).

such as routing (e.g. TOR [3]) or content sharing (e.g. BitTorrent [2]). There is no global definition of the services provided in the overlay network by the participant; they are free to create their own services and provide them privately to others). Furthermore, there is no global notion of who is involved in the overlay network. Each participant will have his own view of the overlay network, which will be formed (to him) by the persons with whom he has a VPL established. That's why we say that we have social overlay networks (one for each person).

1.1 Problem

Bootstrapping overlay networks has been a longstanding problem [7] that is usually solved by one of two ways: using the binding information of a least one node in the network (e.g. for DHTs); or using a centralized directory service (e.g. TOR directory servers [3]). In the first case the binding information can change frequently and needs to be obtained through an out-of-band mode. The second case requires dedicated network infrastructure to aid the bootstrap. Moreover it leaks information about the entire network since the directory server contains information about all the nodes in the network, which besides the privacy implications that it may bring, it provides a single point of failure that can be open to attacks or that can be easily blocked.

Yet another problem with current overlay network designs is that users joining the network have little or no control on the network. Users have no control regarding the nodes they connect to or which nodes connect to them. And even if they had the control to choose that, there is not enough information about the other nodes in the network except for their binding information. In short, overlay networks are cooperative and service-oriented by nature, but not social. This is not what we are looking for, since we want persons to build their own overlay network by explicitly exploring H2H interactions with known persons.

1.2 Contribution

Since we want to bootstrap in a distributed way an overlay network formed by an arbitrary number of H2H interactions, its seems natural in our days to explore social networks for that purpose. This could enable persons to create and manage their personal view of the H2H overlay network (i.e. create their own VPLs) by reusing their previous work in the management of their social graph in Web-based social networks. In other words, we can use social networks to extract existing relationships with persons with whom one may be interested in setting up a VPL.

2 Decentralized Bootstrap for Our Social Overlay Network

Nowadays social networking platforms (Twitter, Facebook, Google+, etc.) have an API that enables applications to exchange private messages with friends within the same social network. This facility enables us to use social networks to bootstrap our overlay network. In particular, we can use social network to send our personal communication endpoint to friends, this way using the social network as a rendez-vous point, or a mailbox, for exchanging this information.

Personal communication endpoints are UDP/IP or TCP/IP transport endpoints that can be used to contact a person in our overlay network. Such endpoint needs to use a public IP address, otherwise it may not be reachable from outside its own network. However, the current Internet architecture makes this difficult, since Internet clients are frequently behind NAT (Network Address Translation) routers that raise many issues regarding the direct addressing of hosts behind them [6].

Currently we foresee three strategies for enabling client hosts to get their public transport endpoint: (i) management of the egress NATs to set up a public endpoint as a forwarding transport port; (i) exploitation of transport addresses of TURN servers [4]; and (iii) exploitation of a TURN server as a service provided indiviadually by participants in our own overlay network.

The first possibility is the preferable one, since it allows the most direct communication between participants. However, in many cases it may not be possible to explore, because existing NAT equipments may not allow hosts behind them to manage port forwarding policies.

The second possibility may overcome this limitation but requires the exploitation of TURN (Traversal Using Relays around NAT) servers. These servers simply relay traffic over allocated, public transport endpoints. A host behind a NAT router can allocate a single TURN public endpoint to receive incoming traffic from several hosts. The identification of the contacting peers is provided in TURN messages that are used to encapsulate the traffic between the TURN server and the TURN endpoint allocator.

The third possibility is in fact a combination of the previous ones. A hosts capable of having a public transport endpoints can run a TURN server and provide this service to friends that may use it to set up their public endpoints.

In any case, for the handshake protocol through a social network direct messaging channel all we need is to send, along with some distinctive keyword, the transport endpoint that should be used to contact the message sender, regardless of being a public address of his own or the public address of a TURN server.

This bootstrap protocol is completely decentralized, since each participant manages the bootstrap of his own VPLs. Furthermore, even for each VPL, which connects only a pair of participants, each of them may take the initiative to propose to the other its creation, just by publishing on a social network his public endpoint.

3   Conclusions and Future Work

In this paper we have presented a strategy for bootstraping an overlay social network of services. Unlike other overlay networks, this one does not target a single service, but rather a H2H personal exchange of services. Each participant in the overlay network has its own view of it, formed by a set of VPLs established with friends. Thus, for bootstraping such an overlay network we may use social relationships established through social networks to make a first handshake towards the creation of VPLs. This is currently facilitated by the fact that the most popular social networks have APIs for sending and receiving arbitrary information, and through which we can send the public communication endpoint that a person makes available to a friends for establishing VPLs.

The next step that needs to be tackled is related with the authentication of the participants in the overlay network. This authentication is fundamental for preventing a person from being fooled by the social network (with fake messages) or by someone else that gets to know his public endpoint without being explicitly contacted. This authentication is also fundamental to perform an authenticated key distribution protocol for deriving session keys for protecting VPLs' traffic.

References

1. Boyd, D.: Facebook's Privacy Trainwreck. Convergence: The Int. Journal of Research into New Media Technologies 14(1), 13–20 (2008)
2. Cohen, B.: Incentives build robustness in BitTorrent. In: Proc. of the First Workshop on the Economics of Peer-to-Peer Systems, Berkeley, CA, USA (June 2003)
3. Dingledine, R., Mathewson, N., Syverson, P.: Tor: The Second-Generation Onion Router. In: Proc. of the 13th USENIX Security Symp. (August 2004)
4. Mahy, R., Matthews, P., Rosenberg, J.: Traversal Using Relays around NAT (TURN): Relay Extensions to Session Traversal Utilities for NAT (STUN). RFC 5766 (Proposed Standard) (April 2010)
5. Marques, R., Zúquete, A.: User-centric, private networks of services. In: Int. Conf. on Smart Communications in Network Technologies (SaCoNeT), pp. 1–5 (June 2013)
6. Srisuresh, P., Ford, B., Kegel, D.: State of Peer-to-Peer (P2P) Communication across Network Address Translators (NATs). RFC 5128 (Informational) (March 2008)
7. Wolinsky, D., Juste, P., Boykin, P., Figueiredo, R.: Addressing the P2P Bootstrap Problem for Small Overlay Networks. In: 2010 IEEE Tenth International Conference on Peer-to-Peer Computing (P2P), pp. 1–10 (August 2010)

Part IV

Keynotes

Enhancing Privacy with Quantum Networks

Paulo Mateus, Nikola Paunković, João Rodrigues, and André Souto

SQIG- Instituto de Telecomunicações and
DM - Instituto Superior Técnico - Universidade de Lisboa, Portugal

Abstract. Using quantum networks to distribute symmetric keys has
become a usable and commercial technology available under limitations
that are acceptable in many application scenarios. The fact that the security is implemented directly at the hardware level, and moreover, relies
on the laws of physics instead of conjectured hardness assumptions, jus-
tifies the use of quantum security in many cases. Limitations include
100 km communication range and installation of quantum channels between each pair of users of the network. Presently, with the current lack
of trust in commercial security solutions, mostly due to the Snowden crisis, there is the need to improve such solutions. In this paper we discuss
how quantum networks can be used to setup secure multiparty computation (SMC), allowing for instance for private data mining, electronic
elections among other security functionalities. SMC relies mostly on establishing an efficient oblivious transfer protocol. We present a bit-string
quantum oblivious transfer protocol based on single-qubit rotations that
can be implemented with current technology based on optics and whose
security relies only on the laws of physics.

1 Introduction

Security is the most important factor for building trust and confidence between
consumers/population and companies/State; this trust has been severely dam-
aged with many recent events such as the "Snowden crisis" and the Open SSL
critical bug, and as such, private companies and state providers are pressured to
improve the security of their products. In this paper we discuss how quantum
security protocols can be integrated in a classical setting to provide multiparty-
secure computation.

Two seminal works have driven most of the research in the area quantum security: the quantum polynomial time factorization algorithm proposed by Shor [7];
and the quantum public key agreement protocol BB84, proposed by Bennett
and Brassard [1]. While Shor's algorithm raises the threat of making widely used
cryptographic systems (via classic communication channels) completely obsolete
by a breakthrough in quantum hardware, the BB84 protocol shows that quantum communication channels allow public perfect security in the context of an
authenticated channel.

Due to Shor's factoring algorithm, research on (asymmetric) cryptography
shifted significantly. Presently, one of the most important problems in the area
is to find one-way functions robust to quantum attacks. Indeed, Shor's algorithm

B. De Decker and A. Zúquete (Eds.): CMS 2014, LNCS 8735, pp. 147–153, 2014.

is able to attack all cryptosystems based on factorization and discrete logarithm, even in the elliptic curve setting, which accounts for essentially everything that is used in practice and is based on asymmetric keys.

On the other hand, BB84 is already commercially available through peer-to-peer optical networks. It is worth pointing out that quantum channels sending an arbitrarily amount of quantum information can already be produced using cheap technology. Moreover, much research is being done to develop quantum networks and routers using traditional optical fibers and laser satellite communications. It is expected that quantum networks will be available much sooner than quantum computers and thus, it is fundamental to understand which security and distributed protocols can benefit from quantum technology.

Secure multiparty computation is an abstraction of many security functionalities, including private data mining, e-voting, verifiable secret sharing, verifiable computing, among others. In general terms, the goal of secure multiparty computation among n parties is to compute a function of n secret inputs, one for each party, such that at the end of the computation the output of the function is known to all parties, while keeping the inputs secret.

It is well known that to setup secure multiparty computation it is enough to establish oblivious transfer (OT) protocol between two-parties using Yao's garbled circuits [8] (see a more modern discussion in [3]). The first OT protocol was presented by Rabin [6] and its security relies on the hardness assumption that factoring large integers is difficult in polynomial time. OT can be seen as a game played by two parties, Alice and Bob. Alice wants to share a number of secret messages with Bob such that, on average, Bob receives half of those messages (the protocol is *concealing*), while keeping Alice unaware to which messages Bob got (the protocol is *oblivious*). A protocol achieving these properties is called an OT Protocol. An OT protocol is made out of two parts: the transferring phase and the opening phase. In the former Alice sends the secret message to Bob; in the latter Alice unveil enough information that allows Bob to recover the secret with probability $1/2$.

The main contribution of this paper is to propose an OT protocol that can be implemented over quantum optical networks using currently available technology. Such OT protocol can then be used to establish a secure multiparty computation using classical infrastructure. We introduce a quantum oblivious transfer protocol for bit-strings, based on the recently proposed public key crypto-system in [5]. Each bit of the string to be transferred is encoded in a qubit (quantum bit), a particular quantum state, in such a way that states corresponding to bit-values 0 and 1, respectively, form an orthonormal basis. The key point of the protocol is that for each qubit, the encoding basis is chosen at random, from some discrete set of bases.

Next section provides a brief survey of quantum information, including basic definitions and important results necessary for understanding our proposal. Section 3 describes our proposal for a bit-string oblivious transfer protocol and discusses its correctness and security. Finally, we summarize the results and discuss future directions of research.

2   Preliminaries

In this section, we provide notation, necessary definitions and results for defining and reasoning about the security of our proposal.

For a complete study of quantum information we suggest the reading of [4]. Here we present some relevant notions. According to the postulates of quantum mechanics, the state of a closed quantum system is represented by a unit vector from a complex Hilbert space $\mathcal{H}$, and its evolution is described by a unitary transformation on $\mathcal{H}$. In this paper we work only with finite-dimensional Hilbert spaces reflecting the realistic examples of systems with finite number degrees of freedom (strings of quantum bits, i.e. qubits).

Contrarily to the classical case where a bit can only have values 0 or 1, in the quantum case, a *qubit* can be in a unit superposition of 0 or 1 denoted by $\alpha \left|0\right\rangle + \beta \left|1\right\rangle$ with complex coefficients α and β such that $|\alpha|^2 + |\beta|^2 = 1$. The Dirac notation $\left|0\right\rangle$ and $\left|1\right\rangle$ denotes vectors forming an orthonormal basis of a 2-dimensional complex vector space. Note that we can define many orthonormal bases for that space, such as $\left\{ \frac{1}{\sqrt{2}}(\left|0\right\rangle + \left|1\right\rangle), \frac{1}{\sqrt{2}}(\left|0\right\rangle - \left|1\right\rangle) \right\}$, but it is common to distinguish the basis $\{\left|0\right\rangle, \left|1\right\rangle\}$ from all the others, and call it the *computational basis*.

The state of two qubits is from the tensor product of single-qubit spaces, that is,

$$\left|\psi\right\rangle = \alpha \left|00\right\rangle + \beta \left|01\right\rangle + \gamma \left|10\right\rangle + \delta \left|11\right\rangle$$

with $|\alpha|^2 + |\beta|^2 + |\gamma|^2 + |\delta|^2 = 1$. The state $\left|\psi\right\rangle$ is said to be *separable* if

$$\left|\psi\right\rangle = (\alpha \left|0\right\rangle + \beta \left|1\right\rangle) \otimes (\alpha' \left|0\right\rangle + \beta' \left|1\right\rangle) = \alpha\alpha' \left|00\right\rangle + \alpha\beta' \left|01\right\rangle + \alpha'\beta \left|10\right\rangle + \beta\beta' \left|11\right\rangle.$$

Otherwise, it is called *entangled*. Although entangled states are particularly important in quantum information, in this paper we only work with separable states. Note that a system with k qubits can be described by a unit vector over a space with dimension 2^k.

One of the most important results of quantum information states that the maximal information that can be stored in a qubit is the same as that contained in a bit. This means that we cannot extract more than a bit of information from a qubit, although there is potentially an infinite number of states available to encode in a qubit. The reason for this is that it is impossible to obtain coefficients α and β from a single qubit in a state $\left|\psi\right\rangle = \alpha \left|0\right\rangle + \beta \left|1\right\rangle$. Indeed, what is possible is to perform a measurement given by an orthogonal decomposition of the Hilbert space $\mathcal{H} = \bigoplus_{i=1}^{d} \mathcal{H}_i$, with P_i being the projectors onto $\mathcal{H}_i$. Then, upon performing such a measurement on a qubit in state $\left|\psi\right\rangle \in \mathcal{H}$, there are d possible outcomes $\{1, \ldots, d\}$, where the probability of observing $i \in \{1, \ldots, d\}$ is given by $\| P_i \left|\psi\right\rangle \|$, and then the state evolves to $P_i \left|\psi\right\rangle / \| P_i \left|\psi\right\rangle \|$. For instance, the outcome of a measurement of a qubit can only take two possible values.

To understand the protocol we need to consider a function that is easy to compute, but, without the help of a secret trapdoor, it is impossible to invert with non-negligible probability according to the laws of quantum physics. One candidate for such a function was proposed in [5] which uses sinlge-qubit rotations and is given by

$$f(s) = R(s\theta_n)\,|0\rangle = \cos{(s\theta_n/2)}\,|0\rangle + \sin{(s\theta_n/2)}\,|1\rangle$$

where, for some fixed n, $s \in \{0, \ldots, 2^n - 1\}$, $\theta_n = \pi/2^{n-1}$ and $\{|0\rangle, |1\rangle\}$ is a fixed computational basis (i.e., f is not a function of a quantum state). Moreover, f can be used to construct a quantum trapdoor function $F(s, b)$, where s is the trapdoor information for learning an unknown bit b [5]:

$$F(s, b) = R(b\pi)f(s) = R(b\pi)R(s\theta_n)\,|0\rangle = R(s\theta_n + b\pi)\,|0\rangle\,.$$

Note that inverting F (learning both s and b) is at least as hard as inverting f. In [5] it was shown that every binary measurement that could be used to infer unknown bit b would outcome a completely random value. Nevertheless, if s is known, by applying the rotation $R(-s\theta_n)$ to $F(s, b)$ and measuring the result in the computational basis, one obtains b with certainty.

Using the properties of f and F a secure public key cryptographic protocol was proposed in [5]: using the private key s, the public key is generated by computing $f(s)$; the encryption of a secret message corresponds to computing $F(s, b)$; and the decryption of the message corresponds to inversion of $F(s, b)$, using the trapdoor information s.

Finally, in order to guarantee that at the end of the OT protocol Bob knows if he got the message m or not, Alice is required to send both m and $h(m)$, where h is a *universal hash function*. A hash function maps strings to other strings of smaller size . Bellow, we present a definition of universal hash function and a basic result.

Definition 1. *Consider two sets A and B of size a and b, respectively, such that $a > b$, and consider a collection $\mathbb{H}$ of hash functions $h : A \to B$. If*

$$\Pr_{h \in \mathbb{H}}[h(x) = h(y)] \leq \frac{1}{b}$$

then $\mathcal{H}$ is called a universal family of hash functions.

Theorem 1. *Let $\mathbb{H}$ be a collection of hash functions $h : A \to B$, where A and B are sets of size a and b, respectively, such that $a > b$. The size of a set A_x of strings $x \in A$ mapped to the same hash value $h(x)$ is at most N/b.*

In our particular case we consider A and B as the sets of strings of length ℓ and $\ell/2$ respectively. Hence, there are $2^{\ell/2}$ different strings for each hash value (for an overview see [2]).

3   Oblivious Transfer

Having set the required definitions and results, our protocol works as follows:

Protocol 1 (Oblivious transfer)

Message to transfer $m = m_1 \ldots m_k$;
Security parameter $n, \theta_n = \pi/2^{n-1}$ and a hash function $h : \{0,1\}^k \rightarrow \{0,1\}^{k/2}$;
Secret key $s = (s_1, \ldots, s_{3k/2})$, where each $s_i \in \{0, \ldots, 2^n - 1\}$.

Transfer Phase

1. Alice chooses uniformly at random a bit $a \in \{0,1\}$ and prepares the following state:

$$|\psi\rangle = \bigotimes_{i=1}^{k} R(m_i\pi + (-1)^a \times s_i\theta_n)|0\rangle \bigotimes_{i=1}^{k/2} R(h_i(m)\pi + (-1)^a \times s_{i+k}\theta_n)|0\rangle$$

   (Note that $h_i(m)$ represents the ith bit of the binary string $h(m)$).
2. Alice sends the state $|\psi\rangle$ to Bob.

Opening Phase

3. Alice sends $s = (s_1, \ldots, s_{3k/2})$ and n to Bob.
4. Bob checks if s is likely to be a possible output of a random process by performing a statistical test.
5. Bob chooses uniformly at random $a' \in \{0,1\}$ and applies $R((-1)^{a'} s_i\theta_n)$ to each qubit of $|\psi\rangle$.
6. Bob applies the measurement operator $M = (0 \times |0\rangle\langle 0| + 1 \times |1\rangle\langle 1|)^{\otimes 3k/2}$.
7. Let $m' \cdot h'$ be the message that Bob recovers. He checks if $h' = h(m')$. If that is the case then Bob is almost sure that $m' = m$, otherwise he knows that m' is not the correct message.

In the following, we discuss the security of our oblivious transfer protocol, showing that: if both agents are honest, Bob will obtain the message m with probability $1/2$ (the protocol is sound); if Alice plays fair, Bob is not able to recover m before the opening phase (the protocol is concealing); if Bob is honest, then Alice is unaware if Bob got m or not (the protocol is oblivious).

To state the results we need the notion of negligible function. $\varepsilon : \mathbb{N} \rightarrow \mathbb{R}$, a nonnegative function is called *negligible* if for every polynomial p and sufficiently large k we have $\varepsilon(k) \leq 1/p(k)$.

First, we provide the reasoning for the soundness of our protocol.

Theorem 2. *If both parties are honest, then with probability $1/2 + \varepsilon(k)$ Bob will get the right message, where $\varepsilon(k)$ is negligible function on the size of the message $m = m_1 \ldots m_k$.*

Notice that if Alice and Bob are honest then the choice of rotation direction of both will differ with probability $1/2$. Only when they are different, i.e., Bob undo Alice's rotation and obtains the states in computational bases, Bob is ensured to recover the message. When Bob rotates in the same direction of Alice, the results of Bob's measurement are random and hence the probability of recovering m in this case is a negligible function on the size of the message m.

We proceed by discussing the concealing property of the protocol.

Theorem 3. *If Alice is honest, the probability of Bob recovering Alice's message before the opening phase is negligible. Furthermore, after the opening phase Bob recovers the message, up to a negligible value, with probability $1/2$.*

The first part of the theorem follows directly from the security of the public key encryption schemes presented in in [5]: without knowing the secret key s and the rotation direction a, Bob's description of a message m is given by a completely mixed state. The second part follows from a similar argument to the previous theorem.

To finish the security discussion we argue that the protocol is unconditionally oblivious.

Theorem 4. *The Protocol 1 is oblivious, i.e., at the end of the protocol Alice does not know whether Bob received the right message of not.*

During the execution of the protocol, there is no information traveling from Bob to Alice. Therefore, in order to increase the probability of learning if Bob received the message m or not, Alice has to perform the following cheating strategy: instead of sending $|\psi\rangle$, Alice sends a cheating state $|\psi_{ch}\rangle$ for which Bob will open the desired message with a probability greater than $1/2$ (possibly with certainty). This is impossible, unless with negligible increase $\varepsilon(l)$, bounded above by $\frac{1}{2}\left(1 + \cos^{2l}(\pi/8)\right)$, where l is the number of s_i's for which $s_i\theta_n \in [\pi/8; 3\pi/8]$.[1]

4   Conclusions

In this paper we proposed a scheme for oblivious transfer of a bit-string message. Its security is based on laws of quantum physics. We reasoned about its security and showed that the protocol is unconditionally oblivious and concealing. Our protocol can be implemented with today's technology using optical equipment. Moreover, the protocol can be integrated with existing classical networks to achieve secure multiparty computation, and promote an extra level of security on such functionality.

Using single-qubit rotations have been proved useful in designing quantum security protocols, such as the presented oblivious transfer and the previously proposed public key cryptographic scheme [5]. This opens a number of possible future applications of single-qubit rotations in designing several secure protocols such as quantum bit-string commitment protocol and undeniable signatures.

---

[1] Since the values of s_i's are required to be random, the expected value of l is $k/4$, with the standard deviation $\sigma = \sqrt{k}/4$.

Acknowledgments. This work was partially supported by FCT projects Com-FormCrypt PTDC/EIA-CCO/113033/2009 and PEst-OE/EEI/LA0008/2013, and SQIG's initiative PQDR (Probabilistic, Quantum and Differential Reasoning). João Rodrigues and André Souto also acknowledges respectively the FCT grants SFRH / BD / 75085 / 2010 and SFRH / BPD / 76231 / 2011.

References

1. Bennett, C., Brassard, G.: Quantum Cryptography: Public Key Distribution and Coin Tossing. In: Proceedings of the IEEE International Conference on Computers, Systems and Signal Processing, pp. 175–179. IEEE Press, New York (1984)
2. Carter, J., Wegman, M.: Universal classes of hash functions. J. Comput. Syst. Sci. 18(2), 143–154 (1979)
3. Lindell, Y., Zarosim, H.: On the feasibility of extending oblivious transfer. In: Sahai, A. (ed.) TCC 2013. LNCS, vol. 7785, pp. 519–538. Springer, Heidelberg (2013)
4. Nielsen, M., Chuang, I.: Quantum Computation and Quantum Information, 1st edn. Cambridge University Press (January 2004)
5. Nikolopoulos, G.: Applications of single-qubit rotations in quantum public-key cryptography. Phys. Rev. A 77, 032348(2008)
6. Rabin, M.: How to exchange secrets by oblivious transfer (1981)
7. Shor, P.: Polynomial-time algorithms for prime factorization and discrete logarithms on a quantum computer. SIAM J. Comput. 26(5), 1484–1509 (1997)
8. Yao, A.C.-C.: How to generate and exchange secrets. In: Proceedings of the 27th Annual Symposium on Foundations of Computer Science, SFCS 1986, pp. 162–167. IEEE Computer Society, Washington, DC (1986)

The Fundamental Principle of Breach Prevention

Rui Melo Biscaia

Watchful Software, Coimbra, Portugal
rui.biscaia@watchfulsoftware.com

1 Introduction

Information has evolved to become a crucial commodity, requiring just as much security as any other tangible asset. People take it, use it, and 'leak' it out and organizations are challenged to protect a growing quantity of valuable digital information against careless mishandling and malicious use. In addition, a growing list of legislative requirements adds to the ongoing task of protecting digital files and information.

For the past decades, vast amounts of money and countless hours have been invested in breach prevention. The order of the day has been to harden network and server access through the deployment and redeployment of an evolving series of firewalls, anti-spam/anti-virus applications and intrusion detection and prevention systems – all of them, in essence, attempts to 'reinforce the perimeter' to protect what lies within.

While this remains good and necessary IT practise, it takes no account of two very important and inescapable truths: a) users are always inside the perimeter, and b) even those authorised users can cause significant damage. By ignoring these, CI(S)Os fail to address possibly the most fundamental persistent threat, that of a breach orchestrated by one or more of their organisation's own users.

Information leaks are all too often caused by trusted insiders, people with the right and credentials to be behind the firewall, who leak information whether knowingly or unknowingly. The sheer numbers and types of external storage media available make it very easy for information to leak out. Moreover, corporations are increasingly being held legally liable for the safeguarding of information they hold on their own employees as well as on their customers.

2 What Is a Malicious Insider?

According to Carnegie Mellon University's CERT Insider Threat Center, which offers comprehensive and authoritative research on insider threats, a definition of a malicious insider is a "current or former employee, contractor, or other business partner who has or had authorized access to an organization's network, system, or data and intentionally exceeded or misused that access in a manner that negatively affected the confidentiality, integrity, or availability of the organization's information or information systems."

Also, according to the CERT Insider Threat Center, the employees that pose the greatest risk for insider threat/theft include:

B. De Decker and A. Zúquete (Eds.): CMS 2014, LNCS 8735, pp. 154–156, 2014.
© IFIP International Federation for Information Processing 2014

1. Disgruntled employee – This is usually the employee who feels personally disrespected, possibly due to a missed pay raise that was expected or a negative encounter with supervisors over benefits, time off, demotions, transfers or other similar issues. In this instance, revenge is the employee's motive.
2. Profit-seeking employee – This is a simple motivation for many people. They work for a wage; however, by stealing information, they can make more money selling the stolen data to organized criminals or modifying the data to steal an identity. The information could be easy to access and steal for the employee, plus the theft can be rationalized because, as a malicious insider might say to himself, "The Company won't even miss it". Motivations in such circumstances could include large financial or drug-related debt.
3. An employee moving to a competitor or starting a business – For someone starting a business in the same field, the theft of customer lists, business plans, and even simple forms or templates can be tempting. Alternatively, imagine the employee leaving to work for a competitor. Perhaps the competitor has hinted that an exchange of information can be made for a better position when the employee comes on board.
4. Believe they own the code or product – In this case, employees feel a sense of ownership over code they wrote or a product they developed. Therefore, they take the code for their future use or even for their next job.

3   Data-Centric Security

The way to effectively and efficiently address those concerns seems to be Data-centric Security, whose focus is to classify and encrypt sensitive or confidential information and ensure that only properly authorized people have the key to decrypt it. Thus, even if an intended or unintended breach occurs, whether the information is sent, left on a USB key or stored on a web drive, the data can't be seen or used by anyone beyond the authorized audience.

The first step to accomplish Data-centric Security is encrypt confidential and sensitive data. This can be done automatically, without the user being involved in the process. Enterprises should develop dynamic global data policies, so that when information is created (be it an email, document, spreadsheet, presentation, engineering drawing, etc.) it is automatically encrypted using a secure wrapper. This protection lasts throughout the lifecycle of the information, regardless of how many times it is sent, opened, stored, saved or edited. The information will always have this classification and encryption wrapper protecting it, even if it's sent, carried or stored beyond the enterprise's secure IT perimeter.

The next step is to ensure that the keys are centrally stored and managed. Each time an attempt is made to use that protected information (to open, print, forward, etc.) the wrapper 'reaches out' to the central server managing the keys (more accurately, a list of who has the rights to what levels of information). Effectively, the wrapper asks: 'has this person the right to use me?'. If the answer is 'yes', the action is allowed. If the answer is 'no', then the encryption stands firm and the object is useless.

Moreover, in effective Data-centric Security, all interactions with the rights management server (requests to open information, to print it, to forward it, to save it, etc.) will be saved for future forensic, auditing, and tracking purposes. The records of interactions will be useful in cases where the attempted breaches were not unintentional.

4 Information Security "Rules of Thumb"

As with most approaches to Information Security, layered defenses need to be implemented to reduce insider threats. As there's no silver bullet, a recipe for success starts with following some simple "rules of thumb":

1. Information should be classified. This can be done in one of two ways: either manually, by the author; or dynamically, according to content and context aware policies established by the company. Advanced data-centric security solutions allow information to be classified as it is created (in the case of documents, spreadsheets, presentations, etc.) or as it is sent (in the case of messages and emails);
2. Information should be protected. Quite simply, the best way to protect information is to have it encrypted. There are many different types of encryption, and people employ encryption at different parts of the equation (on the drive, in transit on the network, etc.). Experts today, however, are agreeing that instead of trying to encrypt the physical media where the information might be stored (the drive, the network, etc.) if you simply encrypt the information itself then it's protected regardless of where it is. If it's on a laptop drive, it's encrypted. If it's in transit across the network, it's encrypted. If it's in a cloud based drive, it's encrypted. If it's on a USB key hanging around someone's neck, it's encrypted. What that means is that this information is persistently secure... regardless of whether it in inside or outside of network boundaries;
3. Information should be accessed based the user's "need-to-know". Users should be assigned appropriate security clearances and access to data should be granted based on the user need-to-know according to his job description and the classification of the data itself. Hence, enterprises should enforce separation of duties and privilege, thus not allowing access to sensitive information that the employee has no reason to view, obtain or download.

In a nutshell, Insider threats can (and probably have) happened to every enterprise. Those organizations that are knowledgeable of the risks and are well prepared for such eventualities will thrive reducing and/or preventing the insider threat.

Author Index